Y0-BZY-576

THANK YOU
Uncle Sam

THANK YOU
Uncle Sam

Calabrian families in America

Niall Allsop

Text © Niall Allsop 2013

All rights reserved.

No part of this book may be reproduced in any form or by any means, electronic or mechanical, including information storage and retrieval systems without prior permission in writing from the author.

The only exception being a reviewer who may quote extracts in a review.

ISBN-10: 1-49275-276-2

ISBN-13: 978-1-492752-76-9

Published by **In Scritto** *Italy in writing*

www.inscritto.com

Photograph Credits

Front cover and page 176: Photography Collection, Miriam and Ira D Wallach Division of Art, Prints and Photographs, The New York Public Library, Astor, Lenox and Tilden Foundations.

Page 108: Palisades Amusement Park; courtesy Vince Gargiulo, www.palisadespark.com

Page 146: American Tobacco cigarette production in Brooklyn; courtesy Dick Elliot.

Page 280: The Barge Office; Print Collection Maggie Land Blanck; *Frank Leslie's Illustrated Newspaper*.

All other archive photographs were supplied by the families I met or are in the public domain.

Cover and book design by Niall Allsop – niallsop@mac.com

Main text set in Sabon

Additional text, headings and captions set in Frutiger and Dead History

Front cover titles set in Broadsheet, back cover text in Frutiger

For all the Calabrians who dared to dream

The words 'Uncle Sam' have been used as a personification of the United States since the Second War of Independence of 1812-13.

The iconic 'Uncle Sam' poster first appeared as an army recruiting tool in the United States in 1917 when America entered World War I.

The image itself was created by artist-illustrator James Montgomery Flagg and is said to be a representation of his own face.

Acknowledgements

I owe a debt of gratitude to many people for helping me complete this book but there are three who deserve special mention:

Kay Bowen was, as ever, always there with support, help, advice, a keen eye for the inevitable typographic errors and occasional refreshments.

Carolina Ventrella's assistance in steering me through the many potential pitfalls in Americanizing the text was over and above the call of duty.

Jennie Cariddi for allowing me to use the title of her diary for this book.

The Calabrian-American families I met are the backbone of this book ... sincere thanks to you all for your hospitality, generosity, time and patience.

The Cubello family in the Bronx: Luigi Cubello, Vilma Cubello and Dora Cubello-Villani.

The Cortese families in Albuquerque: Debi Bartucci, David Cortese, Deborah Cortese, Sue Cortese, Mary De Luca, Mike De Luca, Cristin Fuller, David Fuller, Eli Fuller, Ethan Fuller, David Goodman, Jim Goodman, Monica Goodman, Bert Leyva, Shay Leyva, Anthony Lovato, Jeanne Shaw, Joe Smith, Adam Triolo, Tañia Triolo, Dedi Van Winkle, Grant Van Winkle, Russ Van Winkle and Zane Van Winkle.

The Sculco families in New Jersey: Anastasia Fontaiña, Jose Fontaiña, Manuel Fontaiña, Rose Fontaiña, Jennifer Mandrachia, Anna Rubano, David Rubano, Jonathan Rubano, Joseph Rubano, Sara Rose Rubano, Antonio Sculco, Gino Sculco, Gino B Sculco and Sina Audia Sculco.

The Scida family in Long Island: Pat Scida and Rosalie Scida.

The Piezzo families in Long Island: Joanne Bifulco, Anthony Miriello, Katrina Piezzo, Luigi Piezzo, and Marion Vaccaro.

The Farese family in Long Island: Johnny Farese and Mary Farese.

The Cariddi families in New York and Massachusetts: Mary Bergeron, Frances Brown, Antoinette Cariddi, David Cariddi, Gail Ann Cariddi, Jennie Cariddi Tamasi, Joseph Cariddi, Rose Cariddi, Alice Manica, Louie Manica, JoAnn Maselli, Katherine Mogavero, Christopher Tamasi, Cynthia Tamasi, Kristie Tamasi, Leonard Tamasi, Leonard Tamasi Jnr, Michael Tamasi, Nico Tamasi and Sophia Tamasi.

The Fragale family in Chicago: Anthony Fragale and Pepe (Gerardi) Fragale.

The Ventrella family in Chicago: Carmela (Morelli) Bonocore and Carolina (Bonocore) Ventrella.

The Piro family in Wisconsin: Angelo Piro, Domenica Piro, Ippolito Piro and Ralph Piro.

The Fonte families in Wisconsin: Lucia (Iovine) Fonte, Tommaso Fonte, Dennis McGreal, Patrick McGreal, Sylvia (Fonte) McGreal, Brian Sharkey, Vittoria (Fonte) Sharkey, James Roiniotis, Jimmy Roiniotis, MaryAnn (Fonte) Roiniotis and Tommy Roiniotis.

In addition, the following all gave of their time, energy and support:

In Calabria: Maria Rita Aprigliano, Gino Buba, Dott. Manlio Cappa, Bruno Cortese, Maurizio Cortese, Rosalba Gerardi, Silvana Gerardi, Vicki Kelly, Letterina LeRose, Ciccio Marzano, Denise Milone, Klizia Mirante, Agata Miriello, Anna Miriello, Ornella Miriello, Pasquale Piro, Salvatore Piro, Vittorio Pisani, Mariana Postolache, Ornella Quaranta, Dott. Rocco de Rito, Isabella Scida, Filomina Scida, Giuliano Stoica, Carlo Tigano, Giuseppe Tigano, Gustavo Tigano and Raffaele Vizza.

In Albuquerque: Janice Mundy and Judge James Parker.

In London: Graham Allsop.

In Manhattan: Hélène Arnoult and Sara Ng.

In New Jersey: Matthew Higgins, Daniela Maddaloni, 'Mitch', the Saigon Café (Danny, Karen, Kim & Steve) and Sherrie Vamos.

In Pennsylvania: Carmela Capellupo-Beaver.

In Washington: Eddie Lloyd at Mrsimcard.

Contents

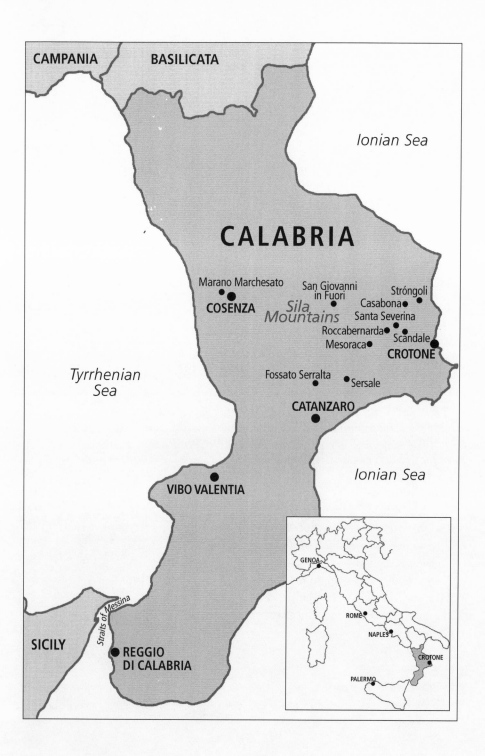

CAMPANIA   BASILICATA

Ionian Sea

CALABRIA

Marano Marchesato   San Giovanni   Stróngoli
                           in Fuori
● ●   ●   Casabona ●   ●
COSENZA   *Sila*   Santa Severina
                     Mountains
                              Roccabernarda ●   Scandale
                           Mesoraca ●   ●
                                          CROTONE ●

Tyrrhenian
Sea

Fossato Serralta
          ●
          Sersale ●

CATANZARO ●

Ionian Sea

VIBO VALENTIA ●
VIBO VALENTIA

GENOA

Straits of Messina

ROME ●

NAPLES ●

SICILY   ● **REGGIO**
                    DI CALABRIA   CROTONE

PALERMO ●

Some notes on the text

Apart from Calabria's five main provincial centers, the map opposite only shows the Calabrian towns referred to in the text, most of which were the birthplaces of emigrants featured in this book.

The smaller map includes the three Italian ports that most of the ships that plied between Italy and New York called at—Genoa, Naples and Palermo. Almost all of the emigrants featured in this book left from Naples.

Most of the stories are straightforward but two have a more genealogical element so in these cases I have appended, in the interests of clarity, my own version of their family tree—in both such cases an incomplete family tree that focusses only on the main players.

As this book is largely about America and Americans, albeit those who were originally Calabrian, I have used American English throughout rather than International English: color for colour; center for centre; trunk for boot; realize for realise, sidewalk for pavement ... and so on. I'm sure most readers will be conversant with the language of both cultures.

I have tried to be consistent in my use of the words 'emigrant' and 'immigrant'. Until people set foot in the United States I refer to them as 'emigrants'; thereafter they are 'immigrants'.

Many of the photographs are old, some are not particularly sharp, others were damaged ... they are no more than embellishments to the text.

Prologue

The pilot tells us to expect a crisp, clear November evening in New York. He is right. It is less than a week since Hurricane Sandy wreaked havoc on this city so a clear, calm evening is particularly welcome.

Still inside the terminal I am heading for the long, serpentine queue that will eventually permit me to step outside into that relative calm that is the United States of America.

While I am waiting my turn, I recall the procedure: I'll hand the officer my passport; expressionless, the officer will scan it to confirm that I have completed my ESTA (Electronic System for Travel Authorization) and that my entry has been 'authorized'; he (or she) will examine the green card I completed on the flight, take my photo and digital thumbprints, ask why I'm travelling to America and how long I'm staying, staple the stub of the green card to my passport and, with a firm flourish, stamp the passport, and tell me to "have a nice day" before waving forward the next person. It'll take no more than two minutes. Life in the modern world.

I think back to my young friend Vincenzo who made this trip twice in one year ... both times with the intention of working in the States with family members from Calabria long-established there. The first time he was back home within a month ... he decided America was not for him, he was homesick, preferring small-town Calabria to Long Island. Four months later he gave it another go, preferring the certainty of construction work in America to the uncertainties of his native Calabria, more prepared to cope with the homesickness and the language. Last time I heard he was working as a *pizzaiolo* (a maker of pizzas) in Virginia.

As the queue moves slowly forward, my thoughts inevitably wander back further in time trying to imagine what it was like for all those other immigrants who, in other ages, queued to gain entry to the United States of America, the land of hope, opportunity and work; the land of the free.

Until the sixties most of these came by sea, and from the late nineteenth century until 1924 nearly all entered the country through the Immigrant Inspection Center at Ellis Island, close to the iconic Statue of Liberty.

For me this is the first time I have come to America alone or without anyone waiting to greet me in Arrivals. I feel a sense of disquiet ... of apprehension, of wondering how I'll cope without either my wife Kay or my occasional travelling companion, Neff, my nephew Graham.

Then, as I shuffle forward another ten paces, I snap out of my melancholy and return to the reality that I am infinitely more fortunate than those who had to queue their way through Ellis Island (and its earlier incarnations on the southern shores of Manhattan) with little more than the clothes they wore and the strong belief that life could not be much worse this side of the Atlantic. For me, when I think of these desperate people it is the Irish who fled the Great Hunger in the mid-nineteenth century that instantly come to mind. I recall someone once saying that if you laid a cross in the water for every Irish emigrant who died crossing the Atlantic, then you could have walked to America.

I am at the head of the queue, one or two quick questions, a few bits of technological wizardry away from American soil. I move forward. My interrogator is female and friendly and I am momentarily embarrassed by my earlier stereotypical speculation ... until, that is, she stamps my passport with extreme force and says, "Have a nice day.".

One minute, fifty seconds.

I am tired and ditch my original intention of taking the shuttle bus from JFK Airport to Manhattan's Penn Station and then a yellow cab down to the Lower East Side, in favor of a more costly alternative—a cab door to door, from JFK to Clinton Street.

The cab passes through Queens, a part of New York I have never been to before, and, as it's dark, will scarcely remember. My cabbie is bemoaning his lot and the fact that he has had to wait in line for up to three hours for gas in the chaos of post-Sandy Manhattan; he is not impressed with the efforts of the powers-that-be to bring fuel to the city.

My mind wanders elsewhere and returns to the notion of walking across the Atlantic on all those crosses. Being from the north of Ireland, I know something about the statistics of the Great Hunger and the number of people who bade farewell to Ireland and its blighted potato at that time in search of no more than food and fair play. Gazing out the window at the reflected lights, I do some mental arithmetic ... number of miles from Ireland to America, average length of cross, estimated number of people (some say thirty percent) who never saw the American shore ... and conclude that it would not have been possible to walk to America. It might just have been possible to jump to America, but not walk ... then again, my estimate for the average length of a cross could have been wildly off the mark.

As the cab approaches Williamsburg Bridge, the link to Manhattan, I see a city skyline that, thanks to Hurricane Sandy and its aftermath, is not looking its usual vibrant and sparkling self. Nevertheless it never ceases to mesmerize and amaze and, as I head across the bridge towards the restorative powers of a glass or three of red wine and a good night's sleep, I am just glad to be here.

Now all I've got to do is find me some Calabrians.

Introduction

The genesis of this book is complex.

Some years ago, as we were planning our first holiday to Calabria, I read Peter Chiarella's extraordinary *Calabrian Tales*, the story of his family's life in Calabria up until the time—in 1920—when his father Raffaele emigrated to the United States.

Calabrian Tales is the fascinating story of a family's trials and tribulations over several generations which concluded when Raffaele and his mother decided to leave their native Calabria and seek a new life in America.

In the book's final chapter, Chiarella describes the scene aboard the *Dante Alighieri*, as it negotiates it way out of the harbor at Naples—on board his father Raffaele looks back at his homeland and wonders if he will ever see it again.

For Raffaele, as for millions of other Italians, mostly from the south and Sicily, this moment was the beginning of a new story.

Then, as now, I was no less interested in what happened next ... in how Raffaele's family fared in the land they chose to be their new home, in how it was Peter Chiarella and *his* family became the people they are today.

In the summer of 2011, almost three years after my wife and I moved to the small hilltop town of Santa Severina in the Crotone province of Calabria, we were introduced to an 'American' sitting outside one of the bars. Gino Sculco spoke like an American and dressed like an American but was actually born and bred in Santa Severina; he and his wife were on holiday. Gino told us that they lived in New Jersey and were back in Santa Severina for a couple of months, renewing old acquaintances and, it so happened that summer, saying a final farewell to some of them.

Our paths subsequently crossed a number of times: at two funerals, outside the Jolly Bar where all his friends gathered and played cards and in and around the town's beautiful *piazza*; we also met his wife Sina in the courtyard of the family home in Via dei Bizantini. For other reasons I was interested in the 'Sculco' name but, Sina explained, although there was another family in the town with the same surname, there were not *parenti* but two separate families.

In the *centro storico*'s one and only restaurant later that same summer we bumped into an acquaintance who introduced us to her friend Elvira Arabia who, it turned out, hailed from 'near Chicago'. Elvira too was on holiday, visiting family and friends in her home town of Santa Severina.

In early April 2012 I received an email from a man called David Brightbill living in north Florida. David had read my book *Scratching the toe of Italy* and had rightly surmised that we could probably see his grandfather's home town of San Nicola dell'Alto across the valley from Santa Severina. Although David and his wife had recently had their Italian citizenship recognized, they had never visited Calabria.

He explained that the current *sindaco* (mayor) and *vice sindaco* of San Nicola dell'Alto both bear the same surname as his grandfather, Basta. He mentioned too family stories about Calabria that revolved around a mysterious feud, land that may or may not belong to his cousin and the sense of loss that he heard in his grandmother's voice when she talked of her Calabrian homeland.

It was a moving story and one day I looked forward to meeting David when he finally fulfilled his ambition of coming 'home' to San Nicola.

By now the idea of finding out more about these Calabrian families and why they made such a dramatic change in their lives was germinating and then two separate events focused my mind.

In the late summer of 2012 I happened upon a website which, among other things, contained potted histories of Italian families who had emigrated to America. The stories were normally written by first- or second-generation 'Americans' and ranged from just a few lines to a thousand words or more. Almost without realizing it, I found myself seeking out the few stories that related to families who had left Calabria.

One in particular, the story of the Cubello family from Fossato Serralto near Catanzaro, I found particularly moving. I made a mental note that one day I might like to get in touch with the writer, Luigi Cubello.

Not long afterwards I was talking with Santa Severina's *ex-sindaco*, Bruno Cortese, and innocently asked him if many people from the town had emigrated to the States. When he told me that he had family there I was more than a little surprised ... I was even more surprised when he told me that his father was actually born in America and he still had close relatives living in Albuquerque, New Mexico. I was particularly fascinated for, in all the years I had known Bruno, neither he nor any of our many mutual friends had ever mentioned the American side of his family; also his persona and his life were so focused on Santa Severina that the notion that he might have such direct American connections seemed almost incongruous.

These different strands—and this latter encounter in particular—served to focus my mind and the next time we met I told Bruno that I was planning a trip to the States to visit some Calabrian families and was keen to visit his in Albuquerque ... it was a few weeks and a couple of reminders later when finally I had an email address.

•

I planned to visit the States in November for two reasons.

First, I was one of those strange people who liked to sit up late every four years and watch the American presidential election results and I was not wont to let the chance of actually being there on 6 November slip by for another four years.

Second, I was curious to see if the annual Thanksgiving holiday (22 November that year) was really the family disaster that many American movies seemed to portray.

In between these two events I hoped to find more about ten Calabrian families that would put up with having me around and answer a few questions.

Finding families proved more difficult than I expected for, generally, I was contacting people cold—sometimes on the phone, sometimes via email, sometimes through a third party. Initially most were skeptical and I found that contact via email was more successful as people had time to think about it and could also check out my website to verify that I was who I said I was. Via email I could also give people a more detailed list of the sorts of things I would like to talk about.

In addition, word had got out that I was interested in families or individuals who had emigrated to the States so I was not totally surprised to receive a call from a friend to tell me that there was an American couple staying at the local *agriturismo*, Le Puzelle, who would like to meet me.

The following morning Kay and I had breakfast at our local *pasticceria* with Luigi and Katrina Piezzo who hailed from Valley Stream in Long Island (New York); they were accompanied by their London-based New Zealand friend, Grace Chan, who prefers to describe herself as Kiwi Chinese.

The *pasticceria* was a fitting venue that morning. It is owned and run by two members of the Quaranta family, Antonio and Paolo, who in turn are related to Luigi through his grandfather. Luigi and Katrina (who also comes from New Zealand) were making their first ever visit to Italy to connect with Luigi's antecedents in Santa Severina.

Luigi was also related to another local family that we knew well, the Miriello family at whose house we had recently celebrated Vittorio Miriello's sixtieth birthday; it was Vittorio's sister Agata who had set up the meeting with Luigi, Katrina and Grace.

We five met several times in the following few days and I arranged to visit them in New York ... as it happened London-based Grace was going to be in New York around the same time so a reunion dinner was added to my itinerary as was an overnight stop in Valley Stream.

Eventually enough families and individuals had agreed to meet me, including Gino and Sina Sculco in New Jersey, Luigi Cubello in the Bronx (New York) and Bruno Cortese's family in Albuquerque; I had hoped

I might get to visit David Brightbill in Florida and Elvira Arabia 'near Chicago' but it was not to be.

Apart from Albuquerque, New Jersey, the Bronx and Long Island, my planned itinerary would take me to Schenectady in upstate New York, Chicago, Kenosha in southern Wisconsin (where I was invited to spend Thanksgiving with a Calabrian family) and Reading in Pennsylvania.

Apart from Santa Severinese, I hoped to visit people originally from Crotone, Roccabernarda, Stróngoli, Sersale and Fossato Serralta, all Calabrese from the provinces of Crotone and Catanzaro.

•

My original plan was simply to visit families and listen to and note their stories, write a book with a dozen chapters or so to tell the story of each. I had no sociological or political axe to grind, I did not have any expectations ... in truth I had no way of knowing whether or not such a venture would yield anything worthy of record. I was just interested in their stories, why they had emigrated, whether the reality and the 'dream' matched up and what life was like now. Of course these areas were no more than the bare bones of what I wanted to find out; it would be the meat that people put on these bones that could be fascinating.

But outside forces such as Hurricane Sandy slowly began to change this basic concept and substituted instead the idea of a travelogue which, as well as documenting my time with these families, would include other encounters that were an inevitable and integral part of my short twenty-two-day journey through a small part of America. In this respect I have, of course, some previous history (*Keeping up with the Lawrences* and *Stumbling through Italy*) and so it is not surprising that almost as soon as I set foot in America I felt impelled to record my experiences.

The result, *Thank you Uncle Sam*, has therefore these two strands which inevitably and inexorably blend into one. That said, the core of the book is the time I spent with families and individuals who shared no more than their common Calabrian ancestry.

Sometimes I spent just a few hours with people; sometimes I stayed overnight or longer.

Some families went to America early in the twentieth century; others as recently as the 1960s.

Some of the people I met were in their, sixties, seventies or eighties; others mere youngsters in comparison.

Some stories are intriguing and intricate; others straightforward and predictable.

Some stories have a complex genealogical element; others no more than a relatively straight line.

Sometimes I knew quite a lot about the family before I met them; usually almost nothing.

Some people I had already met; most were total strangers.

All their stories and experiences are both unique and commonplace—they are no more than people's subjective memories, stories and occasional skeletons, shared with a stranger.

•

While I was already in America two families had to cancel, one in New Jersey, the other in Pennsylvania.

By chance, while I was traveling, I encountered three other families with Calabrian roots and was able to see two of them.

The third—whose story is also included—I couldn't visit; even though I passed close to their Chicago home, it was not possible to drop by. So, on the move and with the help of the internet, I slowly began to unravel their story and embrace the concept of the virtual chapter.

•

One final thought. On two occasions in the days leading up to my departure friends independently asked me if I was aware of the irony of what I was going to do ... by which they meant that my wife and I were also immigrants. Until then it had never occurred to me that I had something in common with the people I wanted to meet, albeit in a different age, in different circumstances and, most importantly, at a different time of life.

The comparison was, I felt at the time, scarcely worthy of note but, that said, almost every Calabrian I met on my travels began our conversation by turning the tables on me and asking me why I went to live in Calabria. On some occasions it was as if I had come to their home to be interviewed by them.

I mention this as, on reflection, the fact that I shared some of their experiences (with the provisos mentioned above) was a bonus and helped me understand more fully both *their* lives as Americans from Calabria and *mine* as a Calabrian from Ireland via the UK.

Santa Severina, May 2013

•

I wrote the above Introduction in preparation for publication in June 2013 but unfortunately unforeseen health-related events intervened and I was unable to complete the book within the time-frame I had set myself.

Following surgery in Rome the health scare is no more and life has slowly returned to normal (whatever that means); more importantly the book is now finished.

This delay had an unexpected bonus in that I was able to meet again some of the families whom I met in the United States in November 2012, families who had returned to Calabria during the summer to visit family and friends. Some of these encounters I have appended as a Postscript to the appropriate chapter.

Santa Severina, November 2013

Acclimatizing

The cab dropped me off in Clinton Street in New York's Lower East Side and I dragged my suitcase up the five stories to the top of the house which would be home for the next five days.

Introductions with my host, Sara, over with, I didn't have the energy to go out in search of sustenance and went straight to bed for a well-earned rest ... there followed instead a restless night where my mind fought off sleep by flirting with the notion that I might just have left one of my phones—a UK phone and the only one that would work in the States—in the cab. I had.

Still, all was not lost. As if aware of this eventuality, I had ordered an iPhone and an American SIM before leaving Italy and these had already been delivered to Luigi and Katrina in Long Island. I was hoping to see one or the other that day for the official hand-over.

But first I had to block the existing number ... no problem, I thought, should be able to do that easily through Virgin's website. I logged on using my iPad. No, despite having a safe username and password, I could not use my secure Virgin account page to block my lost phone ... they had a much better idea ... I was to call them on a special number for those-who-mislay-their-phones-overseas.

I let this notion filter through my tired brain ... I have lost my phone and the only way I can block the phone is to call Virgin on my non-existent phone. The idea seemed somewhat flawed; still, perhaps later in the day when I caught up with my new iPhone, I might give that a try. In the meantime I needed to email Katrina to finalize the arrangements for meeting up with Luigi.

Luigi had already departed for work in Monday's Manhattan and, according to Katrina, was awaiting my call so that we could arrange to meet. I explained the phone situation and Katrina seamlessly took on the role of mission control as she successfully married up Luigi and I for a lunch date near Times Square.

Meanwhile I thought I had a brainwave ... I sent all the phone details, including the exact amount I'd already spent that month, to nephew Graham—Neff—and asked him to call Virgin's UK number and put a stop to things. He did, but they wouldn't let him. They repeated the gloomy message that the only way to do this was if I personally gave them a call on my non-existent phone.

I gave up and decided instead to sally forth into the neighborhood, my neighborhood, to get my bearings before heading uptown. My base for the first five days, an apartment in Clinton Street, was at the southern extremity of the Lower East Side, a vibrant quarter bordering on Little Italy and Chinatown.

Traditionally an area that hosted immigrants, it is gradually becoming gentrified. I soon discovered that my end of Clinton Street was at the partially-gentrified end of the spectrum, a mixed community with both older, slightly-jaded but nonetheless engaging, shops and cafés cheek by jowl with trendy restaurants and bars less than a minute's walk away on the same street. Over the next five days I suspected it would be incumbent on me to become a regular at several.

I found my base in Clinton Street, as I did with all my accommodation, through the Airbnb website, a site where travellers can book reasonably-priced private rooms in local apartments and houses. Later in the week I was going to move across to Jersey City in New Jersey where I would base myself until I returned to Italy.

I suppose I was lucky to be here at all. Hurricane Sandy had not actually caused much physical damage in this part of lower Manhattan but the power had been off for almost a week and people and businesses had only just got back on their feet. Shops, restaurants and bars that relied on fridges and freezers were particularly badly hit and the gas shortages affected deliveries ... for New Yorkers such mayhem was the stuff of apocalyptic movies rather than what you'd expect in the Big Apple.

Having got my bearings, chosen my eaterie for the evening and also my post-prandial bar *and* discovered a shop selling off at a huge discounts all the unwanted paraphernalia for the cancelled New York Marathon, I headed for Essex Street subway station, bought myself a seven-day pass, and headed up to the thriving heart of Manhattan and Times Square.

Strange it was indeed to see Luigi on his home turf. We had only ever met in Santa Severina a few weeks earlier and here we were greeting each other like old friends, Italian-style, on a Manhattan sidewalk. It was one o'clock and people were pouring out of their offices or walking with purpose clutching their take-away coffee cups or speaking loudly into their cell phones, each in his or her own way contributing to the frenetic backdrop that was lunchtime in Manhattan. We joined the throng in search of food and a quieter place to talk.

Over lunch Luigi spoke with strong emotion about his few days in Santa Severina; to say that he saw it as a life-changing experience is no exaggeration. He waxed lyrical about the people he had met, strangers who had welcomed him into their homes and lives in such an open and selfless way. This side of the Calabrian character I was able to relate to for our experiences had been exactly the same and, unlike Luigi, we weren't even family.

More than once I saw him well up as he recalled the many kindnesses he had been shown, as he reflected on individuals, as he paused to picture special moments in his mind's eye. All I could do was nod in agreement and repeat that our experience of Calabrese generosity had been just like his ... we had been accepted into their community with the same unconditional warmth that he, Katrina and Grace had all experienced.

Just before we parted we got down to the main business of the day when Luigi passed over the bag with my new phone which, he said, Katrina had already charged for me. It seemed to me that American generosity was not a lot different from Calabrian.

Finally, we arranged to meet at a Vietnamese restaurant in Chinatown that Thursday at six; Grace would also be there as would another of Katrina's friends from New Zealand.

Back in Clinton Street I immediately set up my new phone only to discover that I hadn't bought the correct SIM to make calls to the UK. A call (and a small payment) to Eddie Lloyd at Mrsimcard, resolved that problem in a matter of minutes and finally I had the wherewithal to give Virgin Mobile a piece of my mind—except that the number on their website for those-who-mislay-their-phones-overseas didn't solicit a response. I kept trying, the number kept ringing, nobody answered, not even a machine.

I was getting annoyed. I called Neff and asked him to call his new friends at Virgin again and explain the Catch 22 situation in which I found myself—earlier I had a no phone so couldn't call, now I had a phone but couldn't get an answer.

Neff's younger, tech-savvy brain came up with a crafty solution. He would set his phone to forward all calls to Virgin's UK number so that when I called him my call would automatically be passed forward to that number ... the one exclusively for those-who-mislay-their-phones-nearer-to-home.

It worked and at long last I got through to a human being who took all my details and blocked my phone before I flew into calm-but-bloody-angry mode and said my piece about their so-called service.

Before leaving Calabria I had resolved that, during my time in America, I would eat neither pasta nor pizza. Eating out in southern Italy it is well nigh impossible to find anything but Italian cuisine and, much as I like it, I was not going to waste the opportunity to try all the wonderful foods on offer from other cultures in America. So, that evening I ate in a nearby Thai restaurant before crossing the street to sample the red wine at the Cocoa Bar where, as you do, I discussed the best place to watch the presidential election results the following evening with Iranian *Huffington Post* journalist, Shirin Barghi, and her co-patriot from London who was working behind the bar.

The suggestion that appealed most was to head up to Times Square where there was sure to be a big screen or three. Despite its attraction, at the time the very thought of it felt like a marathon ... I was fading fast and didn't think Times Square would be on my agenda ... perhaps after a good night's sleep I might feel more energized. At least I had no phones to think about.

•

Election day dawned and, still half asleep, I dragged myself to the kitchen for a glass of water.

Since arriving on Sunday I had not seen my host Sara so I was more than a little surprised when a door opened (which I had assumed was Sara's bedroom) and out popped a complete stranger and proffered her hand. "Bonjour, Niall" she said in perfect French, "Je m'appele Hélène." And then, in near perfect English, "I believe we are sharing the apartment while Sara is at her boyfriend's."

Nice touch that, I thought to myself, Sara's found me a flatmate ... and she's French.

Hélène hailed from San Tropez, delivered yachts for a living and was in New York to support her friend who was running in the Marathon ... or rather her friend who wasn't running in the Marathon.

It was a controversial issue at the time. In the aftermath of Hurricane Sandy to run or not to run, that was the question. The Mayor, Michael Bloomberg, first of all said 'yes' then changed his tune when some of those most directly affected by Sandy, ably encouraged by the media, created a fuss. At the time, just a few days before I left Calabria, I could see both sides of the argument, it was one of those issues where there was no right or wrong, just different perspectives from people effected in different ways by the hurricane. After I listened to the eloquent Hélène talk about her friend, it was a difficult not to think that the Mayor may have made a mistake.

For the runners one of the problems was that the original decision to go ahead meant that most had already arrived in New York from all over the world. Hélène's friend, Justine, only came because she had heard Mayor Bloomberg's initial positive statements—she left France believing the race was on, by the time she landed in New York it was cancelled.

Justine had applied to run on several occasions but actually being chosen is, quite literally, a lottery; there is approximately a one-in-ten chance of being selected. Then there is the rigid training schedule, finding accommodation and traveling. From what Hélène told me, Justine was more than just disappointed by the cancellation, she was devastated ... it was perhaps her only chance of ever participating in the marathon and she was stunned by what had happened.

On the other hand many, many people in post-Sandy New York and New Jersey were more than stunned, their lives were turned upside down and would probably never be the same again. It was a difficult call. It was also difficult to ignore Hélène's passionate support for her friend's situation.

And all this before breakfast.

Hélène and I had separate missions that day but arranged to eat together that evening and watch the election unfold later, assuming, that is, we could find a bar with a television ... though I still hadn't discounted the Times Square option.

•

I was here, after all, to talk to Calabrians so spent the rest of the day preparing myself for visiting Luigi Cubello the following morning in Pelham in the north-east Bronx. I had already worked out that this was about a half-hour train ride from one of my favorite New York landmarks, Grand Central Terminal, itself at least half an hour on the subway from 'home'.

As I had an early rush-hour start in the morning—another reason why I thought a late night at Times Square was not a good idea—I decided to go up to Grand Central, renew my acquaintance with this fascinating place, get my ticket and check out the likely platform ... a 'dry run' I suppose you'd call it.

This was the first time I was ever in Grand Central Terminal with the intention of buying a train ticket and actually contemplating catching a train here. I still found it extraordinary that such a majestic, lavish and monumental place was also a fully functional railway station. I thought back to the time I met two friends here who, although they lived in Tennessee, were from Long Island, New York and had never been to this station; I showed them round. They were in awe that such a place was almost on their doorstep and they'd never seen it before. The reason was probably simple enough—trains from Long Island arrive in Manhattan a few blocks away at Penn Station.

Thankfully in the rush to redevelop in the fifties and sixties, plans to demolish Grand Central Terminal were scrapped; the original Penn Station was not so fortunate.

Ticket in hand, I phoned Luigi and told him what train I expected to be on and arranged to confirm my progress en route in the morning. I also gave him my American number.

Back at base, my travel homework done, I went over what I already knew about Luigi and his mother and sister and prepared myself to meet my first complete Calabrian stranger. I was a little nervous, a little unsure what to expect and, even worse, what might be expected of me.

•

After another splendid Thai dinner, Hélène and I checked out the lack of a television at the Cocoa Bar and headed instead for the Salt bar, literally the building next door to our apartment, even with the same street number. Here there was a television, albeit a television a bit on the capricious side, and it was tuned in to all things electoral ... there were even occasional shots of the festivities getting underway about forty blocks away up at Times Square.

The election results would not have been Hélène's program of choice so, as a seasoned watcher of such things, I was able to explain what was happening and what was being predicted by the exit polls and the pundits. The bar itself was getting busier as things began to heat up; by my reckoning there was just one lone Romney supporter there—as you would expect of New York, and in particular the Lower East Side, the Obama camp was in the ascendency and smelling victory.

By ten-fifteen Hélène had had enough and returned to the apartment while I stayed on till it was clear what the result was going to be. Mentally I finally conceded that I didn't have the energy for Times Square. I also knew I'd always regret it. On the other hand almost everyone in Salt seemed just as happy as those we could see in Times Square ... and we had benefits, a warm environment and a selection of Irish whiskeys.

Before I left Salt I scribbled a note for Hélène on the back of one of the bar's business cards and left it on the kitchen table as I headed to bed. It simply said 'Obama won, Romney zero'. I hoped she'd get the play on words.

I first came across the story of the Cubello family by chance when I happened upon the Italiamerica website, a site with all the hallmarks of being past its heyday.

Luigi Cubello had written eloquently and movingly about his great-grandfather, his great-uncle and his parents and their experiences as Calabrians in America. There were three other stories that I found interesting on the same site but Luigi was the only one who didn't rely for contact on the site's generic email contact form; fortunately Luigi had appended his actual email address.

I emailed four people but only Luigi received his. My suspicions about the website being past its sell-by-date were well-founded for the other three got lost in the ether (though subsequently I managed to trace one of them).

Thereafter Luigi and I exchanged several emails and I arranged to visit him at his home in the Bronx.

My mother's not chasing too many goats lately ...

I arrived at Pelham station just after ten and was met by Luigi Cubello, a distinguished-looking man in his late fifties with close-cropped white hair and matching Van Dyke beard. On the short drive to his home we compared and contrasted two of our favorite movies, *The Taking of Pelham One Two Three* and *The Taking of Pelham 1 2 3*, two versions of the same basic train-hijacking story made thirty-five years apart. We agreed they were both excellent movies but that nothing could eclipse the wry, knowing smile on the face of Walter Matthau in the final scene of the original.

At the house I was introduced to Luigi's mother, Vilma, a short, powerful woman in her eighties. Luigi had already explained that Vilma spoke her own form of English and that I might not understand everything she said. Her unique language was in fact a mixture of Italian and English ... she sometimes started a sentence in one language and finished it the other. I could see that English-only speakers, like shop assistants, might well have had a problem with this but generally I could make sense of it.

So that I could appreciate just what life was like back in Calabria in the mid-fifties Luigi showed me a DVD compilation of old family movies some of which was filmed around their home-town of Fossato Serralto clinging to the lower folds of the Sila mountains, north of Catanzaro.

The occasion was the visit of the descendants of Luigi Calogero, Luigi's great-grandfather, and their family from their homes in New Jersey and the Bronx. Before they reached Fossato Serralto they had visited London, Paris, Rome, Venice and Madrid, they also bought a Jaguar on their travels and had it shipped back to the States.

Great-grandfather Luigi and great-uncle Giuseppe Cubello had both gone to America in 1910 though it is unlikely they even knew each other before they emigrated ... they were from different generations, travelled separately three months apart, and yet from towns only a few hills apart.

Luigi spoke proudly of these pioneering members of his family; he knows they did something extraordinary because they wanted to better their lives. They also did their bit for their adopted land—Luigi was part of the 1500 (mostly Italian) workforce who built the Kensico Dam in upstate New York, even today still crucial to New York's water supply, while Giuseppe fought in the First World War after America entered the fray in 1917.

Like many others both returned to their native Calabria; Giuseppe married and went back to America and remained there while old Luigi returned to Fossato to end his days and I watched as, in his mid-nineties, he emerged from the antiquated family home, was reluctantly

Luigi Calogero in 1955

helped down the stone steps so that he could take center stage with his American descendants and their movie camera. His young helper was his oldest grandson, Domenico, my host Luigi's uncle, the brother of Luigi's father Giuseppe, who, following the death of their father, also Luigi, was effectively the head of the family.

Also in the Fossato footage there is a little curly-haired boy, scarcely eighteen months, first in his mother's arms then scuttling around among the chickens on unsteady legs as he revels in the excitement of that day and these strangers from another place. I looked up at Luigi to see how much he'd changed ... whatever happened to all that hair, I wondered; on the other hand, I marveled at how his mother Vilma, sitting across the room from me, had scarcely changed at all.

So, for the Cubello family emigration was in the blood and I wondered if this visit by his late great-uncle Frank's wife Fiana, her daughter Mary and daughter-in-law Margarita, was the catalyst for his parents' decision to head across the Atlantic less than a year later?

Luigi and Vilma agreed that it was something that was on the cards for some time, the fact there was family already there was a bonus. For a start there was not a lot of work in and around Fossato, and what there was was generally seasonal; Fossato was also succumbing to the elements, with floods and landslides becoming more frequent ... less than ten years earlier the part of town known as Noce had been completely washed away. But most importantly there was the health of Luigi's father, Giuseppe, to take into consideration with the possibility of better health care in America. At the time the family were not sure what exactly what Giuseppe's illness was but with the benefit of hindsight and the internet they are fairly certain he was suffering from rheumatic fever brought on by strep throat.

The family's plans to leave Fossato were shrouded in an element of secrecy to some people. Intertwined with this was the idea, still prevalent in today's Calabria, of the evil eye, *il malocchio*, the superstitious notion that one person, just by a look, can cause bad fortune or worse to another. Vilma would tell her children stories about the blend of good and evil around them and how San Francesco, their patron saint, would protect them and that they should always be on their guard against false praise and protect themselves from envy.

To illustrate their caution before departing, Vilma told me the story of her husband's suit. The suit was bought in secret for going to the States and, as he'd never had a suit before, those that they thought capable of ill-will, of casting *il malocchio*, were kept in the dark about its existence and, by default, the reason for its existence.

In the States they of course had the advantage of family and Vilma had the security of knowing she had a job and an apartment there before they even left Calabria thanks to Giuseppe's aunt Betty and uncle Johnny. In December 1955 Vilma got her passport which included photos of her two children; the family planned to leave in April.

•

Vilma was telling me about their journey when her daughter, Luigi's sister Dora, arrived. For Dora, five years older than Luigi, leaving Fossato and her extended family was more traumatic. Unlike Luigi, seven-year-old Dora knew what was happening and wasn't happy about leaving her friends and family.

Still, leave they did and travelled first of all to Catanzaro then on to

Ha versato tassa speciale confirmed that Vilma had paid the special exit tax

Sant'Eufemia (better known today as Lamezia Terme) where they caught the train north to Naples from where they sailed on 14 April 1956. They paid for their passage with a loan of $200 from Catholic Charities, a loan they had to pay back in full once established in America.

The trip itself was a far cry from what people had to endure in the earlier part of the century. For a start it was much faster (they arrived in New York on 23 April) and the ship was modern ... with bars and dining rooms, even people to look after the children while their parents went to dance in the ballroom. But, the nearer they got to New York, the nearer Giuseppe and Vilma came to facing up to a potential problem.

With Giuseppe in poor health, they knew there was a risk that he might not be allowed to enter the United States. Back in the days when immigrants went through the Immigrant Inspection Station at Ellis Island everyone was scrutinized for potential health problems and it was not unknown for families to be separated at this stage with one member being quarantined while further tests were conducted. Nor was it unknown for people to be sent back to their country of origin. Ellis Island had ceased to process immigrants in 1924 (though it had other incarnations as a detention and deportation center until 1954) but the practice of weeding out those thought to be poorly, both mentally and physically, continued.

To circumvent this possibility, Giuseppe was dressed in his new suit (Luigi believes it was the only suit his father ever owned) and Vilma used her make-up to give him a healthier complexion. Also he never left his wife's side and was using her as support while Vilma in turn carried young Luigi with Dora holding on to her mother's skirts.

Their ruse was successful and on Monday 23 April 1956, Vilma Dornetti, Giuseppe Cubello, Dora Cubello and Luigi Cubello entered the United States of America to begin their new life.

But they never forgot their old life—the things that were precious to them in Calabria came with them as cherished memories.

Vilma would conjure up pictures of cold winter nights, of her family sitting round the fireplace to eat cheese, *sopressata* and chunks of bread cut and passed round by her father ... people were poor but never went hungry.

Over dinner she would tell her two children about life in Fossato, about their grandparents, about the joys and the hardships of growing up poor

Giuseppe Cubello's American aunts and uncles (from left to right) Betty, Johnny, Frank and Rose. Betty and Johnny it was who helped the family emigrate and it was Frank's wife and family who visited Europe and Fossato in the fifties. Luigi was very fond of his uncle Johnny (a barber), less so of his aunt Betty, for though it was she who took Giuseppe to all his visits to the doctor, she never let anyone ever forget how she had helped the family ... she even told Dora and Luigi that they would have amounted to nothing if it weren't for her.

in Calabria. They heard about the earthquakes, the wild storms, the floods and the landslides and the mysterious superstitions.

Most of all Vilma never forgot the day she was out on the steep hillside feeding the goats when one strayed off ... it was while chasing that capricious runaway that she went into labor and Luigi was born shortly afterwards.

And together she and Giuseppe told their children the story of how they first met and fell in love; of how Giuseppe asked Vilma's father for her hand in marriage and told her he was going to be hers for ever.

In the piece he wrote on the Italiamerica website, Luigi put it both simply and succinctly, "I was born poor but I felt so rich with tradition.".

•

Just three days after arriving in America Vilma started work for the upscale, Manhattan-based, shoe manufacturer, Pappagallo where she clocked in at eight in the morning and out at four-thirty in the afternoon. Dora recalled how, at weekends, her mother would bring home loafers that needed some delicate decorative touches such as tassels and they would do the work together.

At this time they lived in a three-roomed apartment in Fulton Avenue in the Morrisania neighborhood of the south Bronx not far from the Zoo. There was already an established Italian community in the area but the Cubello family were never really part of it, instead their ties were generally familial with aunts and uncles and their families always dropping by ... an embryonic Calabrian community in the making.

There were four Calogero families in all, three of whom were born in America, and most were older than the Cubellos. The children's cousins were mostly second generation Americans so Dora and Luigi had first-hand experience of what it was like to be an American and soon assimilated this new way of life and its language. But the Cubellos also clung on to their Calabrian roots and Luigi recalls how, when they visited family, they'd eat, the wine would flow and then out would come the accordions and the tambourines, the prelude to a real Calabrese hoedown ... having shared such evenings myself, I know it to be an unforgettable experience.

Despite having Giuseppe's family close by, Vilma recalls how homesick she felt at the beginning, particularly for her parents, but also for the sights and smells of Calabria ... the cherries, the figs, the olives, the beans, the chickpeas, the hazelnuts, the gingerbread *biscotti*, the *cavaluzzi* (horses made out of provolone cheese). And then there were the annual rituals of the countryside such as the fair at Taverna, the largest in the area, and the winter slaughter of the pig, a family occasion when every single part was used to make something for the table, from *sopressata* to *stinco*, from *salsicce* to *zampone*. And the festivals ... America celebrated Thanksgiving but only Italy had Befana (5-6 January) and Ferragosto (14-15 August). Dora and her family still keep up the tradition of Befana when an old, witch-like, woman on a broomstick delivers presents to the children.

But the Cubello family initiated their own traditions and every summer Saturday and Sunday they and their Calabrian family and friends headed for Orchard Beach. Whoever got there first saved space for the others to transform this place into a little oasis for those from in and around Fossato Serralto. They relaxed, ate and talked until the sun went down and it was

Dinner at the family's Fulton Avenue apartment not long after they arrived in the States. From left to right: aunt Betty, her adopted daughter Violetta, uncle Johnny, the Cubello family (Giuseppe, Dora, Luigi and Vilma) and aunt Helen, uncle Johnny's wife. Uncle Sam, aunt Betty's husband, took the photo.

time to head back to Fulton Avenue. For Luigi and Dora the weekends at Orchard Beach evoke childhood memories they have never forgotten, will never forget. Luigi says he could write a book about those wonderful warm summers at Orchard Beach when all seemed right with the world.

Vilma continued to work at Pappagallo to support the family while Giuseppe fought to regain his health. Luigi recalls how this frustrated his father, a proud man, a man with ambition, a man with a sense of humor, a man the Italians would call *simpatico*. He would make toys for his children ... small wooden chairs for Dora's dolls, wooden wagons for Luigi and little cardboard houses for *il presepio*, the traditional Christmas village next to the Christmas tree.

Giuseppe's health was improving. He went to school to learn English. He looked after his children and prepared the evening meal, anything he could do to ease the burden on Vilma and to help make ends meet. With Vilma making all the children's clothes, the Cubellos were a self-sufficient family; they weren't prosperous but they wanted for nothing.

On his own, in the basement of their five-story walk-up, lived George, the building's janitor, a black American without a tooth in his head. But every Christmas the Cubello family had always enough to give George a meal to thank him for his services. Luigi saw his parents' kindness to, and respect for, George as something that they brought with them from Calabria. In recognizing his need, they were reminded of their own and passed on to George the respect and compassion that had been shown to them in both Calabria and America.

•

By the end of 1960 Giuseppe was well enough to work and had found a job in a local photographic lab; at the kitchen table he talked excitedly about the future and how much better things were going to be for the family. That Christmas Babbo Natale excelled himself and Dora and Luigi had more toys and presents than ever before. It was the best Christmas that Luigi can ever remember.

Five years and two days after he set foot in America, on 25 April 1961, Giuseppe Cubello died; Luigi was seven, Dora was twelve.

Over an extended lunch, a Calabrian lunch prepared by Luigi with some wonderful mixed peppers as I recall, we talked about the years after Giuseppe's death and how Vilma soon got back on her feet and forged ahead, focused on her family. She could have returned to Italy but knew that her children would have a better chance of prospering in America; she could have gone on welfare, but that was not her way.

Her way was to work hard for her family and to do everything she could to finish what she and Giuseppe had started ... there she was, this remarkable woman, sitting across the table from me, the embodiment of the same strength and courage she had shown back then when she sat her two children down and told them that without their father they would all have to pull together. Of course family and friends helped but Vilma was clearly no ordinary woman.

She took American citizenship but she never forgot her family back in Fossato Serralto and regularly sent packages and money back to them. The packages, usually containing Camels (cigarettes) and coffee, Vilma covered in material and hand-stitched it all together so that it was completely encased and secure.

A family photo in Crotona Park taken in the late 50s by which time Giuseppe was in better health; also in the photo is aunt Betty's daughter Violetta (front left). The road top right is Crotona Park Avenue which runs parallel to Fulton Avenue.

The family continued to spend summer weekends at Orchard Beach and also spent two weeks every summer upstate with uncle Giuseppe and his family in Albany. Once too they went for a four-day trip to Washington DC where they visited the grave of President Kennedy.

Kennedy was the family's first real president and like many other American homes there was a photo of Kennedy and wife, Jackie, on their living room wall. For the Cubello family *their* President was charismatic, authoritative and strong.

For Luigi the international events of 1961 and 1962, the Bay of Pigs affair and the Cuban Missile Crisis, were diversions that helped take his mind off the loss of his father. But already he had a sense of country and, even at nine, was feeling sufficiently patriotic that he wanted to fight for it. He had another distraction at this time—the new wave of music that filtered across the Atlantic and in particular The Beatles.

On 22 November 1963, Luigi was in the third grade, That afternoon on his way home from school he and some friends climbed up on the exposed bedrock behind their apartment ... it was here he was playing when he heard that his President had been shot. Like everyone else the family watched the subsequent events play out on television, the murder of Lee Harvey Oswald and Kennedy's funeral.

Other traumatic events shaped his sense of being an American, the assassinations of Martin Luther King and Bobby Kennedy. Like me Luigi felt the loss of Bobby Kennedy even more than his brother but King's death had a more immediate impact on Luigi's life ... they lived in an integrated neighborhood and he felt both a sense of shame and a sense of loss as he walked to school the following day.

It was seven years after the death of their father that Luigi and Dora returned to their Calabrian homeland for the first time; Luigi was fourteen and Dora nineteen. It was the same year that Pappagallo, based on the corner of 5th Avenue and 17th Street, not far from the Flatiron and Union Square, was bought out by the US Shoe Corporation. Listening to this story of their trip I was even more in awe of what Vilma had achieved in just twelve American years.

In 1968, when Vilma and her two children flew from JFK to Rome, they had two itineraries.

The first took them to Fossato Serralto where they visited the families and friends they had last seen a dozen years before. Naturally they

November 2012: Vilma Dornetti, Luigi Cubello and Dora Cubello-Villani

were welcomed with open arms and shown the sort of unconditional generosity and infinite Calabrian kindnesses that Vilma, Luigi and Dora were showing me that very day. But most of all the young, impressionable Luigi was aware of the freshness of the air and the blueness of the sky, that deep Calabrian blue which deserves to be a color in its own right ... there's Prussian blue, so why not Calabrian blue? And the night sky ... crystal clear, a canopy of bright stars overseeing the silence ... alluring and compelling but, above all, Calabrian.

Beneath both the deep blue and the crystal clear, Luigi said he felt at home. All his parents' stories and recollections of their homeland suddenly made sense and he began to understand what made him, Luigi Cubello, who he was: a Calabrian who lived in America; an American with deep roots in Calabria.

Itinerary number two was to visit all those iconic Italian places that, had the family remained in Fossato Serralto, they may never have seen. With their Europass train tickets they travelled to Naples, Pompeii, Rome, Florence, Venice and Turin and even visited Belgium, where Vilma's sister lived, before returning to Rome en route to their home in New York.

When Vilma, Dora and Luigi told me this story I was even more in awe of what this strong, diminutive woman achieved in such a short time, of how, after just twelve difficult years in America, she had the physical and emotional resolve to travel between and across continents with her two children. And, of course, she could also afford it.

It probably took something more than mere resolve to leave Fossato Serralto for the second time ... *and* without a husband. I wished I had asked her about that.

After the relocation of Pappagallo, Vilma got six months temporary work at a local hospital and when her time was up was asked to stay on.

Her children grew up and went to college; Dora became a teacher, Luigi a civil servant. Both have long since flown the nest.

All three know that, as a family, they did the right thing in coming to America. They are humble and proud of their achievements and despite the hardships they endured, particularly the loss of their father, they have negotiated the twists and turns of life and become, like many before and since, Italian Americans. As Dora put it: "We are proud Italians and proud of what Italians have contributed to this country."

And for both Luigi and Dora there is one important bonus—their mother is finally enjoying the fruits of her labor.

Despite his mother's half-hearted protests, Luigi likes to think of it like this: "My mother is not chasing too many goats lately ... but she does feed the slot machines in Atlantic City from time to time."

Ups and downs

An unseasonable nor'easter was dumping huge amounts of snow on New York and New Jersey as Luigi negotiated the Pelham traffic on our way back to the station ... thankfully the trains were till running and I was soon on my way back to Grand Central Terminal.

Grand Central was as elegant as ever; on the other hand its clientele looked the worse for wear. Those heading for their trains were shaking umbrellas, stamping the snow off shoes and boots, slapping hats and caps against coats, anything and everything to brush aside the unexpected change in the weather.

Those, like me, heading out into it did so with little relish. Some took a few minutes by the doors to psyche themselves up for the dash into windswept white wetness while others thought that if they stood there long enough it would go away; some, with time on their hands, turned back and headed for the nearest bar while others busied themselves improvising, with newspapers, briefcases and bags, some form of headgear.

I knew there was no escape and went straight out onto 42nd Street and ran through the snowstorm for four blocks to the M-line subway that would take me straight back down to Essex Street. Another few blocks of running and dodging sludgy puddles and inconsiderate driving got me back to the apartment in Clinton Street. I was wet and bedraggled, a sorry specimen ... must remember to take my hat next time, I thought.

Hélène on the other hand thought it was funny.

The evening before we had been impressed by what we saw of the bar food in Salt so decided that we'd cut out all that walking in the snow and pop next door to eat and drink. We arranged to rendezvous at seven-thirty which gave me time to check through my notes on the Cubello family.

Our final evening (Hélène was heading to Rhode Island the following day) went well apart from the strange local man who seemed to spend much of his time trying to offend the incredibly tolerant bartender in some way, while befriending us and ignoring the woman he had come with and all at the same time and almost in the same breath. He confided in me, though I've no idea why, that he had just been awarded several million dollars in compensation for a motor cycle accident that had left him with a limp. I was going to ask the obvious question, "A limp what ...?" but thought better of it. (I subsequently found out from someone else that his claim to be a limp millionaire was in fact true.)

Anyway, Hélène and I were more intent on trying to empty the jar of sangria and left him to his own devices ... and his millions.

The next morning Hélène left for Penn Station and Rhode Island and I did some more work on my notes before heading uptown again to see if I could find a cover for my iPhone. That turned out to be a fruitless task as my phone was now regarded as almost archaic—not being the latest model, meant that all such accessories had been already consigned to the scrap heap ... or eBay as it's sometimes called. Just before five-thirty I set off for my six o'clock Chinatown rendezvous with Luigi, Katrina, Grace and an unknown friend.

The plan was to catch the J-line train from Essex Street to Canal Street from where it was a short walk to the Thaison restaurant in Baxter Street. Well, it would have been had I not instead gotten on the J-line train going in the opposite direction, across the river to Brooklyn ... it felt like the longest station-to-station journey on the New York subway system, even if most of it was *above* ground.

Running and checking my watch simultaneously, I exited down the stairs at Marcy Avenue station, dodged the early evening traffic as I shot across the road, ran up the stairs on the other side and leapt onto the train heading back to Manhattan and Canal Street just as the doors were closing.

I arrived at Canal Street at one minute to six and, as ever, found it confusing when I got to street level because I'm seldom sure which side of the road I'm going to end up on. I ran across what I assumed to be Canal Street and accosted a woman in the middle of the road, "Excuse me, do you know where Baxter Street is?" I asked breathlessly.

Instead of answering, she threw her arms round me and gave me a hug. ... I thought my luck had changed until I saw, out of the corner of my eye, a Kiwi Chinese woman I recognized laughing uncontrollably in the background. My hugger was Katrina ... out of the context of Santa Severina, where we'd last met, I simply didn't recognize her inside that woolly hat. The laughing Kiwi Chinese woman was Grace; the confused woman next to her was Katrina's friend, another New Zealander, Raewyn. The impatient cars horns brought us back to reality and I was formally introduced to Raewyn when we had regained the safely of the sidewalk ... on the corner of Baxter Street. Two minutes later we were explaining it all again to a bewildered Luigi who had already arrived at the restaurant.

After our meal we finished off the evening by visiting an Italian *pasticceria* in what was left of the area of Manhattan known as Little Italy.

By chance some years ago Kay and I were in this very area, the epicenter of which is Mulberry Street, at the time of September's Feast of San Gennaro, the largest Italian festival of the year. Even then it was apparently a shadow of its former self for, in recent years, the area had gradually become more Chinese and less Italian. As the more-established Italian community had done well for itself and moved out to Queens, Brooklyn, Staten Island and the Bronx, so a newer wave of immigrants, largely Chinese, moved in and now inhabited much of the same area.

The balance had subtly shifted which was why we could enjoy a Vietnamese dinner one minute and tuck into some delicious Italian pastries the next. Over our sweet indulgences we discovered that everyone except Luigi had the same plans for the following morning. It was my last day in New York before transferring across the Hudson to New Jersey and I wanted to walk the High Line; Katrina, Grace and Raewyn had exactly the same plan in mind so we arranged to meet at eleven at its northern extremity at 30th Street off 10th Avenue.

(The High Line is a disused, elevated rail track that, instead of being demolished, as was the original plan back in the eighties and nineties, has been revamped as a linear park, the park in the sky. It was such an unusual concept in an otherwise urban landscape that I was keen to take a look.)

·

It was still early when I returned to Clinton Street—this time without the extra trip across to Brooklyn—more than enough time to say my farewells to my friends at both Salt and the Cocoa Bar. It was past midnight when I eventually staggered back into my apartment ... at the time I wondered whether I'd ever make it to the High Line the following morning.

I even forgot to do anything about an email from AirBnb that I'd picked up earlier in the day which threw up something I hadn't been expecting. AirBnb were reminding me about my *second* booking in New Jersey starting on November 13—I was moving there the following afternoon, staying just one night (but leaving my suitcase) and then returning, or so I thought, on Monday November 12 after my trip to Albuquerque.

I was too tired to think about it ... I decided to sort it when I got to New Jersey and, if necessary, book the 'missing' night somewhere in the Newark area.

·

The High Line began life as a low, street-level, railway running along

10th Avenue but, as non-railway traffic increased in the early twentieth century, so did the number of accidents and deaths associated with the intermingling of road and rail. It became so bad that 10th became know as Death Avenue and safety considerations eventually saw the introduction of so-called West Side Cowboys who rode in front of the trains waving a red flag ... clearly not the most economic way to run a railway. Thus the High Line was conceived to carry the railway *above* ground, mid-block and parallel to 10th Avenue and away from street-level traffic and the associated chaos.

It opened to trains in 1934 and connected directly to factories and warehouses along its route. But within a mere twenty years transportation by road was already on the ascendency and, correspondingly, the High Line's *raison d'être* was fast declining. In the sixties the southernmost section was demolished and the last train ran through the Meatpacking District in 1980 ... its cargo, three carloads of frozen turkeys.

To the powers-that-be the idea of a linear park above street level initially seemed a pie-in-the-sky notion but a decade of persistence and patience paid dividends and in June 2009 the first section opened to the public. A second section was inaugurated two years later and a much shorter third and final section at the northern end should open in 2013. It goes without saying that it has been a great success and the High Line is already a major New York tourist attraction.

The walk from the subway on 6th Avenue across to 10th was almost uneventful ... but I could not help raising a chuckle as I photographed a huge billboard on the side of a building that, only two days after the presidential election, was using Mitt Romney's defeat as an advertising opportunity. I wondered had there been another version on standby with a different name in the frame?

Despite there being more than a nip in the air, the High Line was busy as tourists from almost every corner of the globe took advantage of this free and unusual view of Manhattan one way and across the Hudson to New Jersey the other. Being November, the horticultural aspect was less bounteous with color than it would have been in the spring and summer, nevertheless with a little imagination it wasn't difficult to picture what a glorious place this could be ... perhaps having seen the photos on the website helped.

There were five of us as another friend of Katrina's joined us, an Irish-American woman, Genie, who was more knowledgeable than most about the High Line and its environs.

The High Line runs for almost twenty blocks from 30th Street to Gansevoort Street, one block below 12th Street; between 17th and 16th Street, it crosses 10th Avenue. The area south and west of here (as far as the Hudson river) roughly corresponds to what was called the Meatpacking District which, in its heyday, boasted some 250 slaughterhouses and packing plants. These days you are more likely to stumble across a stylish, high-end, boutique.

But the High Line is stylish too ... to complement the planting there is a creative blend of the old and the new, both in its use of wood, steel and concrete and the way these make something that is essentially linear into a walkway which has curves, corners and character. There are small pockets where the past speaks for itself, there is an abundance of public art and interpretation boards aplenty for those hungry for more information. For those simply hungry there is an excess of seating in addition to exit points where, down a few steps, there is always something to whet the appetite.

Our whetting of choice was at 16th Street where we headed into Chelsea Market, the former home of the New York Biscuit Company. Here you can eat almost anything and buy speciality ingredients from practically every corner of the world. There are a few clothes shops and the odd outpost for

household goods but basically Chelsea Market is about food and eating ... all plans I had for picking up a small suitcase for my flight to Albuquerque the next day were dashed.

Nor is it a market where you can buy all types of fresh produce ... there is some, but this is a not a place for prodding the fruit and vegetables and bartering with the vendor. Indeed the only prodding in evidence was when I inadvertently assumed that the man walking past me with a selection of fine looking *crostini* on a platter was offering free samples ... he prodded me when I tried to take one and told me in no uncertain terms that I was not part of the group who had paid to partake in a tasting tour of the market.

Apart from these exclusive *crostini*, the eating choice was amazingly varied and, being fleet of foot, we were fortunate enough to commandeer a table for five without causing an international incident; we then took it in turns to steadfastly guard the chairs and seek out the cuisine of our choice.

This was November, and a pretty cold November day at that, so the mind boggles at what this place might be like in the height of summer ... if I'm ever back this way then, I'll have to remember to bring my own chair.

Back on the High Line, we paused for a photo-shoot before descending to street level a few blocks later, literally at the end of the line.

The High Line I loved: brilliant idea, tastefully and robustly executed ... and free. Chelsea Market left me ambivalent, I found it both compelling and irritating—compelling because I'm a sucker for all those different food options and irritating because that's how contrived authenticity and rusticity, combined with inflated prices, makes me feel. That said, it would be hard not to visit one without the other.

I wanted to get back to my Clinton Street apartment no later than three-thirty in the hope that I could finish off my packing and be on my way across to New Jersey before the Friday evening rush hour. So, back at street level, I asked Katrina to point me in the direction of the nearest subway station but she went one better, she led me/us there and en route we passed along Bleeker Street where there was still much evidence of the Italian community who settled here before the Mulberry Street incarnation of Little Italy. This was, if you like, Older Little Italy, part of the less well-known West Village.

There were a couple of excellent Italian delis along Bleeker, one of which, Faicco's Italian Specialities, had served the local Italian community since

1900 from its first incarnation on nearby West Houston Street; it moved to Bleeker in the fifties and now serves a more cosmopolitan clientele. Noses-against-the-window was simply not enough and we had to venture across the threshold. For me Faicco's was better than anything Chelsea Market had to offer, indeed as good an Italian deli as I have ever seen.

A little bit further on, we passed John's of Bleeker Street, an award-winning Italian pizzeria that's occupied the same site since 1929 ... the clue to their success is their simple message, "no slices, no reservations, cash only, dine in or take out" ... and, I imagine, pretty good pizzas too.

•

We said our good-byes at Washington Square on 6th Avenue and I headed underground and back to Clinton Street ... I was tired and paying the price for my late night bar crawl there.

The plan was simple: finish off packing; head out onto East Houston Street to pick up a cab to take me to World Trade Center; catch the Path train under the Hudson to Grove Street; finally a short walk to my new 'digs' in Wayne Street ... I guessed around forty-five minutes in total. That, I surmised, would give me time to find somewhere local to buy a small suitcase and a towel, the latter being one of the Wayne Street apartment's house rules. Everything that could go wrong, did go wrong ...

The first part went well—by four o'clock I had manhandled my large case down from the fifth floor and was wheeling it along Clinton Street in search of a cab. I turned onto Houston, crossed the road and began hailing cabs in earnest; it started to drizzle. It took twenty minutes before I was able to say "World Trade Center Path station, please." Still, the rain had stopped.

I paid the cabbie and walked across to the station to be met by two security guards who told me it was closed ... no Path trains would be running to New Jersey for at least another week, maybe longer. The station, it seemed, had been swamped by Hurricane Sandy. Now, I knew that World Trade Center station had been closed but the day before I had overheard two people say it had re-opened. And, besides, my cabbie hadn't said anything about it still being closed when he clearly knew that I was going there to catch a train. I was told that the nearest operating stations were Christopher Street or 9th Street. Walking and dragging, I headed for the nearest main thoroughfare and hailed another cab.

The Path runs north-south under Sixth Avenue which is what I discovered when my second cabbie dropped me by the 9th Street station and explained that one entrance was on one side of Sixth Avenue, the other on the opposite side ... there were no connecting underground links between the stations.

I manhandled my suitcase down to the platform, stopping on the way to buy a ticket from the self-service machine. Just before going through the barrier I checked my route again and I realized I was on the wrong platform ... so I hauled my suitcase back up to street level, crossed Sixth Avenue and descended to the other platform and went through the barrier. I still wasn't absolutely sure about this being the right platform so asked a woman whether the approaching train would take me to New Jersey ... she shook her head knowingly and said I needed the other platform.

I returned to street level, crossed Sixth Avenue yet again and had to buy another ticket as I'd 'used' the first one when I went through the barrier and on to the platform. My suitcase was getting heavier; my arms wearier. But at long last I was on a train.

When the guard announced that the next station was 14th Street, I didn't really take it in but when she said that the one after that was 23rd Street, I began to take notice. I asked the man next to me whether I was heading to New Jersey or Uptown Manhattan ... even before he answered I knew what he was going to say.

Basically I'd spent the previous hour *increasing* the distance between me and my goal, Jersey City, instead of the other way round.

Back at street level at 23rd Street, I crossed Sixth Avenue for what I hoped would be the last time. The Friday afternoon rush-hour had begun in earnest as I descended onto the southbound platform having, of course, bought yet another ticket. To say I was exhausted would be an understatement.

Finally, just before six in the evening, I climbed my last flight of subway stairs and plunked my suitcase on New Jersey soil for the first time. I extended its handle, got my bearings, and, with leaden limbs, set off in search of Wayne Street.

Four blocks and four floors later, I finally laid my suitcase to rest ... it seemed as if a lifetime had passed since I was walking along the High Line in the weak November sun earlier that same day.

•

Less than an hour later, armed with a twenty-percent discount voucher for Bed, Bathroom and Beyond, courtesy of Sherrie my host, I returned to and walked past Grove Street station and then headed off along Marin Boulevard for another six blocks into the unknown in search of a suitcase and a towel. Sherrie had also given me the number of a cab company to book my early-morning ride to Newark Liberty Airport. I called the cab company as I walked along Marin but hit an unexpected snag when the receptionist asked me for my phone number. My mind went blank, it was as if she'd asked me to count from a hundred backwards in Russian.

I explained about the new phone and said I'd call her back. I knew I should be able to find my number but decided that, at that particular moment, I just couldn't get my head round it. Besides, I had another plan.

At the BB&B check-out, I asked the pubescent young man taking my money if I could borrow his pen. He handed me the pen and I handed him my phone. This is the deal, I said ... you find my number for me, I write it down, you give me my phone back, I give you back your pen ... and then I pay for the suitcase and towel. All transactions successfully completed, I shook his hand and thanked him for his techno-savey youth. I booked my cab.

By eight I was back in Wayne Street, having earmarked en route a nearby Thai restaurant where I thought I might eat. With Sherrie's advice, I ate instead at the Saigon Café, a five minute walk away and, according to her, by far the best place to eat in the area.

Sherrie was right and that evening, I unwittingly embarked upon a relationship with a wonderful Vietnamese family, with parents Danny and Kim and their children Steve and Karen, their exquisite cuisine, their excellent Pinot Noir and their friendly customers.

•

Before finally passing out that night I did remember to ask Sherrie about my booking for November 12 or 13; she confirmed that I was booked from November 13 to 26 and that there was someone else staying on November 12. Somehow I had missed booking any accommodation for the night of November 12, the night I would return from Albuquerque. When I told her I'd probably find somewhere in Newark for that night, she advised against it ... she didn't actually say that Newark was like the dark side of the moon but that was the impression she gave.

I didn't know it at the time, but there would be moments to come when I would look back on that conversation and regret the fact that I hadn't listened to Sherrie's advice.

My first contact with the family of my friend Bruno Cortese in Albuquerque, New Mexico did not get an immediate response.

I found out why later from Bruno's brother Maurizio—quite rightly, Mary De Luca and Jim Goodman had contacted him to check out that I was who I said I was.

When Mary replied it was to confirm they were happy for me to visit them and talk about her Calabrian and Cortese connections so I booked my flights and accommodation for two nights.

A few days later another family member from Albuquerque, Tañia Triolo, emailed me and insisted that I stay instead with her and husband Adam.

The arrangement was that Mary would pick me up at the airport, I would eat with her family and then they would drop me off at Tañia's.

The following day, Sunday, there would be a family gathering at Tañia's house when everyone would bring their 'Cortese' photos, documents, memories and questions.

A tale of three families

My flights from Newark to Dallas-Fort Worth and on to Albuquerque arrived on schedule ... they were a revelation only in that I discovered it was clearly possible to pay for and use Wi-Fi mid-flight, despite all the scare stories that some airlines were wont to put about. Ignoring Sherrie's advice, I finally booked my accommodation in Newark for November 12 from somewhere over Tennessee.

Mary and her daughter Monica picked me up at the airport and took me on a whistle-stop tour of Albuquerque. Mary explained that she had booked a table for us at five-thirty at a local restaurant, Antiquity, where we would be joined by husband Jim and Monica's twin, David. After eating they would drop me off with Tañia and Adam.

Our first stop was the house where Bruno Cortese, the grandfather of my friend in Santa Severina of the same name, had lived.

Through a chance encounter in Santa Severina a few weeks earlier with one Judge James Parker and his wife Janice, both from Albuquerque, I already knew that in the early twentieth century there had been significant Italian immigration to the town, mainly from northern Italy and in particular the area around Lucca.

There was always work to be had on the railroad and many Italian immigrants received their first American paycheck from the Atchison, Topeka and Santa Fe Railroad. The railroad was, for many, a means to an end, a way of making good money fast and being able to save some for the future ... a concept almost unheard of in their native Italy at the time.

But it was not to work on the railway that Bruno Cortese came to Albuquerque. Mary explained how it was that Bruno, who emigrated in 1912, settled in Elkhart in northern Indiana where his cousin Francesco lived, married Louise Fortino in 1916, then ended up in Albuquerque, New Mexico.

Louise was born in Albion, Michigan; her father was Italian, possibly Calabrese for Fortino was a common name in the Cosenza area, but her mother was born in Philadelphia, the illicit love-child of a German woman and a married Italian man who had initially emigrated without his family.

Bruno was twenty-eight and Louise seventeen when she became pregnant and there was, apparently, some early opposition to the idea of marriage—possibly because of the age difference. So they eloped ... but only as far as the local Episcopal church where, despite the fact that they were both Catholic, they married.

The home of Bruno Cortese and his second wife, Angela Parisi, on 11th Street NW Albuquerque. Bruno still lived there at the time of his death in 1980 at the age of 91. He bought the property in 1929 with a bank loan of $2000.

Four years later Louise came down with the third, and least deadly, wave of the pandemic Spanish Flu and then contracted tuberculosis. It was well-known that wall-to-wall sun and a high, dry climate could alleviate the condition, hence the family's move to mile-high Albuquerque in 1921 with their two children, Anthony and Mary's mother, Elizabeth.

Indeed many people came to Albuquerque around this time for the same reason and a significant part of the town's growth and economy was fueled by this 'health' industry. There were a number of clinics specializing in treating the condition along Central Avenue which was even given the nicknames 'Lungers Avenue' and 'Tuberculosis Row'.

The following year Louise eventually succumbed to the illness and died in the town's Southwest Presbyterian Sanatorium a year later. In thoughtful mode we drove past its current incarnation, Albuquerque's Presbyterian Hospital ... Louise Fortino was of course Mary's grandmother and nineteen year-old Monica's great-grandmother.

En route from the Hospital to the University of New Mexico I noticed from the roadside signage that Central Avenue had another claim to fame as part of the iconic Route 66 that ran between Chicago and Los Angeles—then as now, Route 66 is an important part of American culture and history.

As we drove round the University campus where Monica's twin, David, is a student, we talked more about Mary's grandfather and how he actually emigrated to America twice, once in 1906 at the age of eighteen and then again six years later in 1912 when he settled in Elkhart, worked as a cobbler, and married Louise.

In 1905 Bruno's older brother Vincenzo was the first to emigrate and settled in Buffalo in upstate New York. Unusually, when Bruno emigrated the following year, he went instead to Brooklyn in New York where his uncle Giuseppe Rizza lived in Box Street. Bruno may well have gone to Buffalo at some stage as the family memory has it but, by the time he returned to Calabria in 1910, he had settled in Cicero, a suburb of Chicago with a large Italian community many of whom found employment at Western Electric.

It seems that Bruno's first emigration in 1906 was not part of his or his family's plan but rather was prompted by pressure to marry emanating from the family of a woman with whom he had become romantically

The young Bruno Cortese and later with his first wife Louise and their two children.

Bruno and Louisa's children, Anthony and Elizabeth, just before they went to Italy in 1924.
Bruno with his second wife, Angelina Parisi.

involved ... essentially he left Calabria abruptly and surreptitiously to escape the possibility of being rushed into a marriage he didn't want.

Exactly what prompted him to return to Italy in 1910 is not known ... perhaps he had received word that he no longer had to worry about marriage, that the woman in his past life was now spoken for.

Likewise, what prompted his return to the States in 1912 remains a mystery though more often than not the economic realities of life in Calabria were the catalyst and Bruno of course had had a taste of life on the other side of the Atlantic.

Following the death of Louise, Bruno continued to make a good living in Albuquerque as a cobbler but then decided to return to Calabria, initially to the family's home town of Mesoraca, with his two children, Elizabeth and Anthony. This was 1924 and Bruno was already an American citizen himself, as of course were the children, so the fact that he soon remarried (in August that year) and later returned to America would suggest that he came back to Calabria with the sole purpose of finding himself a Calabrian bride and a stepmother for the children.

•

We took a break from family history to take in instead the delights of Abuquerque's old town on foot.

Historic Albuquerque is noted for its low-rise, Pueblo-Spanish style adobe architecture, a style that was reflected in many of the newer buildings in and around the University. The dominant terracottas and contrasting chalk blues, the gentle curves and the basic contours, the fact that you can see the sky without having to look up, together give Old Town a unique ambience. It was like stepping into a Western movie set without the horses ... indeed later when I saw some photos of the town as it was around 1920, it reminded me exactly of the stereotypical American Western and I wondered how the Cortese family viewed it back than. Perhaps they hadn't seen as many Westerns as I had.

Overseen by the town's oldest building, the San Felipe de Neri Church, what used to be homes, stores and offices had become restaurants, cafés, galleries, bookshops, boutiques and craft shops as Old Town has become a tourist attraction, albeit one that, it seemed to me, had retained its dignity and was also a place where native Albuquerqueans still liked to shop.

It was getting cold and so we adjourned to the Antiquity Restaurant where we met up with Mary's husband Jim and their son David and where, as I was increasingly getting accustomed to, I was the one on the spot and having to explain why and how I had ended up in Calabria. Not that I minded of course.

As we ate, we put the Cortese family to rest for a while and talked instead about the recent presidential election and American politics in general ... for David this was his subject of choice and I looked on in amazement, fascinated at how someone so young could speak so eloquently and with such confidence and at such speed about the intricacies of the body politic.

When I was first introduced to Monica back at the airport, I had made some reference to the time she spent in my home town at Belfast's Queens University ... she didn't really respond so, ever-persistent, I brought it up again. Even as the words were tripping off my tongue the puzzled expressions on everyone's faces were telling me that I was barking up the wrong tree and I had to explain myself ... I had gotten Mary's two children mixed up with the two children of Maria Cavaliere whom I was meeting in two week's time in Pennsylvania.

After a magnificent dinner Mary drove me to 'cousin' Tañia's house close to the Rio Grande in Los Ranchos, a northwestern suburb of Albuquerque where I would be staying for two nights. Mary warned me that the house was palatial ... but I coped.

Bruno Cortese crossed the Atlantic in 1906 aboard the *Moltke*. The ship accommodated 2,102 passengers—333 first-class, 169 second-class and 1,600 third-class. The German-owned ship was seized by the Italian government in 1915 and renamed *Pesaro*.

•

The rest of the evening I spent sitting at a well-stocked bar with glass after glass of excellent red wine and great company. The bartender, Tañia, was sitting cross-legged on the worktop behind the bar counter, her husband, Adam, was on a bar stool next to me and the setting was their huge living room. I felt completely at home.

After we had dispensed with the obligatory and-how-did-you-and-Kay-end-up-in-Calabria question, I began to come to grips with where exactly Tañia fitted in to the Cortese family history. It was really quite simple: like Mary, Tañia was a direct descendant of Bruno Cortese—Mary through his first wife, Louise, and Tañia through his second wife, Angelina (Angela) Parisi, from Sant'Eufemia (part of today's Lamezia Terme), whom he married in 1924. Tañia and Mary had different grandmothers, but the same grandfather, Bruno Cortese.

We finished the evening talking about the family mystery, the part of this story that has puzzled both sides of the Cortese family in the current generations: the fact that, when Bruno returned to America after his second marriage, he left Anthony behind. He and Angela arrived back in America with Elizabeth only and Anthony never saw his father again.

This story and its ramifications was one I wanted to pursue the next day when we would be joined by many other family members including the descendants of Bruno's brother Vincenzo and in particular his grandson Joe Smith who, Tañia and Adam agreed, was the font of all knowledge when it came to Cortese family history.

We talked too about the uncompromising courage of people like Vincenzo and Bruno who made the trip across the Atlantic in conditions that would be considered primitive and squalid these days.

But even getting as far as the ship presented its own problems: raising the money for the ticket (usually $30), and having the requisite $25 in cash upon entering America; deciding which family member should go first (assuming the plan was for more of the family to follow); getting to the port and than waiting for the ship ... the concept of train and ship timetables dovetailing in some way had not yet crossed anyone's mind.

Vincenzo, the oldest Cortese son, traveled in 1905; his brother followed the next year. Both would have found their way to the station at Sant'Eufemia on the Tyrennian coast by whatever means possible ... it was not unknown for people to walk. From Sant'Eufemia they traveled for a day by train to Naples, the usual port of embarkation for southern Italians. Then they had to answer twenty-nine basic questions (their answers were recorded on the ship's manifest which forms the basis of today's archive at Ellis Island) before being disinfected and vaccinated prior to embarkation.

We knew that Vincenzo and Bruno traveled to America third class, steerage, the lowest of the low both socially and geographically within the bowels of the ship's stern. Those, like Bruno, who came back to Italy and returned to the States often only traveled steerage the first time ... perhaps they had already become American citizens or had put enough money by to return in better style. On the other hand Bruno travelled steerage both times which would suggest that, initially at least, he wasn't intending to

Immigrants on board ship; c1905.

return. Perhaps employment conditions in southern Calabria deteriorated further and he felt America was the lesser of two evils ... perhaps he fell foul of another family wanting his hand in marriage.

Of course he could just have liked traveling steerage though from some of the descriptions of this it was never an easy passage and unlikely that anyone would want to travel that way by choice. There were horror stories aplenty going back to the wave of Irish immigration in the 1850s when at least ten percent never made it to the new world of their dreams.

By the early twentieth century things were slowly improving, nevertheless immigrants talked of dimly-lit, cramped, foul-smelling, unsanitary living conditions with food scarcely fit for human consumption; many, it is said, just huddled up in their berths for most of the voyage, their only diversion a game of cards, occasional musical interludes, endless talking about times past and future hopes and, inevitably, rehearsing their answers to the questions they could expect from the Immigration Officers on Ellis Island.

This nightmare journey—which, depending on the ship itself and the weather, could take anything between nine days and a month—Bruno Cortese did twice. Fortunately for Bruno on both his crossings, on the *Moltke* and the *Sant'Anna*, steerage wasn't full to capacity.

Twice he arrived in New York physically, mentally and emotionally exhausted; twice he was scrutinized by the Medical Inspectors; twice he waited for and boarded the small ferry that shuttled immigrants from their ship to Ellis Island, twice he lined up for a more circumspect medical examination by a doctor and twice his paperwork and health were deemed to be in order and he was admitted to the United States of America.

Eighty percent of those who went through Ellis Island did so without a hitch; the remainder were detained for further medical checks or paperwork discrepancies and of these ninety percent eventually got their landing cards. Overall only two percent were refused admission.

•

In the morning I found Adam in the kitchen browsing the internet to learn how to make coffee using the classic Italian coffee maker that Bruno Cortese's daughter Maria Antoinetta had brought them some years before. This was all for my benefit as he realized, rightly, that I would be used to the real thing and not the American freeze-dried granules that are as close to coffee as a dehydrated Subway egg is to what a hen lays. Together we made a proper cup of coffee, the second real cup of coffee I'd had since leaving Calabria. (For the record, the first real coffee was in a wonderful little café in Clinton Street, Manhattan that I only discovered on my last day there.)

All those tentative plans we discussed the night before of doing a little sightseeing in the countryside around Albuquerque flew out the window and we went out instead for a late Sunday breakfast/early lunch, almost an American institution these days. Over brunch I discovered that the afternoon's family gathering might include up to twenty people and could see that this could be problematic. Adam came up with a neat solution and gave Joe Smith a call and asked him to come over an hour earlier than the others so that we could have a more constructive one-to-one chat.

·

One of the things I wanted to know was how and when the Mesoraca/Sant'Eufemia (Bruno and Angelina) connection with the Cortese family in Calabria became the Santa Severina connection and how this may or may not tie in with why Antonio was left in Calabria and who raised him.

Joe Smith threw some light on who brought Antonio up, it was his Aunt Teresina Cortese, his father's sister, but could not help with how it was that the adult Antonio is associated with Santa Severina.

Tañia found a letter from Bruno to Angelina in December 1923, a little over a year after the death of Louise, his first wife, which confirmed not only that he did indeed return to Calabria in search of a bride but also that he had his sights on Angelina and had already asked her father for his daughter's hand in marriage. This letter also made it clear that somewhere in this romantic chain of events Bruno's brother Vincenzo played an important role, in that he either already knew Angelina's family and/or acted as a go-between for Bruno.

Other letters written at the same time between the two families indicate that both were literate, well-educated families. Of course those who could write at this time wrote in Italian—the local dialects were more often spoken than written. Furthermore, from letters received from his solicitor in America around the same time, it is clear that Bruno already had an excellent understanding and command of English.

Another of these letters was from Angelina's parents to their prospective son-in-law just before Bruno left to come to Italy with his children—it was sent from Santa Severina.

When Mary arrived she had more information about those early years when her grandfather returned to America leaving Antonio behind. Mary's mother, Elizabeth, often spoke about those two years in Calabria and of a particular house where they sometimes stayed in lofty Altilia, one of three *frazione* of Santa Severina.

She described it as an idyllic place with a beautiful garden and horse trails, the *palazzo* of a baron who somehow was a friend of the family, possibly through another of Bruno's family, a priest also named Antonio, who seemed to be close to the baron. Ostensibly young Anthony was left behind so that he could be 'educated' by this uncle, the priest.

When Elizabeth returned to America, she had forgotten most of her English ... for some reason only the word 'bridge' stuck in her mind. In two years she had become used to speaking the local dialect and when she returned to America, recalled being teased by kids at school for speaking Italian which was why she never taught her own children the language.

When Bruno crossed the Atlantic for the third time with Angelina and Elizabeth in 1926, he didn't travel steerage; he was an American citizen and through his lawyer in Elkhart, Frank Treckelo, seems to have acquired all the appropriate documentation that guaranteed Angelina entry as a 'Preferred class' passenger. Also this was two years after Ellis Island closed as an Immigration Inspection Center, four years after Mussolini came to power in Italy ... in the twenty years since Bruno had made his first trip in steerage on the *Moltke*, his world had changed.

•

More people were arriving and the discussion turned to further speculation as to the real reason Anthony was left in Calabria ... some suggested it was because Angelina, Bruno's new wife, simply did not want him and that his sister Elizabeth, now nine, would be of more use around the house than her little brother. This was 1926 and a nine year-old Calabrian girl would have been expected to have a hands-on role when it came to household chores, particularly if she was the eldest.

Whatever the reason, neither Elizabeth nor Anthony ever forgot the day

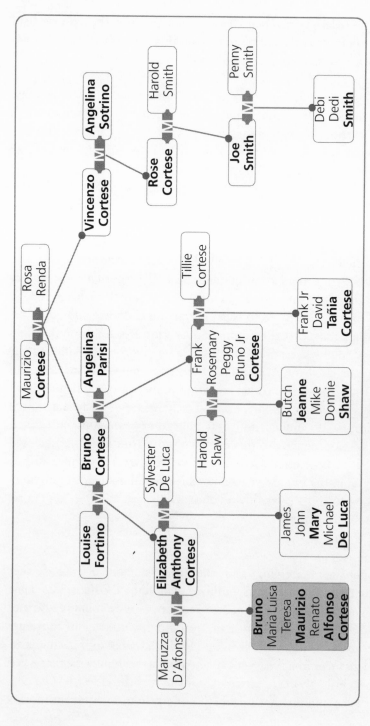

A skeletal version of the Cortese family tree starting from the parents of Bruno and Vincenzo Cortese.

The extant Calabrian part of Bruno Cortese's family, the children of Antonio Cortese, are in the shaded box on the right. The 'M' signifies a marriage and those listed below the dot are the siblings of that marriage who feature in this chapter; those in **bold** generally figure more in the story.

On the American side note that one of the first generation wives has already adopted the American custom of dropping her surname in favour of her husband's name—in Italy the wife always retains her surname while children take their father's name.

the family said its goodbyes. Mary told me how, in later life, both recalled how Anthony threw himself down on the ground weeping uncontrollably as his father, step-mother, and sister departed without him. For Elizabeth this same incident had an indelible and tragic effect on her ... she found the loss of her little brother almost unbearable and also the loss of aunt Teresina who had looked after them both so lovingly for two years. These events, together with the recent loss of her mother, significantly altered the course of her young life. Names changed too—in Italy Anthony became Antonio while in America Angelina became simply Angela.

Brother and sister grew up thousands of miles apart and only ever met once again when, in 1988, Mary and Jim took the seventy-one year-old Elizabeth to Santa Severina to visit her brother Antonio. Antonio died three years later, his sister, Mary's mother, outlived him by seven years.

My initial reaction to the story of these two children being separated in this way had been to see it in terms of Antonio being left behind in a less fulfilling environment while Elizabeth went to the land of opportunity, to a more rewarding life. Ironically, Mary sees it the other way round ... she has no doubt that it was Antonio who had a happier life in Italy than her mother did in America.

Still more people arrived: two of Joe Smith's daughters, Debi and Dedi and Dedi's husband Russ; Tañia's brother, David and wife Sue, her cousin Jeanne and husband Anthony Lovato, Mary's brother Mike and innumerable children. Tañia had decided to set apart a small study with a large table for all the photos and related documents that people brought. Not what I was expecting at all but great fun and people did actually discover things relating to both sides of the family that they hadn't previously known.

More than once I stepped back and watched this family, the family of my friend in Santa Severina, eagerly looking into their past and the people who through economic need and audacity had crossed from one continent to another in search of a new life. These people in this house in New Mexico, the personification of the different strands of the same family who came together that afternoon to eat, drink, talk and laugh with a total stranger, were *all* Americans, all second- and third-generation Americans.

To varying degrees they were interested in their Italian heritage but essentially they were Americans with family and roots in Calabria. The fact that they were in Albuquerque at all went back to just one small episode in the lives of a young Italian-American family ... back to the time when Louise Fortino caught Spanish Flu and then contracted tuberculosis.

Their Calabrian family they visited as often as they could—many of the people I met had been to Santa Severina, some several times; they had a connection with Santa Severina that was important to them ... as I looked round, I wondered would the next generation feel the same.

Only one family member from Santa Severina had been to Albuquerque, Bruno Cortese's daughter Maria Antoinietta who, unwittingly, made sure I had a proper cup of Italian coffee that morning.

I was mulling over these thoughts when Tañia handed me a letter written in a child's hand and asked me if I could translate it ... she said she thought it was from my friend Bruno Cortese to his grandfather of the same name, the grandfather he had never met.

The short letter was dated Christmas 1960 at which time Bruno was almost eight. It read as follows:

Dear Grandfather,
In this happy Christmas season my first thoughts are of you and I send you much affection even if I have never met you. My father has spoken of you often as we have with him. I would dearly love to meet you and my father has promised me that some day soon we will go together to America. I will write to you often and would like to thank you for the things you sent me. With lots of love and greetings to you, my grandmother and all my aunts and uncles in America.
Lots of love and kisses,
Your Bruno

For a short time there was silence in that small room in Albuquerque as everyone privy to that moment saw in their mind's eye that small child writing to the grandfather he had never met and expressing with such simplicity his fervent desire to come to America and meet him. We all knew how the story ended; despite the fact that his grandfather lived another twenty years, we all knew that it never happened.

Tañia found an envelope for the letter, wrote Bruno's name on it, handed it to me and charged me with taking it back to Santa Severina to return it to Bruno with a simple message ... please, please come and see us.

It was an emotional moment; and it remains so.

•

A photo of a bar brought the conversation round to the Prohibition era (1920 to 1933) when Bruno Cortese, like many other Americans, dabbled in the noble art of do-it-yourself alcohol or, as the law-makers liked to think of it at the time, they dealt in illicit liquor. The story goes that Bruno was a maker and repairer of fine footwear during the day at his shoe-shop on 2nd Street but a maker of fine whiskey in his basement at other times. Unfortunately the local law found out and his basement was raided. Just like in the movies, the barrels were manhandled up into the street and the police ceremoniously smashed them up and watched as all that hard work literally went down the drain.

Meanwhile, so the story goes, brother Vincenzo was up in Santa Fe making and distributing beer; in the parlance of the time, he was a bootlegger.

There was another story, typical of the times, that several family members recalled. It involved 'somebody', possibly from New Jersey, hiding out in an outbuilding for a short time in the early thirties. For a few days this unnamed fugitive was being guarded by armed henchmen who saw to it that he stayed put and also that no harm came to him. The name 'Capone' was mentioned ... not necessarily as the individual concerned but in the sense of the notorious 'Scarface' being in some way involved in these bizarre events.

Mary hadn't heard this story before and initially felt it had little validity; but for Tañia and Jeanne it was a family story they'd both grown up with. Jeanne recalled that her mother (Rosemary) had remembered her grandmother Angela being angry with Bruno over the episode and all Bruno could say was that he owed him ... though the 'him' remained nameless. Joe Smith also confirmed that he had heard the same story from Tañia's father Frank.

Mary's brother Mike added fuel to the story when he recalled an article in the *New Mexico Magazine* a few years earlier which talked about how Capone used to come to New Mexico from time to time where it was said he had a hideout in the Jemez mountains. Rumors and speculation aside, Capone was known to have been in Abuquerque in 1927 when seemingly the police and the media hounded him and his cronies out of town.

As far as I could see, apart from his small-scale liquor sideline, the only

A rare photo of all of Bruno Cortese's children in America. Bruno took this photo in Jemez ... a part of New Mexico he particularly liked because it reminded him of Italy. Frank, Elizabeth, and Angela are in the top row, then Rosemary, Peggy and Bruno Jr.

connection that Bruno had with the world of Al Capone was Cicero part of Chicago. For a couple of years Bruno lived and worked in Cicero but at a time when the young Al Capone was making a nuisance of himself in and around his native Brooklyn. It wasn't until the early twenties that Capone moved from Brooklyn and set up his headquarters in Cicero. (Of course, Albuquerque and Cicero have something else in common—they are both on Route 66, the so-called Main Street of America, which was commissioned and completed, coincidentally, between 1926 and 1928.)

The only clear association that Bruno might have had with the world of Chicago-based gangsters is that perhaps he still kept in touch with friends and work-mates from his Cicero days—perhaps he 'owed' one of them and he called in the favor.

Wherever the truth lies, it's an intriguing family story, the sort of tale that inevitably gets embroidered with each telling.

•

Between 1927 and 1935, Bruno and Angela had four children, one of whom, Bruno Jr, died of spinal meningitis in 1939 at the age of eight; apart from Mary and her immediate family and Joe Smith and two of his daughters, most people at Tañia's that Sunday were descendants of these three children, Peggy, Frank and Rosemary. Frank Cortese was Tañia's father.

Of course there was a fourth child in the family, the oldest child, Mary's mother Elizabeth; and arguably there should have been a fifth, Anthony, who was left behind in Santa Severina.

Everyone acknowledged that, particularly following the premature death of Bruno Jr, Elizabeth was not treated well by her stepmother ... a relationship best illustrated by the fact that almost all photos of the family which included Elizabeth had been mutilated ... Elizabeth was metaphorically and literally cut off by Angela.

In later life, when Elizabeth had children of her own, Angela made it difficult for Mary and her brothers, to see the grandfather they adored. He too felt the loss of contact with his grandchildren from the Fortino side of the family but, Mary argues, some of this was his own fault in that he should have been more assertive with his new wife from the very beginning when she persuaded him to leave Anthony in Calabria.

•

Bruno and Angela in 1949 with their three children: Peggy, Frank and Rosemary.

Three servicemen—one family:
An unnamed Italian Cortese nephew the time of the Italo-Turkish War in 1911.
Bruno's son, Frank Cortese, was in the US Navy during the Second World War.
His other son, Antonio Cortese, was in the Italian army during the same conflict.

We came across three photos of men wearing uniforms, two from the Second World War, the other from an earlier conflict, probably the Italo-Turkish War—sometimes also referred to as the Libyan Campaign—of 1911. The latter was clearly a Cortese though, at the time, unidentified; later Joe Smith came to the rescue and suggested it was probably one of his uncles, a nephew of his grandfather Vincenzo Cortese, the brother of Bruno.

The other two were more easily identified as Tañia's father Frank Cortese in his US Navy uniform and Antonio Cortese in the uniform of a lieutenant Picket Officer in Italy's 3rd Tank Regiment. Antonio had sent the photo to his sister Elizabeth with the message "To my beloved Elizabeth" written on the back.

It set me thinking about how quickly immigrants became prepared to fight for their host country. I recalled Luigi Cubello telling me how, at the time of the Cuban Missile Crisis and after only six years in America, he was feeling sufficiently patriotic that he wanted to fight for his country. He was, it must be said, only nine years old.

At that time Luigi's enemy was Russia but in conflicts such as the Second World War, Italy was part of the enemy alliance. The United States entered the fray in December 1941 but it was almost a year later when American servicemen first encountered combat in north Africa which involved Italian enemy forces. For many Italian-Americans this meant that they could well have ended up fighting against family.

It seems, however, that, like Frank Cortese, they either never doubted the justice of the allied cause or simply never gave the possible dilemma a moment's thought. Most likely both. Most first generation Italian-American soldiers, sailors and airmen, were already emotionally Americans when it came to this particular war ... most would not even have thought about the possibility of fighting against family and those who did, probably dismissed it. They had clearly made their choice; they were Americans.

For Frank such allegiances were not something he ever had to consider—he saw action only in the South Pacific.

Nevertheless, side by side, these two photographs, both taken in the 1940s, both mementos for their loved ones of their service for their nation in its time of need, are of two men who shared the same father, half-brothers who, unknowingly, were prepared to take up arms against each other.

From 1951 to 1959, Bruno rekindled his interest in the liquor business

Bruno Cortese In the 1950s with daughters Rosemary and Peggy and at home in Frank's Bar in Central Avenue.

when, in partnership with his son Frank, he opened Frank's Bar in Central Avenue. For Mary and her brothers this venture had an unexpected spin-off in that the bar was the one place where they could legitimately go to visit their grandfather Bruno. She recalls that he would give them cokes and some snacks and would hug them and talk to them about their grandmother, their mother's mother. He was also a bit of a cynic and Mary still recalls word-for-word some of his home-spun philosophy such as "All politicians are crooks, but the Republicans are crooks for the rich and the Democrats are crooks for the poor" and "Believe only half of what you see and none of what your hear".

Their step-grandmother, Angela Parisi, died in 1968 after several battles with mental illness during which, sporadically, she acknowledged how she had mistreated her step-daughter Elizabeth.

Twelve years later Bruno died not long after having been hospitalized with a broken hip ... not the sort of thing that would stop any self-respecting Calabrian from climbing over the bed railing and flirting with the nurses.

As I have already mentioned, in 1988 Mary and Jim eventually persuaded Elizabeth Cortese to return with them to Calabria to visit her family there. First she had to overcome phobias about flying and leaving America ... the last time she had done so, in 1924, was still associated with so much loss and pain. It was sixty-two years since she left Calabria with her father and his new wife, sixty-two years since she had seen her dear brother Antonio and her aunt Teresina.

And there was another reason to make such a trip at this time ... it meant they could attend the marriage of Antonio's son Maurizio to Adele in Vibo Valentia on the beautiful Tyrrehenian coast of Calabria.

Mary recalled the emotional reunion at Lamezia Terme airport: brother and sister hugged and wept as did most of the extended Cortese family who had turned out to welcome them. For everyone, except Antonio, it was the first time they had ever met their American aunt.

There were the same emotional scenes when they visited aunt Teresina in Crotone who then observed, *Elisabetta, che vecchia!*, Elizabeth, how old you've become ... and this from a woman in her nineties.

Initially for Elizabeth the language was a problem; what little Italian she still recalled was actually the local dialect of sixty years earlier and

Elizabeth Cortese (right) returned to Calabria only once—for the wedding of her nephew Maurizio Cortese to Adele Guarascio in 1988. Elizabeth's daughter Mary De Luca is second from the left next to her husband Jim Goodman.

Antonio Cortese had six children, three of whom, Bruno, Maurizio and Alfonso, still live in Santa Severina. In this photo taken at Le Castella in 2010—when members of the extended Smith and De Luca families visited Calabria—Bruno is on the far right, Maurizio third from right and Alfonso left of centre behind the two youngest children, his son Bruno and Maurizio's daughter Elisabetta.

such dialects are notoriously far more flexible and prone to change than the Italian language itself. Indeed it is likely than Elizabeth never actually spoke Italian as we know it today.

Together they also revisited the remnants of the *palazzo* in Altilia, the place where she last felt at peace and which, although old, rundown and divided into multiple dwellings, had not lost its enchantment ... time could never erase their childhood memories of being there together, playing at the top of the world.

When Mary first mentioned this place to me, I knew exactly where she meant as I recalled walking up there with friends on a warm spring afternoon ... a place where, despite the ravages of time, the derelict house and its abandoned environs still exuded a charm, still commanded glorious views over the valley of the river Neto.

I could understand how this place would forever live in the mind's eye of a nine year-old girl.

•

As afternoon crept into evening people began to leave, to venture out into the sharp November air, to make their way to the many parts of Albuquerque and beyond that they called 'home'. Each of these families could trace their line straight back to a young man from the Calabrian town of Mesoraca, to Bruno Cortese who, back in 1906 and again in 1912, was bold enough to cross the Atlantic in search of a better life.

In the twenties and thirties Bruno went on to spawn three different and remarkable families—two in America and one in Calabria—and I was fortunate enough to have been the recipient of many kindnesses and courtesies from all three.

I was also aware that there was a fourth Cortese family there that day, the descendants of Vincenzo Cortese, Bruno's brother and the first to test the waters and emigrate from Mesoraca to the United States in 1905. The story of Vincenzo's wife, Angelina Sotrino, their daughter Rose and her son, Joe Smith, is a story no less appealing than the strand I was focussing on. It is a story that, had I had more time, I would have liked to have pursued with Joe and his daughters Debi and Dedi.

I knew that, for Debi and Dedi, Vincenzo's daughter Rose was the grandmother they adored on their father's side; but they shared her with Mary, Tañia, Jeanne and others for whom she fulfilled the role of a surrogate grandmother, the grandmother they never had. Likewise for Tañia's father Frank, Joe Smith was like the brother he had lost and for Tañia the 'uncle' she was especially close to.

•

Everyone who emigrated, no matter where they came from or where they went, left behind family and loved ones; they took the chance that they may never see them again. But the story of how Anthony Cortese (as he then was) came to be born in America and left in Calabria is not only unique but truly poignant.

Ironically had these events not happened in this way, Santa Severina might well have been the loser. For ten years until 2010 another, younger Bruno Cortese was, just as his father Antonio had been, the town's mayor and is credited locally and even further afield with having been a leader and innovator *par excellence*. One of the reasons my wife and I moved to Santa Severina was because, on holiday there, we had observed how well the town was administered.

Some of Vincenzo and Bruno Cortese's descendants in Albuquerque.

It is therefore also conceivable that this book might not have been written if, in 1926, Anthony Cortese had returned to America with his father, his sister and his stepmother.

Better that it should not have been written.

POSTSCRIPT

Not long after returning to Santa Severina from the United States, I pass on to Bruno the envelope that Tañia had given me containing the Christmas letter he had written to his grandfather so many years ago.

It is just before Christmas 2012.

Bruno reads it in silence. For some time he says nothing ... it is clear he is struggling to control his emotions. Courteous to a fault, he stands up, shakes my hand and thanks me for bringing it to him. I can see he is lost for words and does not want to prolong the conversation.

A month later, the same evening I finish writing the above paragraph, I happen upon Bruno Cortese in Santa Severina's *piazza*. I tell him that I have been writing about his family that day and reiterate what Tañia, Mary and the rest of the family want more than anything—that he should visit his two families in Albuquerque. He tells me he knows now that he has to go there ... and adds that perhaps we might go together.

As good as it gets

The next morning, before taking me to Albuquerque airport, Adam treated Tañia and me to his wondrous specialty breakfast—sadly I can say no more as I am sworn to secrecy. Mind you, I did try it when I got home and I reckon, like all crafty cooks, he never told me the full story.

Four hours later I fastened my seat-belt ready for take-off on the second leg of my journey, from Dallas-Forth Worth back to Newark. I opened my bag to take out my iPad and went white ... it wasn't there. The iPad was not only my link back to Kay (who was in England at the time) but also contained all my contacts for the rest of my time in the States ... everything relating my trip was on that iPad.

People were still filing on to the plane as I was trying not to panic but to focus on where I might conceivably have left it and what I should do next. There were two possibilities—I could have left it on the in-coming flight from Albuquerque or I could have taken it out of my bag while I was in an electronics shop in the terminal where I was considering buying a stylus for it. I decided that if it was on another aircraft there was little I could do about it at this time; if it was in a shop a few hundred yards away, then, it was the least I could do to return there before the flight took off.

People were still moving down the aisle in search of their seats and among them I spotted a flight attendant going with the flow. I got up and said, "I need to get off and go back to a shop in the terminal where I've left my iPad". I expected an argument but instead he shrugged his shoulders and indicated that there were still people coming down the aisle and that not only would I have to hurry but that I'd have to 'swim against the tide' for much of the way ... by which he meant push past everyone coming in the opposite direction, looking for their seat and somewhere for their hand-luggage.

I went for it. I struggled back up the aisle, "Sorry." "Excuse me." "Sorry, excuse me." "Excuse me, sorry." I reached the door just as the last passenger got on and quickly told the steward hovering by the cockpit that I'd be back in a minute, my iPad was in the terminal. I didn't give him a chance to answer. I just ran.

I shot back up the tube, round and up, up and round, till I arrived back at the gate inside the terminal; I ducked under the blue-tape barrier beside the desk and ran round the curve of the terminal, all the time looking out for the store I'd been in, all the time hoping I was going in the right direction.

I spotted it, Airport Wireless, ran in and asked breathlessly "Did I leave my iPad here?" The guy behind the counter was talking to another customer. He continued talking as, slowly, he reached out with his right hand to a shelf behind him, lifted an iPad off it and handed it to me. He never said a word or doubted that the iPad was mine.

I snatched the iPad, shot out of the shop, dashed back round the terminal looking for my gate, ducked under the tape once again as I waved my iPad at two surprised employees, then down the tube I ran and launched myself back onto the plane and almost into the arms of the same steward I'd dashed past no more than ninety seconds earlier.

"Got it!" I said as once more I brandished my iPad like a trophy before heading back to my seat as if nothing had happened. The last passenger on was still looking for his seat.

Apart from which the flight was uneventful.

Uneventful it may have been but, after I'd finished lovingly caressing my iPad and promising it that I would never let it out of my sight again, and I was once again online somewhere over Texas, I made a momentous decision.

I had been studying a map of Newark and located where I was staying overnight in relation to the airport and realized that without my trusty navigator—my wife Kay—it was not going to be easy to find. Against all my instincts I was going to have to bite the bullet and ask that the car I was picking up at Newark be fitted with GPS (Global Positioning System/ Sat Nav/Tom-Tom/Garmin et al ... I never know what to call it).

For years I had successfully traversed America and Europe with my own version of GPS already built into my brain—I simply called it the being-able-to-read-maps part of my brain—but, five miles up and approaching Tennessee, I realized that I was going to need further assistance on this trip.

Still not sure if I should, or could, give in to such thoughts, I back-tracked for a few moments and wondered if I could remember the route to 8th Street from the airport ... before finally conceding that there was nothing else for it but to hire a car with GPS. What's more I'd have to learn how to use it pretty damn quick ... baptism by fire I think they call it.

At Newark I picked up the shuttle bus to the off-airport car rental base. The young woman behind the counter was obviously new to the job but after a few false starts we seemed to be going along nicely ... she had my print-out confirmation, my credit card and my driving license ... my Italian driving license.

She was busy punching in numbers when the door behind her burst open and a young, fresh-faced, well-dressed, upwardly-mobile man emerged; he strode purposefully in my direction.

"Are you Italian?" he asked

I didn't respond immediately.

"I saw your Italian driver's license on the monitor in the back." he continued.

"I live in Italy," I said, "but ..."

"So you're Italian then?"

He didn't give me a chance to reply. "I'm Italian too, my family's from Spezzano, you've probably never heard of it, it's ..."

" ... in Calabria?" I said.

"Yes," he said, "yes, it's in Calabria. How do you know Calabria?"

"I live in Calabria," I said, "in Santa Severina in the province of Crotone. Spezzano's next door in Cosenza, isn't it?"

My new best friend, Carlo, or Charlie as he preferred, went on to give me a potted history of his family and how they 'had to' leave Spezzano and come to America. He didn't explain the 'had to' part but I was fairly certain that somewhere along the line 'had to' spelled 'trouble', the sort of trouble some Calabrians don't like to talk about.

I told him why I was in the States and that I would love to meet his 'had to' parents and find out some of the family's history in Spezzano and New Jersey. He seemed interested though I suspected his 'had to' parents might not be.

While this was going on in one ear, in the other the woman processing my rental was, as always happens, trying to upgrade me to a larger car. From years of experience of renting cars in the States I knew that if you order the smallest 'economy' car they invariably try to get you to pay for the next one up because rental companies rarely, if ever, actually have the 'economy' models. If you stick to your guns and insist on your beloved 'economy' car, they have no option but to give you a car from the next range up for the same price. An old trick but it works every time.

As Charlie was writing out his email address and telephone number for me, I asked if I could have GPS as well and was told what the extra charge would be for my eight-day rental.

Charlie abruptly took command of the transaction and told his colleague that I was to have the Chrysler, the one with the built-in GPS.

"But ...", she protested, "he only wants an economy car."

But Carlo would have none of it ... I was to have the Chrysler for the same price. After all, we were both from Calabria, we were almost family.

We shook hands, I said I would email him later and was looking forward to meeting his 'had to' parents. I thanked him for what I guessed was some sort of modest upgrade, which I would have probably had anyway. He wished me well, said he would call his 'had to' parents and disappeared into the back office to monitor some other transaction.

The paperwork finished, I was handed my keys and the young woman took me outside to the car.

It was black, looked like a car but in reality was the size of a small house. It was clearly the largest and most expensive car in the place which was why the woman, now effortlessly demonstrating the car's features, balked at such an upgrade *and* for the same price.

Initially the only feature that I was interested in was how the GPS worked. I gave her the address where I was going, she showed me how to enter it into the system and I was ready to go. She had wanted to program my iPhone to speak to the GPS (or something along those lines) but at the time that was a technological step too far. If I'd been thinking more clearly I might have asked how I filled it up with gas ... but more of that later.

Alone at last, and finally in the driver's seat, I was ready to go ... but two minutes later was back in the office looking for someone who might show me, a shorty, how to move the seat forward. I was also shown how to lift it, tilt it and heat it.

I tried again. I switched on and put the car's joy-stick into what I thought was driving mode. It wouldn't move. I tried again. Nothing. I returned to the office and asked if someone could show me how to make it go.

You'd think that I'd never driven in the States before but I had, many times ... I just didn't remember that D was for drive and N was for neutral. I was trying to drive with the joy-stick in the N position. I have no idea what I thought it stood for.

I tried again and slowly moved out of the parking lot but every time I braked the car shook and stopped abruptly ... this one I eventually worked out myself I was using my left foot for the brake and my right foot for the accelerator (as I did normally on my 'stick' car back home) instead of my right foot for everything. I say I worked it out but the whole car was shaking and vibrating to a halt every time I stopped for the first quarter of an hour until the penny dropped and my heavy clutch foot was finally laid to rest.

I wondered if Charlie, who I could see was surreptitiously watching my antics, was already regretting his extravagance?

As well as the erratic braking I was trying to get used to the GPS and the other voice in the car, a woman who kept telling me what to do next or what to do in three hundred yards, or that the next turn would be to the left but not for ages yet. When she said 'turn right in fifty yards and then left', I discovered she was actually telling me that the next turn *after* the right hand one would be to the left and *not*, as seemed logical to me, that I should turn left immediately after turning right. I can't tell you how many times I did that before another penny dropped and the woman stopped saying 'recalculating, recalculating'.

Eventually I found myself outside the correct house in the correct street in Newark. The short street seemed pleasant enough as did the house when, finally, after a call to my host, I found out where he'd hidden the key and actually got in. He also told me that I would have the place to myself and could choose whichever bedroom I liked. I was weary and all I wanted to do was wash the tiredness away and eat. I also thought it best to email Charlie, to say that the car was still in one piece and that I was still keen to meet his folks. As I suspected might happen, I never heard another word.

Within half an hour I stepped back out again into the world that was Newark, re-energized and eagerly anticipating finding a good restaurant and an even better bottle of red wine. All too soon my enthusiasm abated when I discovered that this 'pleasant' street was a little oasis of normality in what was otherwise an area that did indeed resemble the dark side of the moon ... Sherrie's advice about some parts of Newark was ringing in my ears.

Still, I found two places to eat ... one was a small and, frankly, not very inviting pizzeria tucked away near some shops that looked as if they'd seem better times. The other one was a desolate-looking Burger King on the other side of the main road. Neither jumped out as the answer to my hunger but the Burger King seemed the lesser of two evils.

I thought that perhaps I could get a cab to take me somewhere that might be a bit more inviting but there wasn't much traffic about and certainly I never saw a single cab. Perhaps they don't come this way except by invitation, I thought. I gave in to my hunger pangs and crossed the road heading for the Burger King but couldn't quite bring myself to go in; I hovered a while outside still keeping an eye out for a cab that had lost its way.

I heard a car pull up in the part of the Burger King parking lot that I couldn't see so, ever hopeful that it just might be a cab, I wandered over to take a look when around the corner came a huge, seven-foot tall Hightower-lookalike policeman. He walked with a rolling, don't-mess-with-me swagger, just as if he'd stepped off a movie set ... for a moment I did actually wonder whether or not he was a real policeman. Don't-mess-with-me swagger or not, he seemed friendly enough and didn't immediately go for his gun when I approached him.

"Excuse me, officer," I said in true I've-watched-thousands-of-American-movies style, "but where can I get a cab around here."

"No problem, sir,"—he'd obviously watched the same movies—"I'll call you one," was the reply I was not expecting.

I thanked him profusely as he took out his cell phone, punched a few keys and put it to his ear as he continued on his way into the Burger King. A few moments later he reemerged and said that my cab was on its way and that I was to wait round the corner in the parking lot. I followed him there where I discovered that he was indeed a real policeman ... unless, that is, he'd stolen the large black and white patrol car from the movie set along with a uniformed buddy.

At last, I thought, this day is taking a turn for the better ... I must learn never to think such thoughts.

Five minutes later my cab arrived and I asked the driver if he knew of any place to eat within a reasonable distance that was neither a pizzeria nor a Burger King. He pondered momentarily and then said he knew of both a Japanese and a Chinese joint not too far away. The clue should have been in the word 'joint' but at the time my expectant stomach and tired brain didn't pick up on it. I opted for the Chinese.

En route, I noticed that perhaps the area around where I was staying wasn't so bad after all. We seemed to be heading into more gloom and doom ... the sort of place they make movies about where people get lost in a terrifying no-mans-land and have to rely on their baser instincts to survive. I'd watched all those movies and was ahead of the game ...

Survival-in-Newark Tip Number One, I thought, get the cabdriver's phone number so that you can call him when you need to get back to base.

He dropped me outside the Chinese 'restaurant' and I promised to call him ten minutes before I was ready to leave. Actually I would have fared better if I'd called him immediately and forgotten all my prejudices and gone back to the Burger King.

The word 'restaurant' didn't apply to this place ... it was a Chinese takeout with a few tables and chairs and no alcohol. I wondered how come, bearing in mind all the programs they make about Health Inspectors visiting and closing down restaurants, cafés and takeouts worldwide ... how come they'd missed this place? And that was before I'd even tasted the food.

I ordered sweet and sour chicken ... what I got was a massive plate of boiled-for-ever rice and a bowl of chicken-like meat drowning in a vile-looking and—it was no surprise to discover—vile-tasting, sticky, fluorescent-orange sea.

I ate enough of the chicken to satisfy my hunger and left most of the rice and the orange liquid for another unsuspecting customer, though I couldn't imagine that anyone else would actually eat here by choice. There was in fact another customer ... well, a customer of sorts. He sat alone at his table and played with his phone, he never spoke to anyone or ordered anything. Perhaps he had already eaten and was digesting, perhaps he was a friend of the family ... perhaps, my increasingly vivid imagination surmised, he was casing the only other customer.

When that thought crossed my mind I decided it was time to call my cab-driving friend who, clearly impressed by the speed with which I ate, said he'd be there in no more than ten minutes.

Paid up, I went to the door to survey my surroundings. Across the road there was a liquor store and parked outside was a cab from the same company that had brought me here. He got here quick I thought and crossed the road but soon realized it was not the same driver. I headed instead for the liquor store ...

Survival-in-Newark Tip Number Two, I thought, always make sure you buy a bottle of wine with a screw-top just in case there isn't a corkscrew in the house.

Back outside, the other cab was still there ... I wondered whether they'd sent someone else and that he'd got there early and *was* actually waiting for me. So I asked him and, between bites into his burger, he said, yes, he was indeed waiting for me. Even though his car's livery said he worked for the same company, I didn't believe him.

Survival-in-Newark Tip Number Three, I thought, never get into a cab when the driver is eating, is clearly lying and protests vociferously when you walk away.

With my fare-stealing cabdriver still protesting his innocence, I started to cross the street with the intention of taking up my post outside the Chinese joint but never got that far as another cab drew up and I could see a friendly face poking out the window.

On the way back I told him about his burger-munching, so-called colleague who had tried to steal his fare ... to say he was not best pleased would be an understatement.

Back in what was clearly the better part of Newark I toyed with the idea of getting some takeout fries from Burger King to go with the fine wine I'd bought ... I just didn't have the energy to cross the road. That bottle of red wine and a good night's sleep beckoned and I succumbed.

That night I dreamt about the Saigon Café in Jersey City where I knew I would eat the following evening. I couldn't wait.

•

I woke up to a drizzly morning, packed and headed out to the small-house-mobile. It was still where I left it and all four wheels seemed to be in place. I typed my Jersey City destination into the GPS and renewed my acquaintance with 'the voice'.

After several wrong turnings and 'recalculatings', I finally found myself going in roughly the right direction and eventually arrived back in the Wayne Street area where I began the search to find somewhere to park the small-house-mobile that wasn't restricted in some way which would inexorably lead to it being towed away. All I wanted was a parking lot, normally no big deal in America.

I went up and down and across street after street for almost an hour before I stumbled upon my first parking lot ... only to be told that I couldn't leave the small-house-mobile there overnight. But the guy was helpful and said he thought there was one lot where I might be able to leave it overnight; he gave me directions to a street not far from where I was staying, indeed much closer than his lot would have been.

Here I met young Mitch who said I could come and go with the small-house-mobile any time of day or night ... at nine dollars a day. He had one space left and, as it didn't look big enough, he said he would park the small-house-mobile for me ... I knew he just wanted to drive it, he probably had never been behind the wheel of something like this and clearly enjoyed the experience. And so began a great working relationship with Mitch over the next two weeks—I had no-hassle parking day and night and Mitch sometimes got to park or move the small-house-mobile.

I returned to Sherrie's apartment and, as I had a free afternoon and I didn't want to lose that parking space, decided to walk to the large mall, the Newport Center, she'd told me about a few more blocks further out of town than I'd ventured before when I bought the suitcase and towel.

En route, I happened to pass Saigon Café and noticed it was open and so, in an effort to expunge all memories of that awful meal the night before *and* make up for the fact that I hadn't had any breakfast, I decided that a bowl of Vietnamese soup would be the perfect antidote. And it was.

By the time I got to the mall, via a few other interesting retail outlets, I was tired and decided I'd come back the next morning in the small-house-mobile and do some serious shopping ... among other things I had to buy presents for three children in Santa Severina.

That evening I returned to the Saigon Café and took up residence at what had now become 'my' table. I got to know all the family members by their Americanized names, mother and father, Kim and Danny, and daughter and son, Karen and Steve. Steve I got to know quite well and thereafter we talked a lot about all sorts of things ... but mainly computers.

Also, that evening was the first time I vacated my table and headed, glass in hand, for the small bar to finish my wine and possibly partake of another ... and to chat to Steve. Just as I was leaving, Kim came over to me with a small package containing a 'takeout' bowl of the soup she

The people who make the Saigon Café special: Steve, Karen, Danny and Kim.

knew I liked and said it was for my lunch tomorrow ... just pop it in the microwave, she said. At the time I wasn't even sure if Sherrie's apartment *had* a microwave.

That was the moment, an unexpected and warm-hearted moment, the finale to what had been two difficult days, that I decided to write this book as a travelogue ... I foolishly thought it couldn't get any worse.

•

The next morning, after a very late breakfast of wonderful Vietnamese soup, I was heading back to the Newport Center in the small-house-mobile and, for the first time, I didn't need any help from 'the voice' ... or rather I thought I didn't.

I turned right off Marin Boulevard; the next left I knew would take me into the area between the mall and its multi-story parking lot. Unfortunately I found myself in the wrong lane to make a left-hand turn and there was traffic coming up behind so I couldn't change lanes easily.

I spotted a bank to the right and pulled into its car park, turned round and headed back to the exit where I would be able to drive straight across the two lanes of the dual roadway and be right next to the mall's parking lot.

I crossed the first roadway (with traffic coming from the left), the roadway I had just left, and went on to cross the next (with traffic coming from the right). Only problem was that, for some reason, I just didn't check whether anything was approaching from that direction.

With all the force I could muster I stamped both feet onto the brake pedal as the other driver, hand on horn, swerved round the front of the small-house-mobile and got clear before I, shaking, continued across the road as quickly as I could, turned left into the car park, snatched the ticket from the machine as the barrier lifted, raced up several stories, and hid inconspicuously—if indeed it were possible to hide the small-house-mobile inconspicuously.

I sat there for several minutes, still shaking, pondering the enormity of what I had almost done ... the car I had almost broadsided was a New Jersey Police patrol car.

I did my shopping with little enthusiasm, ever-watchful for two burly policemen scouring the mall for a diminutive, white-haired fugitive. When

I got back to the small-house-mobile I half expected it to be the focus of a stakeout ... at the very least I expected some sort of note behind a wiper telling me to report to the nearest precinct headquarters.

The small-house-mobile was such a difficult car to conceal that I was more than a little relieved that I would be heading out of Jersey City for the rest of the day and wouldn't return until late.

•

I was heading up-state, to Fairview, to meet the Sculco family, but first I had to make a slight detour to find an Italian *pasticceria* in Hoboken that I'd located on the internet. I thought I should take Gino and Sina some traditional Italian pastries.

Thanks to 'the voice' I parked up a few blocks away from Washington Street and soon found the *pasticceria*. It was not quite what I was expecting.

For a start it was rather gloomy, nothing like the brightly-lit emporium that I was used to in Calabria. The display cabinets were a bit sparse, not crammed with the wonderful delicacies I was expecting; there were no cream pastries at all, just tray after tray of almond-based cookies. Still, they were Italian almond-based cookies.

At the sound of the door bell a man's head had emerged from below the counter at the far end of the shop. Slowly, shakily even, he made his way round to where I was standing. His features weren't as old as his demeanor and gait suggested ... just a little world-weary, I thought.

Pointing to the display cabinet, I asked him for a kilo of mixed cookies. He seemed a little taken aback.

"That's a lot," he said. "Perhaps this size would be better," he continued as he slowly turned and selected a tray from the shelf behind and held it up.

"No, I'll have the larger tray," I said pointing.

"Are you sure?" he persisted still brandishing the smaller one.

"Yes," I said, "the larger one please."

He shrugged his shoulders in silent recognition that the customer is always right and set about selecting a kilo of cookies for me.

A door opened and a young woman dressed in white overalls and matching hair-net popped out as if to see that things were going smoothly in the shop.

"Checking up on me," he said as if reading my mind.

As he continued with his selection, I asked him where he was from and he said he had been born in Naples but had lived in the States for over forty years. I told him that I had been in Naples a few times and we exchanged a few anecdotes about that frenetic city before I explained that I lived in Calabria and what I was doing in the States. His mood was changing and I could see he was warming to our brief conversation.

I asked him how much Hoboken had changed over the years and he made a typical Italian gesture to an accompanying, barely audible, aspiration which I understood to mean 'more than I could possibly ever describe'. I asked him about Hurricane Sandy which, from all accounts, had wreaked havoc with parts of Hoboken and I knew his shop was only a couple of blocks from the Hudson River. His response left me momentarily speechless.

"We didn't really take much notice ... my wife died that week."

Clutching my gift-wrapped cookies, I shook his hand, thanked him for his two-dollar discount, reiterated my condolences and headed out into the sunlight.

I first met Gino and Sina (Benito and Anastasia) Sculco when they were on holiday in their native Santa Severina in the summer of 2011. They had lived in New Jersey for nearly fifty years.

Gino was related to the family of our neighbor and friend, Raffaele Vizza, so I was not surprised to meet him again that summer at the funeral of Raffaele's father, Ciccio.

I heard from their many friends in Santa Severina that they would not be returning in 2012 as planned as Gino had not been well.

However, from a mutual friend, Claudia, I got their home phone number and spoke to Sina about coming to visit them in November. She agreed and I said I would call her nearer the time from the States to arrange a date.

I contacted Sina the morning after I returned from Albuquerque and arranged to go to their Fairview home the following day at three in the afternoon.

The man who emigrated twice

Despite my near miss with the patrol car and my detour to Hoboken, I arrived in the Fairview area over an hour ahead of schedule. Something struck me about my short journey: because I was relying on GPS and not reading a map I didn't really know where I was ... for the first time I had no real picture in my head of this place or where in relation to everything else it actually was. I had been taken there by 'the voice', I had not found my own way there; it was very disconcerting.

I checked out where Gino and Sina lived and parked up in the main street nearby and did all manner of strange things to pass the time. I went for a walk and stumbled upon a small Spanish café-bar where I decided to have a snack. I returned to the small-house-mobile, fed the parking meter and started to play Sudoko on my iPad. I fell asleep.

Fortunately I woke at five-to-three and arrived at the house right on time.

I was good to see Gino and Sina again in their own environment and I was humbled by the welcome they gave me, someone they had only met a few times in Santa Severina more than a year before. I was not family and I was not a friend in the same way as many of the people in Santa Severina and wondered if, like the descendants of Bruno Cortese in Albuquerque, they'd had few visitors from Santa Severina? On the contrary they'd had a dozen or more visitors over the years, with the Sculco family the traffic was definitely two-way. I made a mental note to check this out with other families that I was meeting.

I gave Sina the cakes and apologized for the lack of variety; I also explained about the recent death in the family by way of explanation.

I knew that Gino and Sina had married in Calabria and then moved to the States. What I did not know until we started to talk was that, just like the Cubello family from Fossato Serralto, the Sculco family had a previous history when it came to'emigrating to America.

Carlo and Giuseppe Sculco, taken in America before Giuseppe returned to Calabria.

•

In 1913 and 1920 two brothers, Carlo and Giuseppe Sculco, left their home in Santa Severina (they were actually born in nearby San Giovanni in Fiore) in search of a better life in America. At the time Carlo was eighteen, his younger brother was twenty-two when he followed in his footsteps seven years later. Both were shoe-makers and, unusually, both could read and write. Indeed, on their respective ships' manifests these brothers stood out from their fellow travelers as being neither laborers, peasants or illiterate; both had a trade, both were literate.

When Carlo sailed from Naples in December 1913 he crossed the Atlantic on the *Principe di Piedmont*. He was fortunate in that on that particular crossing there was more room than usual for steerage passengers—over eight hundred fewer people traveled than the ship's official capacity of nineteen hundred. Had he crossed earlier in the year it would have been a different story; in March, according to the ship's manifest, the *Principe di Piedmont* carried more steerage passengers than it should have, a hell on earth. These manifests—viewable on the Ellis Island website—also tell another tale in that saloon and first-class passengers were classified as having embarked at Genoa or Naples while steerage passengers on the same ship embarked at Genova or Napoli; English for the middles classes, Italian for the proletariat.

One brother, it seems, was not intent on emigrating permanently to the United States as, in the late twenties, Giuseppe returned to Calabria; it is said he had twelve thousand dollars sewn into a body suit when he arrived in Santa Severina ... most of it earned at the Israel Millar shoe factory where both brothers worked and where you could make a hundred dollars a week.

Israel Millar, himself an immigrant from the Polish-Prussian border, was an iconic maker of shoes, a true *fashionista*. Millar worked initially for another fine shoemaker, an Italian immigrant called John Azzimonti, before going his own way. At first he imported shoes but then began manufacturing his own designs at a factory in Long Island City. Like Azzimonti he specialized in designing footwear for theatrical productions and then for performers who bought from him direct ... from where it was but a short leap to supplying the well-heeled ladies of New York society with sophisticated, classy and elegant footwear.

In 1929, at the junction of Broadway and 46th Street, he opened a new store, a building designed to be as elegant as his footwear, its façade incorporated four niches each with a statue of a famous actress of the time and below the cornice, etched in marble, the slogan, 'The Show Folks Shoe Shop Dedicated To Beavty In Footwear'. It's all still there, albeit a little worse for wear.

Carlo continued to work at Millar's, indeed when he registered for the draft in 1942, he was still an employee of Israel Millar. At the time he was living in East 124th Street, now Spanish Harlem but an Italian enclave back then, where he and his wife Vincenza Merignano and their three children had lived since the early twenties. Vincenza, a dressmaker, was herself an immigrant; she and her brother came to America from their home town of Seminara, north of Reggio Calabria, in 1921.

•

Our conversation was briefly interrupted when a door opened and a tall, genial man joined us, his spectacles balanced precariously halfway down

Not long married, Rosa Scalfero and Giuseppe Sculco.

his nose ... he looked over the top of them as we shook hands and was introduced as Gino and Sina's Spanish son-in-law, the artist Jose Fontaiña; he and their daughter Rose and their two children, Manuel and Anastasia, lived in the upstairs apartment. Anastasia joined us and then Jose went off to pick up Rose from the school where she taught. Of Gino and Sina's four children, Rose was, I was assured, the most knowledgeable about the family's history.

Gino and Sina continued with the story of Gino's father, Giuseppe Sculco and how, back in Santa Severina, he met and married Rosa Scalfaro who lived in Via Miseria, a narrow street one level down from the Sculco home in Via dei Bizantini. Today, as then, these two streets are connected by narrow nameless alleyways just made for courting couples.

So, although Giuseppe Sculco spent many of his formative years in America, he ended up back where he started in Santa Severina, in Via dei Bizantini just down from the town's square. There, in the years running up to and during the Second World War, he and Rosa had eight children, one every two years, as regular as clockwork, only the last, Raffaele, broke the sequence.

For all their children it must have been an unorthodox upbringing with a father who had experienced living in a modern urban environment that was so alien to life in a small hilltop Italian community ... *and* a father who spoke fluent English and had become an American citizen in 1926.

Giuseppe, erstwhile maker of classy shoes for Manhattan's elite, now made a living as Santa Severina's maker of shoes. He had a small store in the town's square where he not only made and repaired shoes but also sold *alimentari*, groceries, including alcohol ... ironically at the time something he could not have done in America.

This was the background that Sina married into when, in 1963, she said *si* to Gino in Santa Severina. At the time Sina and her family had moved from Santa Severina to Lodi in Lombardy and Gino had followed them there to work and it was while living and working in Lodi that they got engaged. At the time emigrating to the States was not on their immediate agenda ... even though another member of the Sculco family had done so a few years earlier. In 1960, in his early sixties, Gino's father Giuseppe left Santa Severina for the second time and emigrated to America to spend his days there; he was accompanied by his son Antonio.

The original plan was hatched in the mid-fifties when Giuseppe first tried to return and planned to take the eighteen-year-old Gino with him. Not unrelated with this venture was that fact that if Gino left for America at that time he wouldn't need to do the two-year army conscription (the draft) that was compulsory at the time. They were planning to travel in July 1956 aboard Italy's largest, fastest and safest liner, the *Andrea Doria*, plying the north Atlantic route between Genoa and New York ... but there was a problem with Giuseppe's paperwork.

Despite having lived in America for almost ten years and having become a US citizen, he had no paperwork to confirm any of this. Today, online, it takes no more than a few seconds to verify both his arrival in 1920 and his citizenship documents in 1926 but the mid-fifties American bureaucracy was a suspicious and uncompromising body. Italy was also, as Cold War

An engagement portrait of Benito (Gino) Sculco and Anastasia (Sina) Audia taken in Lodi (in Lombardy) shortly before their wedding in 1963.

rhetoric and burgeoning McCarthyism would have it, a country with too many people on the political left who might influence or even damage American institutions.

So, no paperwork, no entry ... and two year's conscription for Gino.

All of which, as it happens, was fortuitous for, off the coast of Nantucket, Massachusetts the *Andrea Doria* was involved in a collision with the Swedish ship the *MS Stockholm*. The *Andrea Doria* sank within eleven hours and, although most passengers and crew were rescued, fifty-one people lost their lives.

It was not until January 1960 that Giuseppe's paperwork was finally deemed to be in order and he and Antonio, two years Gino's junior, set off for America where they were met and sponsored by Giuseppe's older brother Carlo who still worked at Millar's. Two years later Giuseppe's wife Rosa joined her husband bringing with her another three of their children Concetta, Gisella and Raffaele.

In May 1967 another of the Sculco children, Carlo, headed across the Atlantic but it was not until later the same year that the emigration bug eventually overwhelmed Gino and Sina and in October, with Sina just over seven months pregnant and their fourteen-month son, Joseph, in their arms, they too left Santa Severina and set off on their American adventure.

But Gino and Sina had an additional motive for joining the rest of the family in America in that Joseph had an allergy to milk and they were hopeful that in America his health might improve.

The family went in style. They flew Alitalia from Rome to New York where they were met by their sponsors, Gino's parents, with whom they lived in Cliff Street, Fairview, New Jersey for the first three weeks.

Less than two months later Joseph's little sister, Rose Sculco, was born in Saint Mary's Hospital Hoboken, New Jersey.

•

Sina broke off to check something on the internet and her young granddaughter was eager to give her a hand. For me this was an interesting moment: Sina, a spritely seventy-something from Santa Severina, was *au fait* with the internet and even had her own email address ... while her nine-year old granddaughter was more than *au fait*, young Anastasia was internet *savvy*. I didn't have the heart to tell them that at that moment in time, Santa Severina still didn't have broadband ... though it was supposedly 'just around the corner' where it had been lurking for at least five years.

Just after Jose returned with his wife Rose, Sina turned her attention to a more normal activity for Italian women of a certain age—she started to prepare dinner.

Rose introduced herself as the child of Santa Severina that everyone forgets, the child made in Italy but born in America ... then quickly went on to explain. She and her younger sister Anna had been to Santa Severina many times ... it's where their parents lived and for Gino and Sina it was important that their children should know this place and feel at home there. But, Rose explained, whenever they went there, their parent's friends and family always seemed to remember Anna better because she looks like her father and are less sure who she, a mixture of both parents, is.

I made a mental note to call her Carla if I ever met her in Santa Severina.

Sina was on automatic ... on the one hand she was busying herself with preparing dinner while on the other she was filling in the gaps to the story of what it was like when they first arrived in the States.

Sina said she was both apprehensive and downright frightened when she thought of making such a move. On the other hand Joseph's health was worrying her and the possibility that his problems might be alleviated in America had cancelled out her personal fears.

It was ironic therefore that the one person who ended up in hospital the day after they got there was Sina herself—she'd arrived with fevers and bronchitis but it was a bad reaction to an antibiotic injection that saw her hospitalized for the day. She remembered feeling very frightened because of what she thought would be a communication problem but needn't have worried ... she soon found herself in the capable hands of Italian-American doctors and surrounded by other Italian friends and patients.

For Gino the whole emigration process was easier. He had grown up with stories of life in America from his father who had always told him that there was plenty of work there and that his family could be assured of a better future in America. And Gino and his siblings had of course seen it with their own eyes ... their father was living proof that Uncle Sam paid well and that if you worked hard anything was possible.

And so it was, with Sina back home, Gino was straight off to work on a construction site to start earning all those dollars his father had told him about.

•

Initially for Gino and Sina 'home' was, of course, the home of Gino's parents, Giuseppe and Rosa, who had emigrated in the early sixties.

At the time she emigrated to join Giuseppe, Rosa Scalfaro was fifty-seven. Unlike her husband, this was her first time in the States; a momentous decision but then she knew that she would be surrounded by most of her children, three of whom traveled with her. Rosa wasn't a stay-at-home person and so she soon found a job in a clothing factory where she worked until her late sixties.

Unlike her husband, Rosa never learned to speak English ... a revelation that gave me some succor.

My wife and I emigrated to Italy when we were sixty and sixty-four respectfully; at the time our Italian language vocabulary was somewhere along the meet, greet and eat continuum. We expected to assimilate the language pretty quickly but this did not happen ... gradually we realized that we were probably too old to become even close to fluent. Had we moved in our twenties or thirties it would have been a different story.

Recently a man in his sixties asked us why we didn't speak the language better and I tried to explain the difficulties ... we spoke English at home and we were of an age that worked against absorbing the language in the way that the young do. I could see he wasn't convinced ... and I was tempted to say at the time that he should try going to the States or the UK himself for a few years and see how he got on.

There may well have been other reasons that Rosa Scalfaro didn't learn to speak English but, at her time of life and surrounded by most of her Italian-speaking family, it would not have been easy.

I asked about the Scalfaro surname as, at this particular time, Santa Severina's *sindaco*, the mayor, was one Diodato Scalfaro ... like everything and everyone in Santa Severina there is invariably a connection. There was: Rosa Scalfaro was *il sindaco*'s great aunt, Diodato's father, Raffaele was her nephew.

Despite the fact that Giuseppe Sculco—who now preferred to be known by one of his other names, Francesco—was in his early sixties, he got himself a job back at Millar's where he'd last worked in the late twenties. But times were changing and Millar's closed down a year later and so he tried his hand at something completely different and joined the staff at the famous Palisades Amusement Park in Cliffside Park, New Jersey.

The park was originally conceived in the late nineteenth century as a much smaller-scale linear 'trolley' park, the 'Park on the Palisades'—the Palisades being a high verdant area adjacent to Fort Lee in New Jersey—but it was bought in 1909 by Joseph and Nicholas Schenck who renamed it the 'Schenck Brother's Palisades Park'.

The brothers added more rides and attractions to the park, including a massive swimming pool, complete with wave machine and waterfall and filled with salt water pumped directly up from the Hudson River, and three roller coaster rides—Big Scenic Railway, Cyclone and Comet. Palisades Park was an instant success and gained a reputation far beyond its New Jersey home; in late 1931 this was further boosted when the George Washington Bridge was opened and with it a link from uptown Manhattan almost to the front door.

Palisades Amusement Park in its heyday.

The post-war period saw the Park's heyday as Palisades became a local and a national institution. But its success was also its downfall for, during the sixties, the thousands of people who flocked there increasingly did so by car rather than public transportation and neither the Park itself nor its environs could cope with the volume of traffic, the corresponding lack of parking and the litter.

In 1971, following local protests, Palisades closed its doors for the last time; the rides were dismantled, the pool was drained and, for the first time in over seventy years the 'Park on the Palisades' grew silent ... until, that is, the bulldozers moved in and this prime piece of real estate was redeveloped.

And Giuseppe (Francesco) Sculco, a native of a small Calabrian hilltop town, was still working there right to the end.

Both Francesco and Rosa Sculco returned to their native Calabria in 1974 with their son Ralph and two years later Rosa returned for the last time to be at Ralph's wedding to Francesca (Franca) Arabia

They both died in New Jersey surrounded by most of their children who, like them, sought new horizons across the Atlantic. The only difference was that Giuseppe emigrated twice, two times, forty years apart and the second time when he was in his sixties.

●

Our conversation returned to the young Sculco family and how they fared in New Jersey. They were, of course surrounded by Gino's family—his parents, two sisters and three brothers—but they wanted to have a place of their own and within three weeks they found somewhere to rent in Cliff Street where, in July 1969, their second daughter Anna was born.

Gino and Sina took typical Italian pride in creating a home for their growing family so it was not surprising that they decided to paint and redecorate. Their landlord liked it so much that he figured it would be absolutely perfect for his sister and the Sculco family was given one month's notice. Gino argued that this was not long enough ... experience told him that it would take longer to find somewhere with three children and reckoned that it would have been easier if they'd had two dogs.

Instead, in three months of hard work, Gino earned the money to put a down payment on the house that they now own and where they still live, no more than five blocks away from that first apartment.

•

It was time to eat so we all adjourned to the dining room where, as I had come to expect of both Americans and Calabrians, the table was set for a small banquet. We were joined by Rose's brother Gino and fiancée Jennifer, both of whom lived next door. When Gino told me he was a police officer, I couldn't resist telling him the tale of how the small-house-mobile and I had tried unsuccessfully to assassinate two of his Jersey City colleagues. He promised not to tell.

As we were eating I noticed that Sina had dispensed with the array of plates that accompany most Calabrian meals—a plate for the meat, a plate for the potatoes, a plate for the salad and so on—in favor of the British-American way where meat, potatoes and salad are allowed to share the same plate, just as they share the same stomach. When I asked her how this cultural innovation in the Sculco family's eating habits had developed, she simply said that it was obviously such a neat idea as it saved on the washing-up.

We talked about some of the other cultural differences and in particular the celebrations that are either uniquely Italian or uniquely American. As I'd already discovered with other families, neither Befana (5-6 January) nor Ferragosto (14-15 August) figured in their calendar ... except when Gino and Sina happened to spend the summer in Santa Severina of course. In their place there were two uniquely American occasions that the family celebrated—Independence Day on 4 July and Thanksgiving on the fourth Thursday every November.

On Independence Day there was always a family barbecue which Rose and *her* family missed out on every year as they were always in Spain visiting Jose's family in Galicia. But, as far as Rose was concerned, Santa Claus ruled in the extended Sculco family, adults and kids alike, even the non-believers. And, as Calabrian custom would have it at this time of year, her mother still made a mean *pitta ccu passuli*, a traditional Christmas nut and raisin or currant dessert usually cooked in a tray around eight inches in diameter.

When Rose mentioned *pitta ccu passuli* it brought a nervous smile to my face and an ache to my long-suffering teeth. Somehow I resisted the temptation to launch into my eccentric theories about this Calabrian dish as to do so might imply that Sina's version was like many of its less appetizing incarnations. Perhaps another family might yet give me that opportunity, I thought, by actually having some on the table.

That said, having experienced Sina's cooking that evening, I have no doubt that her *pitta ccu passuli* would have been a cut above the rest.

•

Dinner over, young Gino and Jennifer left and we were joined by two of Gino's brothers who also lived in New Jersey, Antonio and Raffaele or Tony and Ralph as they now were. Tony it was who travelled to America first with his father back in 1960.

Ralph told me that his wife Franca had just travelled to Santa Severina and that she would still be there when I got back and that perhaps we might meet up.

Until that moment I didn't realize that Ralph's wife was from Santa Severina and even when he told me her Italian surname, Arabia, I still didn't make any connections. And even when Ralph went on to remind me that he thought I had met his wife's sister, Elvira, I still was none the wiser. It was only when he mentioned that this Elvira lived near Chicago that the wheels began to turn and I recalled the woman I had met the previous year and whom I'd tried unsuccessfully to contact just a few months earlier ... Elvira Arabia from 'near Chicago' whom I mentioned in my Introduction.

This 'near Chicago' turned out to be Kenosha, Wisconsin where I was going to be the following week and where I would spend Thanksgiving with the Fonte family from Roccabernarda. I made a mental note to find out if Tommaso Fonte knew Elvira Arabia ... I might get to see her again after all.

Rose decided that it was time for me to speak to the sister that everyone remembered; she called Anna, and handed me the phone.

Anna apologized for not being able to be there but hoped that we might meet at her daughter's fifth birthday party that Sunday. At the time I was anticipating a long drive to and from Reading, Pennsylvania, on the Saturday and so said I would do my best to get there ... it would depend when I got back to Jersey City and how I felt.

•

Briefly we brought the story of the Sculco family up to date.

I wondered if Sina, the only non-Sculco in that flurry of emigration from Santa Severina in the sixties, had felt the loss of *her* family more. She was philosophical ... of course she missed her own family, and particularly so around holidays and festivals, but she was among friends, people she had known for most of her life back in Santa Severina. And besides she was busy bringing up her own young family: absorbing the American way of doing things, taking the kids to the doctor, doing the shopping, helping out at the local school and, of course, learning the language.

The family returned to Santa Severina for the first time in 1974 by which time both Gino and Sina were naturalized American citizens ... and Sina had an American driving license.

For nineteen years Gino worked as a bricklayer in the construction union and often he worked two or three jobs every day. In December 1986 he fell off the scaffolding from four floors up and landed in the rubble below. By chance his son Joseph, an electrician, happened to be working the same site and found him.

Gino retired from the bricklayer's union after the accident and it took a few years to recover. It saddened him when he realized that he could not do what he loved doing most ... build. Nevertheless, back on his feet, he did a few smaller jobs but never alone, always with the help of laborers looking for some extra cash. Later he and Joseph build a duplex home in Cliffside Park together which they then sold.

These days Gino tends to the two gardens he cultivates and grows tomatoes which Rose insists are the tastiest in the so-called Garden State (New Jersey) where the tomato is the designated state vegetable of New Jersey—even though it's a fruit.

Gino has retained more of his Italian accent than Sina but they and their family and home are as American as apple pie ... apart from Rose's Spanish husband, Anna's Irish husband and Gino's Italian-German-American-Indian fiancée. But then that is the essence of what America has become, a melting pot of cultures and races that, generally, are unconcerned about people's origins, ethnic or cultural. That is not to say that they have forgotten their roots, only that they are growing new, more culturally diverse, roots and are the better able to do so because they never forget that 'other' part of their upbringing.

Because their parents want it to be so, Manuel and Anastasia will always have homes in Spain and Italy but essentially they are and will always be Americans.

The evening was drawing to a close and I was chatting briefly to Ralph and said that I thought that the people who had made the decision to emigrate were very brave. He disagreed and said he didn't think they were brave but had done so out of necessity. I still wasn't sure. While I was mulling this over, I checked again on the dates when his wife would be in Santa Severina and promised to make a point of seeing her.

Only the immediate family was left but before I too departed Jose took me outside and down into his studio to see his body of work.

Many years ago, in another life, I used to design catalogs and books for artists and photographers, usually in support of an upcoming exhibition of their work. So when I say that I found Jose's work both exceptional and inspirational, it is because in the past I had worked with many exceptional people—and a few, it has to be said, less than exceptional—that I think I grew to recognize the difference.

I instantly could see the castle at Santa Severina as a potential venue for an extraordinary exhibition only to be told that I was not the first to come up with the same idea but that, without outside financial support, the cost of transport and insurance would be prohibitive. Such a pity, I thought, such a great pity

•

On my way back to Jersey City, apart from a few interruptions from 'the voice', I was thinking about what Ralph had said about emigrants having no option, that they were not brave, that they had to leave.

I still wasn't convinced that this was so ... I could see it more in relation to the Irish emigration of the mid-nineteenth century when people were fleeing from a country where many were literally starving, indeed many had already died of starvation. *Those* people, it seemed to me, had no option.

And Ireland and Italy were different places when it came to what nature provided for those who had nothing. Even today there are those in Calabria who, out of preference or custom rather than need, can be found out in the countryside gathering edible wild plants and herbs for the table. Every March and April many people, myself included, scour the old, abandoned country lanes and other people's fields in search of wild asparagus.

From the two families I'd already visited in America, it seemed to me that to emigrate or not was an individual choice that people made because they knew that things could be better across the Atlantic and, for those unique individuals with the intellectual and emotional drive to better themselves within a generation, maybe there was no choice but to give it a go. Perhaps that is what Ralph meant.

But I believe they were also brave ... of that I have no doubt.

I also thought of Giuseppe/Francesco Sculco, the man who, at two different times in his life, forty years apart, emigrated to the United States. The first time when he crossed the Atlantic aboard the *Regina d'Italia* he

Sina and Gino Sculco with daughter Anna and her family and two of Gino's brothers.

was one of one thousand, three hundred and fifty-four Italians crammed into the ship's steerage quarters. It was winter 1920 and though conditions were always improving aboard such ships, it cannot have been an easy passage, particularly as he was traveling alone and not, as was more common, with family or friends from his home town. His second crossing was an altogether different experience, both in terms of the conditions— he traveled on the sleek trans-Atlantic liner, the Italian Line's new flagship, *Leonardo da Vinci*—and his expectations. The only point of similarity was that on both occasions he was met by his older brother Carlo.

Francesco Agostino Giuseppe was born in the same year as my father ... it was a good year for I believe they were, in their own distinct ways, extraordinary men.

I wished I had known both.

POSTSCRIPT

I am sitting outside in a bright winter sun in Santa Severina's *piazza*; it is early December 2012 and people are making their way across the square from the church. I am looking for a particular woman whom I know to be a close friend of Franca Sculco, Ralph's wife. I spot my friend Vittoria Barone with a woman I don't recognize but know must be Franca. I shake Franca's hand and we talk briefly about my visit to New Jersey and her sister Elvira.

And another piece of the Santa Severina jigsaw falls into place.

And not long afterwards another piece ...

Kay and I are lunching with Raffaele Vizza and Silvana Gerardi, our friends and whose first marital home we live in; they are our landlords.

We are talking about Rose and Jose as, in the distant Calabrian sense, Rose and Raffaele are 'cousins'. From our conversation it becomes clear that it was Raffaele who also saw the potential for an exhibition of Jose Fontaiña's work in Santa Severina's castle and who spoke to Jose about it when the family were last here.

Raffaele goes on to mention a painting hanging in our dining room and asks me if I had ever noticed the signature.

I hadn't ... but I know exactly what he is going to say.

When I was somewhere over Tennessee on my way back to New Jersey from Albuquerque I received an email from a man who introduced himself as Pat Scida, a Calabrian and relative of the Cariddi family that I would be visiting the following weekend in Schenectady. It was his cousin Jennie Cariddi who had passed on my email address to him.

Pat hailed from Oceanside, Long Island, a part of New York that had been particularly badly hit by Hurricane Sandy, and said that he would like to meet up with me if it fitted in with my schedule.

So, because it was already my plan to visit and stay with Luigi and Katrina Piezzo on the Thursday in Valley Stream, just a few miles from Oceanside, Pat and I arranged to meet that same morning.

He agreed to pick me up at Lynbrook station and offered to drop me off in Valley Stream later in the afternoon.

My father realized that he wasn't Italian any more

I arrived late back from Fair View the night before and was out early the next morning heading for Penn Station where I had breakfast and bought my ticket for Lynbrook.

Like Grand Central Terminal a few blocks to the north-east, Penn Station was an iconic architectural structure but, unlike Grand Central, it survived the remodeling of the sixties in name only. At the time both were controversial projects but these days Penn Station lies beneath the Madison Square Garden complex, the demise of its magnificent pink granite façade described at the time by the *New York Times* as a "monumental act of vandalism against one of the largest and finest landmarks of its age, of Roman elegance".

Elegant it might well have been but today's subterranean incarnation is dismal, rundown and characterless, a monument to nothing other than blind folly.

When I arrived at Lynbrook, Pat was nowhere to be seen ... of course I didn't know what he looked like but there was nobody hovering round a car expectantly. Every time a car drew up I stepped forward in anticipation ... only to withdraw in resignation.

I was about to give him a ring when I recalled how the station at Pelham had two exits and entrances, one for trains arriving *from* New York, the other for trains *to* New York. So I walked round to the other side just as a man was getting into a car ... I called and waved and was rewarded when Pat didn't pull out of the car park after all but instead walked over and shook my hand.

Pat was a large, jolly man and wanted to be reassured that I didn't mind that he'd hijacked a bit of my time. Of course I didn't mind ... I knew from some of the things he talked about in our brief exchange of emails that this was going to be a unique story and, besides, I thought it might be interesting for me to see two different strands of the same family. Ten minutes later we were sitting at his kitchen table drinking coffee and devouring some fine Italian cream cakes ... the sort I'd been looking for in Hoboken the day before.

Like his relatives, the Cariddi family in Schenectady—whom I had not yet met—Pat's family came from Stróngoli, an impressive, fortress-like, hilltop town north of Crotone close to the Ionian coast. Apart from its fine Cirò wines, Stróngoli has another claim to fame in that it was to this slab of rock, at the time called Petelia, that the rebel slave Spartacus fled when things got a little difficult for him and his rebel army. For a while the Roman army managed to confine him there but he and his army slipped

Stróngoli: still as high and impenetratable as ever.

away and fled north before finally succumbing to an inevitable defeat.

It was in 1912, the month after the *Titanic* went down, that Pat's father, Pasquale, first came to America; he was twenty-six and had already completed two stints of military service—conscription.

At the time it was compulsory for eighteen-year-olds to serve two years but Pasquale, a glutton for punishment, did an another two years in lieu of his brother who was a sickly child. I wondered if this story was true as I had always thought that the infirm were exempt from conscription but Pat says that the power-that-be gave his mother a choice ... each son had to go or one could go twice. Then again, perhaps Pasquale just liked the service life and read the political runes and saw trouble around the corner.

Wherever the truth lies, he seemed to do well and served in the cavalry as a houseman for officers in northern Italy for whom he cooked and generally kept their quarters in order. Seemingly the officers took a shine to the young Calabrese so they taught him how to read and write and to appreciate the better things in life ... at the time not normally part of the upbringing of the son of a farm worker, even an overseer like his father.

By the time he'd finished his second tour of duty Pasquale Scida had learned enough to be considered literate. Pasquale realized that, in learning to read and write, he had acquired an important skill. It was his experience that the only other people in most small towns with such skills were the local priests and the church in general and these they were inclined to use as a means of control.

So, because of his two terms of military service, young Pasquale had not only glimpsed how the other half lived in the north of his homeland but could speak and even read and write their language; in addition he was disillusioned with the poverty he saw around him in Calabria and how the status quo was maintained by both the government and the church.

For such a man there seemed only one option ... it was time to go, time to take a chance on what the other side of the Atlantic had to offer.

Pasquale had a friend, Vincenzo Scigliano, eight years his senior and also from Stróngoli. Apparently both Vincenzo and Pasquale had had the same dream ... that one day they would go to America. In 1902 Vincenzo fulfilled that dream. It was ten years and two terms of military service before Pasquale was able to do likewise.

Twenty-six year-old Pasquale was met at Ellis Island by a cousin living in the Bronx but then moved to the Williamsburg district of Brooklyn where his friend Vincenzo Scigliano lived. Later he moved to North Adams, Massachusetts where there was already an established Italian community. Initially he lived there with Raffaele Cariddi and his brother Francesco— Francesco Cariddi had arrived in America just a month before Pasquale with the purpose of setting up home there before returning to Stróngoli two years later to marry Pasquale's sister Antoinette.

Unusually, when Francesco and Antoinette returned as a couple to America in May 1914, they travelled with documentation which showed that Antoinette was already using her husband's surname which, of course, was the custom in America ... and almost unheard of Stróngoli or any other part of Calabria for that matter. In less than two years in America, Francesco had already worked out how to cut down on the paperwork. (The story of Francesco and Antoinette can be found in the chapter entitled 'Thank you Uncle Sam' on page 183.)

For the moment we abandoned Pasquale Scida living and working in North Adams for it was at this point that Pat Scida jumped back in time to tell me the story of another family from Stróngoli and the curious events surrounding Domenico Pirrotto, his wife Maria Mazza, their daughter Carolina and another young girl. The two stories, he assured me, were not unconnected.

•

It was 1902, at the age of twenty-nine, Domenico Pirrotto left his pregnant wife Maria Mazzo in Stróngoli and emigrated to America. The plan was for him to get work, establish a home and send for his wife and the daughter he had never seen. It didn't quite happen like that.

Both Domenica and Maria were illiterate. If either wanted to communicate with the other, then they either had to have someone write a letter for them or had to confide in someone who was going to or returning from America in the hope that they would be able to pass on the message. At the time other Italians and Calabrians tended to live together in established communities so this was not as difficult as it might sound.

After more than a year with no direct contact from her husband, apart from second-hand news that he was alive and mention of him in letters received by neighbors and friends, Maria realized that it was a distinct possibility that Domenico had no intention of sending for her in the immediate future and that he could even be abandoning her. Illiterate she might have been, but she was not stupid.

Such a scenario was not an uncommon story. Many Italian married men emigrated to the United States with the intention of getting established before sending for their wife. And sometimes such good intentions did not match up to the reality ... in my own family there is such a skeleton. Whatever the truth, Maria decided that she wasn't going to take any chances and determined that somehow she would go to America with her young daughter Carolina.

In the meantime a situation presented itself in her home town that Maria used to her advantage. One of her friends was looking after an orphaned niece of about eight years; the woman had a sister in America to whom she wished to send the child. This was another not an uncommon occurrence: parents often did die suddenly and their children sent to live with aunts or uncles in other towns, other parts of Italy and even America. But this particular woman had a built-in advantage ... her brother was a priest.

For Maria Mazza it was not rocket science to see how she could expedite her own desire to go to America to join her husband Domenico by volunteering to take the eight-year-old niece and deliver her to her aunt. There was method in her madness for she realized that she could use the priest's letter-writing skills to speed up the process of applying for and completing all the necessary documentation for the passage ... he could also write letters to her unsuspecting husband to inform him of her imminent arrival and, of course he would pay for everyone's passage.

The priest went along with Maria's proposal and so it was that, in January 1905, Maria Mazza presented herself at Naples with her two-year-old daughter Carolina and another child of eight, Paresena Telelli, on the first stage of their journey to a brave new world on board the *Città di Napoli.*

Only problem is that there is no record of Paresena Telelli ever having arrived in America; nor did any other child travel with Maria and Carolina.

We returned to the mystery of Paresena after Pat told me how these two stories, that of Pasquale Scida and Maria Mazza, were connected ... in the early twenties, when Pasquale was forty-three, he married Maria's daughter Carolina, now called Catherine; she was nineteen at the time.

Maria Mazza is Pat Scida's grandmother; he was one of five children from the union of Pasquale Scida and Catherine Pirrotto.

•

What happened to Paresena has no bearing on Pat Scida's story, nonetheless it is a mystery for, as Pat is sure she did make it to America with his grandmother and that she used to visit his her home, how she actually got there when there appears to be no obvious extant documentation, did rattle my investigative gene. It was a tangent worth going off at and at the time I could see only one possible explanation.

I wondered had Paresena Telelli traveled on the *Città di Napoli* without paperwork ... that somehow she was smuggled on and off the ship? In simple terms, Paresena Telelli could have been a stowaway.

This threw up two questions. Why? How?

If this is indeed what happened then the reason would forever remain a mystery. Perhaps Maria thought she could put the money set aside for Paresena's passage to better use; perhaps something happened in Naples with Paresena's paperwork.

How Maria might have managed such a subterfuge would also never be known for certain but it was not an uncommon story ... bribing one of the ship's crew was not unheard of and, once on board, it would have been

The *Città di Napoli*, launched as the *Republic* in Belfast.

easy for an eight-year-old to become inconspicuous among seven hundred others in steerage on the *Città di Napoli*, particularly if she appeared to have a mother and baby sister.

In 1910 the *New York Times* reported on the story of a fifteen-year-old, Maria Cavallero from Messina in Sicily, who entered the United States as a stowaway in search of her father.

The 1908 earthquake which devastated both Reggio Calabria and Messina in equal measure also wreaked havoc with the Cavallero family— Maria's mother, sister and brother died and she was left in the care of relatives while her father headed for America to start again. Maria got fed up with her new life and decided to follow her father ... she later told officials that she put on her best clothes and slipped quietly out of the house. She did not know where America was exactly but somehow she got herself to Palermo, mostly by foot, and slipped on board the *San Giorgio* in Palermo harbor with the other emigrants.

Among some of her fellow steerage passengers she aroused some suspicion because she was seen to be by herself and this filtered through to the ship's officers who alerted Immigration officials when they arrived at Ellis Island. Maria had no address for her father but she thought that he lived in Brooklyn. An effort was made to find him and, at the time, officials and Maria were all confident he would soon be located; if not Maria would be sent back to Sicily.

A quick look at the Ellis Island archives showed no record of anyone with the surname Cavallero from the Messina area having travelled to America between 1908 and 1910 and of the right age to have had a fifteen-year-old child. I thought that perhaps, unlike his daughter, Maria's father never made it to Palermo and if he did he may have changed his mind and stayed there or gone somewhere else. Then again, perhaps Maria made the whole story up.

In the case of Paresena Telelli from Stróngoli, what seems certain is that she left Naples and arrived in New York; what is also certain is that there appears to be no extant evidence to support the story that she travelled with Maria Mazza and her daughter to America.

But what is known for certain is that, in 1911 for example, 274 stowaways were discovered trying to enter New York illegally; there is, of course, no official record of those who succeeded.

•

Having been deflected by the story of Maria, Carolina, Paresena and others, Pat and I returned to North Adams where we left the young Pasquale a few pages back living with his future brother-in-law Francesco.

In the North Adams area Italians had played a major role in the construction of the Hoosac Rail Tunnel, at the time the second longest tunnel in the world and many had settled in the town, close to the tunnel's western portal.

Work on the tunnel had long since finished but its legacy was a strong and significant Italian community and one which made the young Pasquale welcome.

Over the next seven years or so—before a move back to Brooklyn—he actually worked on the railroad for a time but also chopped wood and was a gopher-tender on a fabric printing press—at the time western Massachusetts was the fabric-printing capital of the world with dozens of mills and one of the largest, the Arnold Print Works was in North Adams.

Pasquale also worked in a bowling alley as a so-called pin-boy—mindless and repetitive work, sometimes even dangerous, but in the days before automated bowling alleys somebody had to put the pins back on their spots.

At the same time Pasquale was learning English and while he was still

Pin-boys at work in Brooklyn around 1910.

in North Adams he had mastered the language sufficiently to gain his American Citizenship and, according to Pat, spoke with almost no trace of an accent.

In August 1918 this young, well-dressed young man returned to Brooklyn to visit some of his co-patriots who were living there, including, of course, his friend Vincenzo Sciglaino. The occasion was the religious festival to celebrate the Assumption—it is what is now called Ferragosto in modern Italian culture—on 15 August.

By this time Domenico Perrotti and his wife Maria were running a small bar and restaurant in the neighborhood and for the Festival had erected a small stall where their daughter Catherine helped them sell their wares—food, beer and wine. It was here, Pat believes, that his father Pasquale first ran into the fifteen-year-old Catherine, his mother-to-be.

Pasquale spoke to his friend Vincenzo about the Perrotti family and Catherine in particular and decided to stop on in Brooklyn for a few months ... he stayed with another friend from Stróngoli closer to his own age, Antonio Grillo.

At this time, unknown to Pasquale, this raven-haired buxom beauty had another suitor, also called Vincenzo, who was considered a good enough match by her family even though he didn't speak much English. Another incentive from Catherine's parents' point of view was that they now had five other children, three of them girls and none of them yet married.

Like Pasquale, Domenico Perrotti also recognized the value of education and made sure all his children could speak English so in that sense Carolina and Pasquale were well matched.

Finally Catherine rebuffed Vincenzo's advances and he returned to Italy while the persistent Pasquale continued wooing Catherine to the point that their engagement seemed imminent. Then word filtered back from Stróngoli that the thwarted Vincenzo had found himself another young girl to woo ... Pasquale's sister (also Catherine but known as Kikina).

Pasquale feared that this was more than mere coincidence; it was common knowledge that Vincenzo had been rebuffed and Pasquale's mother was fearful that, should Vincenzo hear that, back in America, his prospective wife's brother (Pasquale) was intending to marry his old flame Catherine), Kikina could find herself left at the altar.

So Pasquale made an executive decision and decided to postpone all talk of engagement to Catherine and headed back to North Adams. He left his

Pasquale Scida and Carolina Pirrotto in 1954.

friends Vincenzo Scigliano and Antonio Grillo to deal with the fall-out and in particular the anger of Catherine's parents, Domenico and Maria Perrotti.

His two friends were also under strict instructions not to divulge the real reason for his 'disappearance' ... he didn't want anything he might do or say to stand in the way of Kikina's impending marriage to Vincenzo back in Stróngoli. Pasquale was aware that, were his intentions towards Catherine to become common knowledge, it would only be a matter of time before it would filter back to Calabria. Quite simply, until Vincenzo and Kikina were wed, he (and his mother) couldn't be sure whether or not Vincenzo's intentions were honorable or part of some revengeful scheme.

The misjudged Vincenzo was as good as his word and, when he and Kikina finally married in Stróngoli, Pasquale returned to Brooklyn to weather the storm from Catherine's parents.

He and Catherine were married in 1922.

Later Vincenzo returned to America with his wife Kikina, Pasquale's sister; the family settled across the street from Pasquale and Catherine and had five children. Pasquale and Catherine also had five children, the youngest of whom, Pat Scida, was helping me demolish some more cream cakes.

But the story and its five protagonists—Vincenzo, Pasquale, Domenico, Maria and Catherine—was not quite finished; there was another twist in the tale.

Vincenzo Scigliano also married and had nine children, the oldest of whom, Pasquale, died in 1975. Pasquale had children of his own, one of whom popped into the kitchen to say 'hello' ... Pat introduced me to his wife, Rosalie, the daughter of Pasquale Scigliano, the grand-daughter of Vincenzo Scigliano, his father Pasquale's best friend from when they lived in Stróngoli over a hundred years earlier.

•

Introductions over, Rosalie was off again on another errand ... Pat explained that she didn't have the same passion for the past as he had.

But before we returned to the story of his father's life in Brooklyn, and lest I hadn't made yet another connection, he went on to point out that Jennie Cariddi—the woman I was going to visit that weekend in

Schenectady—was the daughter of Pasquale's sister, Antoinette, and her husband Francesco with whom he had lived in North Adams when he first came to America.

Life in Brooklyn was good to Pasquale. He found employment at several different jobs before getting what he really wanted—steady employment which he knew was the key to a better and consistent standard of living for his growing family. In the mid-twenties he embarked upon a thirty-seven-year career with Brooklyn's Department of Sanitation ... as a garbage collector for the first twenty-seven years and then as a street cleaner for the last ten.

Pat recalled how his family were intent on being American above all else. From the start they copied the American way in everything: from the language they spoke to how they decorated the house; from the food to the politics. His mother even listened to a radio station, WOV, which included a program for Italian-Americans on American etiquette ... every week she would listen intently as presenter, Diana Baldi, explained how things were done in America.

Of course they recognized and kept up many Italian traditions but did so in an American landscape. Nevertheless, as tradition demanded, the first five gallons of the each year's new wine harvest, the *vendemmia*, went to his mother to make *vincotto*, literally 'cooked wine', wine reduced slowly through many hours of slow cooking to produce a thick, dark and sweet condiment. I assured Pat that in today's Calabria, the same tradition persists; nothing has changed.

During the Prohibition era Pasquale and some of his friends, like many of their fellow-countrymen, Italian or otherwise, made a barrel or two of the red nectar for home use ... they reasoned, not unnaturally, that the law in this case was a total ass. Unfortunately someone told the police who arrived yielding axes to break up the fun ... and the barrels.

More than anything Pasquale was embarrassed to have been seen to be breaking the law, albeit a law as stupid as it was unenforceable. For Calabrians such as Pasquale it would have been difficult to see the making of wine as any sort of crime ... they weren't making it *because* of Prohibition they were making *despite* Prohibition because that's what they did every fall, that's what their families drank round the dinner table, that's what they'd done for generations. Wine-making was as much a part of their normal life as was the preserving of tomatoes or eggplants or making *sopressata*.

Nevertheless Pasquale waited until the American legislature came back to its senses, and Prohibition was repealed, before turning his hand once more to wine-making. In the late thirties he and his brother-in-law from across the street, Antonio, dug out a wine cellar, a *magazzino* where they made and kept their wine in barrels and preserved all the other traditional foods you might expect to find in any Calabrian *magazzino*, then as now: jars of peppers and eggplants (aubergines) in vinegar, dried tomatoes and hanging hams and sausages.

•

Around 1938, Pasquale returned to Stróngoli to see his aging mother for the last time. He spent three months in Italy during which time he won a substantial amount on the lottery and, as war loomed, was able to finance sending three of his brothers to Argentina. The Stróngoli of the late thirties he could still relate to, it was still the small hilltop town, the town of his birth, a place where the people and culture were almost frozen in time.

It was a different story in 1961 when Pasquale and Catherine returned to Stróngoli for the last time and, like Giuseppe Sculco the previous year, they traveled aboard the *Leonardo da Vinci* ... light years from life, steerage-class, aboard the lowly *Moltke* which had taken him to his new life in America half a century earlier.

Pat talked about how this trip upset his father ... yes, he knew it was unlikely he'd ever see the place of his birth again, but it was more than that ... for the first time this septuagenarian understood that he wasn't Italian any more.

And so on to Pat himself and the lives of his siblings ... bearing in mind that their grandmother and mother were illiterate, they'd all done well for themselves. He told me a bit about his own working life and how his parents' respect for education had paid dividends. By the seventies he was working in the financial world and twenty years later had moved to Wall Street to work for Morgan Stanley; by the time he retired in the early nineties he was a senior Vice-President with the firm.

Pat's memories and stories went back once again to Maria Mazza and we talked a little more about the extraordinary life of quite an extraordinary woman. Not only did she successfully get herself, her young daughter and an eight-year old virtual stranger to Naples in winter, but she embarked on the fifteen-day crossing in circumstances that, for a single woman, were often difficult, hazardous even.

I remembered reading a Report on the conditions that unaccompanied women traveling in steerage sometimes had to put up with on ships plying between Europe and New York. The 1909 Report said the following:

Pat Scida at home in Oceanside, Long Island.

"Everything was dirty, sticky, and disagreeable to the touch. Every impression was offensive. Worse than this was the general air of immorality. For fifteen hours each day I witnessed all around me this improper, indecent, and forced mingling of men and women who were total strangers ... women steerage passengers were compelled to submit to insults ... not one young woman in the steerage escaped such experiences."

Certainly Maria (Mazza) Pirrotto, was an extraordinary woman but, Pat recalled, there was another side to her. Although he had no conscious memories of his grandmother, he recalled photos of an unsmiling, grim countenance; this was a woman, he believes, that never forgave her husband for seeming to abandon her back in 1902.

Similarly, years later, she never forgave her son Luigi for marrying a girl from the Lower East Side against her wishes. When Luigi and his wife had a baby son, they wrote to his parents in Brooklyn to share the good news with them ... Maria tore the letter up and sent it back. Even on her death bed Maria never forgave him for going against her wishes.

But Pat's mother, Catherine, didn't inherit this side of her mother ... Catherine was a much happier and outgoing woman who, even though she was illiterate, spoke perfect English without a trace of an accent.

That said, there was a tough side to her too ... it was said, of all her five siblings she was the most like her mother in her determination to acquire the things she wanted for her family.

Sitting across the table from me, her son, Pat Scida, was living proof of this.

•

It was time to eat and so we left the past behind and ventured out into Oceanside in search of lunch. But first Pat took me on a tour of the area, a place that in just over two weeks had changed beyond recognition.

The culprit: Hurricane Sandy.

On the evening of Monday 29 October 2012 there was severe flooding in Oceanside as well as downed trees and power lines and unimaginable damage to boats, cars and buildings. Pat put it succinctly, "Hurricane Sandy has been a bitch."

He and Rosalie had been suffering from 'survivor's remorse' by dint of being unscathed by the storm apart from being without power for nearly two weeks.

Some form of flooding occurred as close as six houses away from them. On the other hand many of their friends and family had their basements flooded with several feet of water driven up through sewage drains while others watched as the ocean and/or creeks, overflowed into the streets, flooding and devastating basements, even as far as the first floor. Some people had had their houses condemned.

He told me how, several days after the storm hit, he went to nearby Rockaway to his niece's house because he couldn't get in touch with his brother by phone. When he got there they were using a couple of generators for light and were cooking breakfast on the barbecue grill. The water was lapping at the top of the basement stairs and they were just beginning to dig out the sand that the ocean had deposited in the street. They needed to clear paths in the sand to the street-level sewers before they could begin to pump water out of the basement.

After a while his brother looked at him and said, "There's a quarter of a million dollars worth of cars out front and not one of them will start."

That statement, he said, just stuck in his mind—these cars were in four to five feet of water for three or four hours which rendered them totally destroyed. His brother's car and five others stood incapacitated in the

Oceanside in the aftermath of Hurricane Sandy and a boat that thinks it's a car.

street—two relatively new Range Rovers, a Mercedes Benz, two Cadillacs and a two-week old Audi.

I could see it for myself: the contents of houses were piled up on front lawns—chairs, tables, cushions, fridges, carpets, the detritus of one night of mayhem on America's east coast. The front lawn was but a staging post between house and dumpster as young men, sporting masks to protect them against who-knows-what, laboriously shifted the remnants of people's lives from one to the other. I wondered who they'd be thanking for what come Thanksgiving.

Seeing it on television is nothing like seeing and smelling its reality. I could see why Pat and Rosalie suffered a form of remorse ... they had been so close and were fortunate that they were so far.

POSTSCRIPT

For months the story of Paresena Telelli, the eight-year-old from Stróngoli that supposedly travelled to America with Maria Mazza has been bugging me. I don't like loose ends.

Because people who travel together or come from the same town or village are normally listed together on a ship's manifest—and as Paresena was supposed to be just eight and in the care of Maria Mazza—it seemed logical that they would be listed together. Experience told me to look no further than those names above or below Maria Mazzo and her daughter to find the mysterious eight-year-old Paresena.

So I return to the story of Paresena Telelli and recall that the name Telelli—and all its possible alternatives—doesn't seem to exist on the Ellis Island website. I decide instead to focus on this little girl's unusual given name, Paresena, a name I've never heard before; the only way I can do this is to check the names of every passenger who boarded the *Città di Napoli* in Naples ... all 626 of them.

At the bottom of the sixth page I notice the name of passenger 298, Mastimissa Fuisenda, and am intrigued both by the unusual name and the fact that 'she' comes from Stróngoli; then I spot a similar surname a couple of lines below—number 300 is recorded as Parisino Fusenda and is also from Stróngoli.

For a moment I sit in silence, staring at the name Parisino ... but I soon get my act back together and there follows a flurry of further delving into the ship's manifest to find out more about these two Stróngolesi. I discover that they are brother and sister and that their different surnames are both incorrect—they should be Frisenda; their given names are also incorrectly transcribed—'Mastimissa' is male and therefore Mastimisso and finally 'Parisino' is female and therefore Parisina.

For three reasons I know I have finally found the illusive 'Paresena Telelli'. Firstly, the name Parisina is almost identical and equally unusual; secondly, this Parisina Frisenda came from Stróngoli; and, thirdly, she is traveling to America on the same ship as Maria Mazza. These three connections with Maria's story cannot just be coincidences ... nevertheless I check the rest of the passenger list just in case there is another 'Paresena' lurking there. There is not.

Family stories can take on a life of their own and details can easily succumb to the passage of time, fading memories and sometimes a little embroidery. I realize now that the story Maria Mazza passed on to her family is one such tale. The protagonists and the framework of the story are all in the right place at the right time but the detail has become blurred— there is no intent to mislead, it just happened that way. And now I know that the story that Maria passed on to her family happened this way ...

Parisina did indeed travel on the same ship as Maria Mazza and Maria's daughter Carolina but she travelled with her older brother Mastimisso. Both might well have been orphaned as Maria's story suggests but they were scarcely children ... Parisina was seventeen, her brother a year older. There seems no reason to doubt that Maria did offer her services as a kind of chaperone on the voyage and that the local priest, a relative of Parisina and Mastimisso, did help fund Maria.

Once in America these two young orphaned adults did not join their sister as Maria's story had it but went instead to live with their brother Attilio who had emigrated two years earlier and now lived in Brooklyn.

But how do I explain the surname? However hard I might try there seems little mileage in looking at Telelli as a misspelling of Frisenda. I can only think that it is either a genuine mistake or that perhaps Parisina married quite soon after she arrived in America and took her husband's name and everyone soon forgot that she started life as a Frisenda.

I find the extended Frisenda family listed in the 1910 US Census data on the Ancestry website; they are now living in Myrtle Avenue, Brooklyn. Only Parisina it seems has flown the nest so perhaps my theory about her having married is indeed what happened. That said, at first I cannot find anybody in the same census with a name that remotely resembles Telelli and so I gradually widen my search until I come up with Tellelo and find, living in Park Avenue, Brooklyn, Parase Tellelo and her husband John. Park Avenue is a block away from Myrtle Avenue. John sports two alternative surnames, Tellebo and Tellelo.

On the 1940 census, I see that the Tellelo family name has morphed to Tilleli; John is sixty-five and Parssia is fifty-two. The family has now bought a house in Sanford Street and three of the Tilleli children are still living at home; one of them is called Attilio.

I just can't resist finding out a little more about John, or Giovanni as he would have been when he emigrated—I am, of course, assuming he was an emigrant. Naturally I start with Tellebo and Tellelo, the two surnames he was credited with in 1910—nothing. I start widening my search backwards to where I had originally started when I was looking for Parisina and eventually find Giovanni Tilelli who left Stróngoli in 1902 to join his brother Francesco in Brooklyn. I feel I have come full circle.

•

Having solved one riddle, my thoughts return to the *New York Times* story of the stowaway, Maria Cavallero and her errant father, and I decide to dig deeper once more.

The Ellis Island archive shows that there were 149 males with the surname Cavallero who entered the United States through Ellis Island but, as I had already discovered, none has the right profile to be Maria's father—none left Sicily post-earthquake, between 1908 and 1910, came from the Messina area and was born around 1877 (or earlier).

So I change one letter in the surname and Cavallero becomes Cavallaro. Now there are 1241 men to search through and it is soon clear that the majority are Sicilian and that there are many who could have been young Maria's father.

I realize I did Maria an injustice when I suggested she might have made the story up.

I first met Luigi and Katrina Piezzo in Santa Severina in early October 2012 when they were visiting, for the first time, the descendants of Luigi's distant family in Santa Severina.

We met again several times over the next few days and arranged that I would visit them at their Valley Stream home in November and stay overnight there.

At the time they didn't tell me about the other couple who lived in the apartment below them.

Of all the people I would visit, I had spent more time with Luigi and Katrina *before* coming to the United States than with any of the other families and, of course, we had already met up a couple of times the previous week in Manhattan.

A place to call home

After we'd eaten, Pat Scida drove me the few miles to Valley Stream and dropped me at the home of Luigi and Katrina Piezzo.

Before Katrina and I sat down to catch up on my travels since the last time we met on and off the High Line, I handed her my bag of laundry that she'd so kindly agreed to do for me ... it was fortunate that this visit to Valley Stream was exactly halfway through my trip. Truth be told we swapped bags ... part of the deal was that I would take gifts back to their Calabrian families from the Piezzos and their friend Grace Chan.

Having caught up, we went downstairs to talk to the couple who lived in the apartment below though at the time, apart from their names, Johnny and Mary, I didn't really pick up on any connection with Luigi and Katrina. Johnny was retired and when I asked what he had done for a living he told me he'd worked in the paper and cardboard industry where he used to design and make dies. I could tell he was used to people not knowing what a die or a die-cut was. As it happened, I did.

As a retired graphic designer, this was a field where I had some knowledge and experience and so Johnny, having at long last found someone who spoke his language, immediately ushered me down into his den where he showed me the tools of his trade. In the paper and print trade a die, for those still in the dark, is the outline made with small, sharp metal blades that cuts out the irregular, non-rectangular, shape of, say, a folder with a pocket or a box after it's been printed. In the past I had designed several of these and then my design went to someone like Johnny who would actually make the form, the die, that would do the cutting and any scoring for folding.

My initiation into the world of die-cutting over, Katrina and I returned upstairs; I still thought of Johnny and Mary as the downstairs 'neighbors' and still hadn't sought or been offered any other explanation ... the only connection with Luigi that I noted was that I recalled him saying once that his father had worked in the paper industry.

While we waited for Luigi to arrive home after his day's work in Manhattan, Katrina and I looked at some family photos and felt it was only right that we should make a start on the red wine just to be absolutely certain it was good enough to accompany our meal.

Luigi and Katrina, a New Zealander, had only been married a few years and for much of that time Katrina had helped Luigi nurse his father. His

The Santa Severina that Giuseppe Piezzo left behind.

father, also Luigi, died in 2012 which was why later that year they made the trip to Santa Severina to find out more about Luigi's family there. Katrina had taken up the research reins from where Lou had left off and together they slowly pieced together the story of the family's Italian ancestry and when and how grandfather Giuseppe first came to America.

In the interests of clarity, there being more than one Luigi in this story, I have decided to call Katrina's husband Luigi by his Americanized name, Lou and his father Louie.

Lou arrived home and over a wonderful oriental dinner we raced back in time to 1910 when Giuseppe Piezzo decided it was time to leave Santa Severina and seek his fortune in America. As we did so, it occured to me that, unlike all the other people and/or families I had or would meet, the story of the Piezzo family was likely to be the result of genealogical research, in this case by Katrina. In other words, although Lou was aware that he had family in Santa Severina and both the Miriello and Quaranta families knew that they had American cousins somewhere, they really did not know each other until Katrina and her investigative gene got to work on the computer.

•

Parts of this story I already knew. I was with Lou and Katrina in Santa Severina when Lou asked me to ask my friend Ciccio, the husband of Anna Miriello, one of his Calabrian family, if he knew what old Giuseppe did when he lived in Santa Severina as a teenager.

We were standing on Ciccio's verandah at the time, having just eaten a satisfying Calabrian lunch, and he pointed north-west to a nearby hill, halfway between Santa Severina and Altilia and said, "He worked up there in Almirò, guarding oranges."

Like Altilia, Almirò is a *frazione*, a disjointed part, of Santa Severina and, Ciccio explained, at one time the hillside facing us was resplendent with orange groves and, such was the demand at that time, these oranges needed guarding from would-be poachers. Apparently the young Giuseppe Piezzo had a small cabin on the hill and was paid to watch over his orange constituency. Mind-numbingly boring work it must have been and so it is little wonder that, in between scouring the countryside for would-be orange snatchers, his flights of fancy took him across the Atlantic and to a more demanding life.

For the record, the art of fruit poaching still lingers on in and around Santa Severina ... to my certain knowledge, two consecutive year's crops of kiwifruit have disappeared in the days just before harvesting and last year (2012) the grapes of a particularly fine local maker of wine vanished just before his planned harvest.

It goes without saying that I would be willing to offer my services as a guardian to all and sundry if they could only guarantee internet access to my watch-tower.

•

Giuseppe Piezzo was born in 1892, the only son of Francesco Piezzo and Maria Nicoletti, he of Santa Severina, she of San Giovanni in Fiori,

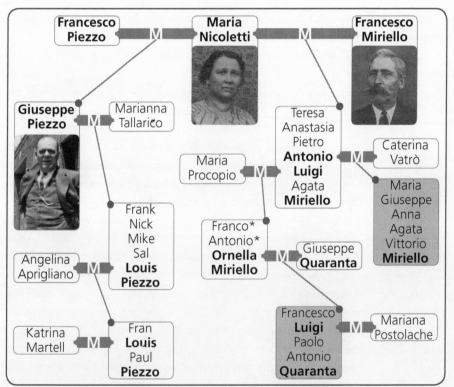

The Miriello and Quaranta families in shaded boxes are members of Lou Piezzo's family who currently live in or close to Santa Severina.
(*Franco and Antonio Miriello both emigrated to the States in the sixties and it was Antonio who helped Lou and Katrina organize their American trip in 2012.)

twenty-five kilometers to the west. The record of his birth—ironically the same year as his father died—has his surname as 'Piezzi' but variations of this sort were not uncommon at the time; everything was hand-written and names often got pronounced incorrectly, heard incorrectly or transcribed incorrectly ... or indeed any combination thereof.

It is a myth that such mistakes were made when they entered the United States via Ellis Island, that language confusion between immigrants and American officials resulted in names and other details getting changed. Any such inaccuracies arose on the home front for the ship's manifest was based on documentation completed by local clerks in Italy *before* departure.

It was incumbent on emigrants to have the correct paperwork when they purchased their passage, just as it was incumbent on the shipping company and their representatives to check such documentation before embarkation. This is where any written error—such as names, dates of birth or towns of origin—almost certainly originated.

In the case of the Piezzo family surname there are at least four variations, each of which appears on at least one document relating to the family: Piezzo, Piezzi, Pezzo and Piezzio. In the interests of consistency, I will use Lou's family surname as it's written today—Piezzo.

Katrina clarified for me how the two families they visited in Santa Severina, the Miriello and Quaranta families, fitted into the story.

Giuseppe Piezzo's father (Lou's great-grandfather), Francesco, died when Giuseppe was an infant and his mother, Maria Nicoletti, remarried a man by the name of Francesco Miriello and they in turn had six children who of course were Giuseppe's half-brothers and half-sisters.

One of these children, Antonio, in turn had seven children and it is some of these children who still retain the Miriello surname in Santa Severina. Another of their (Maria's and second husband Francesco's) children, Antonio's brother Luigi, had a daughter Ornella who married Antonio Quaranta ... the other related family in Santa Severina.

Both of these families, Miriello and Quaranta, I knew well but never realized they were related ... and their connection with Lou from Long Island is that, in Maria Nicoletti, they shared either a grandmother or a great-grandmother.

•

Marianna Tallarico and Giuseppe Piezzo married on 11 April 1915 in Brooklyn.

Marianna Tallarico and her younger brother Alessandro.

It was in 1910 that Giuseppe had had enough of looking after oranges and decided to head for America. On his mother's side there was already family there, he had an uncle, Saverio Nicoletti, who sponsored him and paid his passage. Giuseppe started his new life in America with $9 in his pocket and a home in Park Avenue, Brooklyn.

About a block away, in Skillman Street, an area of Brooklyn to where many southern Italians gravitated, there lived Marianna Tallarico, a striking young woman who, in 1911, had emigrated from Casabona—a small town in the hills north of Santa Severina and due west of Stróngoli—with her fourteen-year-old brother, Alessandro. Marianna was twenty-three at the time and she and Alessandro had gone to Skillman Street to live with their older brother, Andrea.

Katrina and Lou explained how, in her twenty-three years, Marianna had experienced much sorrow and hardship. Her parents both died when she was young and initially she and her two younger brothers, Alessandro and Giuseppe, were cared for by relatives until family funds ran dry and they had to fend for themselves for a time.

Her brother Andrea had already emigrated ... twice in less than a year. The first time, in 1906, he was sent back, possibly a problem with his documentation as his health details seemed in order. Andrea was one of seven young men from Casabona aboard the *Italia* that spring—all of whom were heading for Skillman Street—and the only one to be sent packing. In 1907 he tried again and this time successfully entered America.

Four years later, when Marianna and Alessandro crossed the Atlantic, coincidentally also on the *Italia*, they were detained overnight under the Immigration Act of 1882 which authorized those who might be Liable to become a Public Charge (LPCs)—and, as such, a potential financial burden to the United States—to be scrutinized more closely. High on the list of such LPCs were unmarried pregnant women and even women of childbearing age. Whatever the reason, upon further investigation Marianna was allowed to enter the country the following day.

It is not known when and how Marianna and Giuseppe bumped into each other—they lived close enough for that to have been literally a possibility—but it is also possible that their union was a convenient arrangement between two families, possibly with the help of a matchmaker, whose antecedents were from the same part of Calabria. Such arrangements were not uncommon but were generally only 'arrangements' in the sense that the young couple were introduced to each other and it was then up to them if they wanted to pursue a relationship that might lead to marriage. Clearly they may also have been an element of wanting to please parents and families but such unions were seldom arranged marriages in the sense of the 'forced' marriages still prevalent in the Indian sub-continent.

Marianna and Giuseppe married on 11 April 1915 at St Lucy's Church, a couple of blocks west of the intersection of Park Avenue and Skillman Street and then moved a couple of blocks the other way to a rented house in Walworth Street, midway between Brooklyn's Clinton Hill and Bedford Stuyvesant districts.

In the years just before Prohibition, Brooklyn had become a slightly safer place ... one of its sons, Alfonso Capone, had already decided there were better job opportunities for gangsters in Cicero, Chicago and headed north, closely followed by his new Irish wife, Mae.

When Prohibition did come, Joe Piezzo, like most self-respecting Italian immigrants continued—as tradition demanded—to make his own wine in the cellar where he also stored it alongside all the other traditional

Women working in an ATC cigarette factory, probably in Brooklyn, in 1917.

Calabrian preserved vegetables and fruit that most families still made. However, unlike many other Italians, Joe seems to have got away with his wine-making ... there are no family stories about axe-yielding police and broken barrels.

•

I asked Lou about his grandparents' life in Brooklyn and how easy or difficult it was for them to assimilate the language, particularly as they were living in a largely Italian community. It seems that Marianna took to it better; according to the 1930 census she could speak, read and write English whereas Giuseppe only learned to speak the language. At that time both worked ... Giuseppe in the fur factory in southern Brooklyn that his brother-in-law Alessandro owned and Marianna, in addition to being a housewife, was employed at the American Tobacco Company's factory in Brooklyn where they made Lucky Strikes.

At this time the Lucky Strikes brand was expanding and the company had just moved from it's Penn Street factory in Brooklyn (where Lucky Strikes were first manufactured in 1916) to a new site on Park Avenue. It is said that the slogan for which the brand was famous 'It's Toasted', was first coined when ATC president George Washington Hill had noticed the sweet aroma of the burly tobacco which was being 'cooked' as part of the manufacturing process at the Penn Street factory. Later he mentioned this to other company personnel, one of whom, Gerson Brown, said that it reminded him of his morning toast ... and an iconic slogan for the advertising campaign was born.

In the mid-thirties Marianna and Giuseppe finally bought their Walworth Street home but a few months later Marianna died. They had had six children but their only daughter, Maria, died of spinal meningitis and bronchial pneumonia in 1923 at the age of three. The youngest of their five sons, Louie, was Lou's father; Giuseppe and Marianna were his grandparents.

Not long after the death of his wife, Giuseppe married another Calabrian, Rose Bisignano, a widow with four daughters who, it is believed, originally came from Stróngoli, north-west of Crotone.

Quick off the block this may seem but it was not unusual for men, particularly immigrants, to seek a new wife hot on the heels of losing the first. Unlike life back in Calabria, Giuseppe would not have had the same family support network that would rally round and look after the children; there were no grandparents, no aunts and no older daughters to take over the reins. Similarly, his new wife Rose had all the help she wanted but no earner, no income ... truly this was a marriage of convenience.

Curious to a fault, I asked Lou how Rose's first husband had died and, straight-faced, he said that she had poisoned him. It took a few seconds for me to realize that he was kidding but the notion that she *could* have poisoned him was central to how Lou's father viewed her ... seemingly Rose was nobody's favorite person. I could see that, although Lou was casting Rose as the stereotypical wicked step-mother on behalf of his father, there was a more serious side to what happened for she did not treat his father well and this hurt him a lot.

I asked about the relationships between the five boys and the four girls in this extended family and Lou singled out Catherine, one of Rose's daughters, who was by far the closest to his father and his uncles. Catherine also took care of his grandfather 'Joe' in his old age; she viewed him as a father figure and the two were very close. Ever mindful of how she cared for his grandfather, Lou still keeps in touch with his feisty aunt Catherine, now well into her eighties.

It was interesting to me how quick the family's Italian names were Americanized. Giuseppe had become Joe and his five sons were Frank, Nick, Mike, Sal and Louis ... of these only Sal (Salvatore) had to make do with a name that didn't really have an English equivalent.

All these first generation boys spoke both Italian and English; such families tended to mix socially, work and even live side by side with other Italians including other Calabrese. But the next generation did not see it like that, they, were Americans and wanted to be fully assimilated into American culture. For Louie Piezzo, Lou's father, it was a conscious decision that his children should learn only English at home—that, as he saw it at the time, they should not be disadvantaged in the way that he felt he was; he wanted them to have the same opportunities for advancing themselves and be successful. All Louie's brothers used the same rationale with their children.

Lou understood his parents' thinking but nonetheless regrets that he has no Italian. When he and Katrina were in Santa Severina this was initially a problem and Lou in particular found it particularly frustrating that he couldn't speak the language of his extended Calabrian family.

But help was at hand in the shape of Mariana, the wife of 'cousin' Luigi Quaranta, who just happened to be the best English-speaker in Santa Severina—apart from Kay and I, that is. Indeed Mariana is an exceptional linguist—she is Romanian she therefore speaks both her native tongue and Italian, also English and French.

Of course even if Lou's parents had spoken to him in 'Italian', it would not have been the national language but rather the local Santa Severinese dialect ... even then, as Elizabeth Cortese discovered, over the years it would have mutated almost beyond recognition. As a young adult Lou did study some Italian in university and, when he went to his father for help, his father laughed for he had no idea what Lou was talking about. For Louis Piezzo the Italian his son was learning was like a foreign language to him.

•

Lou showed me some emails he'd received from a 'cousin', Marion Vaccaro, the granddaughter of Alessandro Tallarico's who was Lou's great uncle and ran the fur factory where his grandfather, Joe Piezzo, used to work. The company was called NuWest and had its origins at another furrier's in Brooklyn where Alessandro worked.

Alessandro had the idea of dyeing Australian rabbit skins and fur to create look-alike seal but couldn't come up with the correct formula for 'fixing' the dye so that it didn't rub off on people's clothing and skin. He lacked the chemistry background but knew that his employer at the time had the know-how but was not inclined to share it—indeed he tormented Alessandro with his so-called 'secret formula' and even called him 'ignorant' for not being able to work it out.

But his employer had a weakness ... he liked to partake of Alessandro's home-made red wine and from time to time Alessandro would bring him a five-gallon demijohn. One evening Alessandro suggested they have a drink together but this was to be no innocent socializing ... Alessandro had a game plan. Subtly he brought their inebriated conversation round to his employer's fine achievements and masterful skills and, having stroked his ego thus, it was but a short intoxicating step to the illusive 'secret formula' ... and fine Italian wine did the rest.

The dyeing formula tried and tested, Alessandro raised the money to start his own business and soon NuWest was up and running in the Mill Basin area of south Brooklyn. Despite the Depression, NuWest soon became a success story for, not only were their coats and accessories considered elegant, but they were also much less expensive than mink and fox.

Alessandro Tallarico was, by all accounts, a firm but fair boss, the latter trait best illustrated by the time when he did not resist when outside Union representatives made a presentation to the workforce—mostly Italians who lived in the same Downtown Brooklyn area—about representing them in negotiations with the management. The workforce had to vote for the proposal but nobody put their hands up; not surprisingly the Union representatives thought that they might have been threatened in some way and tried a second vote after reassuring them that they had nothing to fear, they would be protected.

Still not a single raised hand ... just the sound of muffled laughter. Then someone did speak up ...

NuWest furriers in the late 1930s.
Alessandro Tallarico, a hands-on boss, is fourth from the left.

"You don't have to protect us," he said, "Mr. Tallarico already pays us more than you said you would get us. He gives us more holidays and benefits than anyone else in the industry gets ... what would you be protecting us from?"

At the end of the war, Alessandro retired and shortly afterwards NuWest was merged with two other companies; though several years his senior, Joe Piezzo continued working and moved to another Brooklyn-based furrier, Meisel & Peskin, who still operate today out of Scholes Street.

•

Talk of the war years brought us to the subject of loyalties as three of Louie's brothers, Frank, Mike and Sal, served in the American forces, two in the army one in the navy; Louie himself also tried to sign up but was given what was called a 4F, an exemption because he had poor eyesight. From what Lou said, it was unlikely that his uncles gave a moment's thought to the possibility that they might find themselves, metaphorically if not physically, face to face with family members in the Italian forces, the enemy.

Like Frank Cortese, their American gene had long since kicked in and was ever in the ascendancy; for the moment their Italian gene was hibernating.

All the same, they were only first generation Americans and though they could fight and die for their adopted country, there was still an expectation that they should marry within their ethnic group. All Joe's sons did so ... it was not until Lou's generation that things changed. Lou recalled the time his cousin married an Irishman and how she was almost excommunicated by some family members. Mind you, back in the bad old days there was no love lost between the Italian-Americans and the Irish-Americans ... unless you were Al Capone, that is.

Also back in the bad old days, both the Irish and the Italians had their nicknames but, it has to be said, Mick and Paddy are less abusive than some of the names the Italian community had to put up with. Lou told me how, when he was called a 'wop' by another student on his way home from school, he had to ask his father what it meant. Having explained, his father told him that he should never tolerate being called such names ... a stance, I suspect, borne of bitter experience.

•

As we talked, we were enjoying wonderful oriental cuisine, courtesy of Katrina, so it's not surprising that we started talking about food and Italian food in particular.

I recalled the day we spent with them in Santa Severina when we breakfasted together at Le Puzelle, the *agriturismo* where they were staying, had lunch with Anna Miriello and husband Ciccio, then ate in the

Louie Piezzo and Angelina Aprigliano, Lou's parents.

evening with Luigi Quaranta's family—his parents, his wife Mariana and their daughter Alessandra.

Lou, Katrina and Grace Chan, Katrina's friend, had already been in Santa Severina for four days and were pretty sure that they had put on pounds ... each new family member they met and ate with had prepared enough food to feed a small army. They realized it was the Calabrian way and for that they were grateful; nonetheless, that morning Lou was determined to get some exercise in before each eating marathon. He knew that on this, their last day in Santa Severina, he would have to pace himself. We all would.

That morning the situation was made even worse when, as we were light-heartedly bemoaning the fact that bacon and eggs was never an Italian option for breakfast, our waiter, Le Puzelle's eagle-eared Giullano, sped off and returned with his version of said dish ... and this *after* we'd already eaten the normal breakfast.

Aware that in Calabria the Christmas-New Year-Befana feeding fest was fast approaching, I wondered if Italian-Americans had the same traditions, whether Befana and Ferragusto had found a place in American life in the same way as the American Halloween has been exported worldwide. As I suspected, Lou had never heard of either Befana or Ferragosto but said that his mother used to prepare the usual seven fish dishes on Christmas Eve ... I hadn't the heart to tell him that many Calabrian families think the number is thirteen.

Generally at home Lou's mother Angelina cooked Italian-American food though, increasingly, American dishes became part of the daily diet. Lou made the distinction between authentic Italian food (such as he had eaten in Calabria) and the Italian-American variety. Not surprisingly when Italians first came to the States they couldn't find all the ingredients they were used to back home and so American ingredients were incorporated into their diet—and Italian-American cuisine was the result. As an example he cited Chicken Parmesan, a favorite among Italian-Americans but virtually unheard of in southern Italy. For the record, as a kid Lou's favorite dish was *pasta pagioli* ... and it still is.

It wasn't just with food that Italians gradually absorbed American traditions ... Louie, for example, was one of many accomplished baseball players of Italian stock in the mid-forties. He was even fêted by the legendary Brooklyn Dodgers which, at the time, was a really big deal. The

Dodgers were so impressed by young Louie that they wanted him to join a Triple AAA 'farm' where he could continue training until he was good enough for the major league. However, Louie's father Joe soon put the kibosh on that as he wasn't too impressed with the idea and particularly the pay—$50 a month—and so he was 'encouraged' instead to get a job and earn some money.

Had Louie gone for the baseball option, instead of meeting his son Lou and daughter-in-law Katrina in New York, I would probably have had to travel to California for, in 1958, amid much local and national controversy, the Brooklyn Dodgers moved from their beloved Ebbets Field home and relocated to Los Angeles to became the LA Dodgers.

I feel certain that Louie would have had something to say about that.

It was in the late sixties that old Joe Piezzo felt that the Walworth Street neighborhood was in terminal decline and the family moved down to the Cypress Hill area close to Prospect Park. He died not long afterwards.

•

Two of Louie's uncles from Santa Severina, Pietro and Luigi Miriello—sons of his grandmother and her second husband—also emigrated to America but initially the two strands of the family didn't seem to socialize much ... Lou recalls only one occasion when Pietro came to dine with his parents. Pietro had emigrated first and then in 1968 his younger brother Luigi came over with his two sons Franco and Antonio—their sister was Ornella Miriello, the mother of the four Quaranta brothers still living in around Santa Severina. In 1979 Luigi Miriello returned to Santa Severina where he lived out his remaining years; his sons, Franco and Antonio, both well-established in America, stayed there and became America Citizens.

The younger generations of the Piezzo-Miriello families saw more of each other than did their parents and Antonio Miriello it was who was largely instrumental in inciting Luigi and Katrina Piezzo to visit Santa Severina for the first time in the fall of 2012—after all, both American sides of the family have ended up living round the corner from each other in Long Island.

•

It was when I was shown a photo of Lou's mother and father, Louie and Angelina, that the penny dropped in relation to neighbors Johnny and Mary. It was clear from another photo I'd seen in their apartment that Mary and Lou's mother, Angelina, were sisters. In fact they were twin sisters and, by coincidence, their family hailed from Casabona in Calabria, the same small town where Lou's grandmother Marianna Tallarico, was born.

Lou's father and Johnny had known each other since they were thirteen. As adults they both worked for separate companies in the paper industry but they were also business partners and ran a small die-making business. They fell in love with and married twin sisters on the same day in a double wedding; five years later both couples moved to the same house in Valley Stream where they each had an apartment—Johnny and Mary still live downstairs, Lou and Katrina now live upstairs. (The story of Angelina and Mary Aprigliano can be found in the next chapter, 'The Neighbors' on page 157.)

Lou's cousin, Joanne Bifulco, joined us for a short time; Joanne was the daughter of Sal, Lou's uncle. Joanne was a woman that, if you hadn't know about her Italian ancestry, you would probably have guessed. Everything about her said "I am Italian. No, I am Calabrese". Until she spoke, that is, and then it was clear she was American, no more than an Italian in disguise.

Johnny and Mary popped in too ... now that I knew where they fitted in to the Piezzo family, I saw both in a completely new light, I wanted to know more. I was warming to this enchanting duo, both descendants of immigrant families, both kind-hearted and affable and with sharp-as-a-razor memories. I could see that they had some good stories to tell so was pleased when they invited me down for breakfast the next morning—they knew that both Katrina and Lou would be out first thing and I would probably wake to an empty house.

That evening an additional chapter was born which also meant that I could find out about Lou's mother's side of the family, also Calabrian, through the eyes of her sister Mary.

•

As we downed the last of the wine, I was thinking back to the day I met

Lou in New York's Times Square and how I realized that discovering and sharing just a few days with his extended Calabrian family continued to impact on his life; it had been a powerful and moving experience.

As yet I had not experienced quite the same emotions with other families and I guessed it was because all the others already knew about their Calabrian cousins ... like embryonic explorers, together Lou and Katrina had 'discovered' theirs still going about their daily routines in

At home ... Lou and Katrina Piezzo

Santa Severina, the small Calabrian town Lou's grandfather had left over a century earlier.

For Lou his childhood memories of sending clothes to family in Santa Severina, to a place where, he believed at the time, the people probably lived a life inferior to his in America, were shattered in the fall of 2012. In Santa Severina he found instead a place that was, in his words "charming and well-preserved", a place that surpassed his expectations. Like his grandfather Giuseppe, Lou had found a place he could call home.

What began as a genealogical trip into the unknown, ended in a small hilltop town nearly four thousand miles away where people who had never met before, laughed and shared, ate and drank.

It was as if they had always known each other.

But for Lou and Katrina, that end was clearly just the beginning.

POSTSCRIPT

It is a warm summer's evening and I am sitting outside Santa Severina's *pasticceria* waiting to meet another member of the Piezzo-Miriello-Quaranta family jigsaw ... Antonio Miriello, who helped Luigi and Katrina organize the Santa Severina end of their 'home' visit the previous year, is himself back in Santa Severina.

Antonio is able to add some detail to the story and tells me how, when he and his father (Pietro) and his brother (Franco) emigrated in the fall of 1968, he was initially very much against the idea of going to America. Antonio was nineteen at the time and such a life-changing move was not on his agenda. It was only when his father said that if Antonio didn't go with him and Franco, then nobody would go, that he changed his mind.

Now a restaurateur in Long Island and frequent visitor to Santa Severina, Antonio tells me he now knows his father made the right decision for him and his brother.

I reflect on the vagaries of life and my own particular jigsaw ... if Antonio had stuck to his guns back in the late sixties, I probably would never have met Luigi and Katrina.

He's not the only one glad his father remained adamant.

The neighbors

This is the chapter I never expected to write ... but it makes up for another one that never got written.

As I knew I would, I woke to an empty apartment and had just finished dressing when a friendly voice called from below—it was Mary telling me my breakfast was at the planning stage.

Pre-breakfast soon became an inquisition as I wanted to hear more about this lively couple who never seemed to stop having fun, Johnny with the wise cracks and Mary with the wiser ones. For some reason they reminded be of George Burns and Gracie Allen—close, but no cigar.

Johnny Farese was not Calabrian, a cross he's always had to bear. His mother Carmela was born in America of parents who probably came from the Lombardy region; his father was from Sant'Arcangelo Trimonte, in the province of Benevento, north-east of Naples. On the other hand, the parents of Mary and her twin sister Angelina (Lou's mother) came from Casabona, the same small Calabrian town where Lou's grandmother on his father's side, Marianna Tallarico, was born.

In 1914, at the age of twenty-one, their father, Vincenzo Aprigliano, emigrated to the United States and was met by his cousin Salvatore Felice who took him to his first American home on Skillman Street, Brooklyn. A year earlier Francesca Scutifero had also emigrated to join her husband Leonardo Curcio; she was accompanied by their fourteen-year-old daughter Vittoria. According to family memories, supported by the 1930 census, the couple married in 1903, Francesca was Leonardo's second wife—and the story was that his late wife had been Francesca's sister. It appeared therefore that he emigrated to America just a few months after their marriage and had already been in America ten years when his wife Francesca and daughter Vittoria joined him.

Like countless other Calabrian families, they too moved straight to an apartment on Skillman Street so it is not surprising that Vincenzo Aprigliano and Vittoria Curcio should have bumped into each other. At the very least the families, being both from Casabona, would have known one another and probably given the young couple a helping hand to find each other.

That said, by 1915 the Curcio family had already moved to Franklin Avenue which further supported my embryonic theory—based solely on the observation that some apartments appear frequently on the Ellis Island archive as being the destination address for immigrant families— the notion that some apartments in Skillman Street were no more than clearing houses for immigrants ... they went straight there from Ellis Island and, it seemed to me, quickly moved on.

Vincenzo and Vittoria married in 1920 and moved to nearby Kent Avenue, to a house they shared with other members of their extended Casabona family—Vittoria's parents Leonardo and Francesca and their other children. In the late thirties they bought a house in Lafayette Avenue.

The woman frying my bacon in her dressing gown and returning to the table every so often with a flourish to respond to my questions was Mary, one of Vincenzo and Vittoria's twin daughters born in 1930. The other, her late sister Angelina, was Lou Piezzo's mother.

As I was tucking into my breakfast, I was doing the math and wondered if young Vittoria was really Francesca's daughter ... the copy of the ship's manifest gave her age as fourteen and yet, according to the census of 1930, Francesca and Leonardo were not married until 1903 when she would have been four ... an unusual scenario for the time. I wondered was she instead the daughter of Francesca's late sister or were the dates wrong?

Mary was sure that she was her grandmother Francesca's daughter, though admitted that the figures didn't make sense. She was even less enthusiastic about the suggestion that Vittoria had been born out of wedlock ... she recalled how strict her mother (the same Vittoria) had been when she and Johnny were courting when they were scarcely allowed to sit next to one another.

Nevertheless, with breakfast on the table, Mary went off in search of documents that might throw some light on the discrepancy and came back with a copy of her mother's birth certificate which did indeed show that she was born in 1899 and therefore possibly out of wedlock since the Census confirmed the marriage of Leonardo and Francesca in 1903. But the same census did indicate that this could have been Leonardo's second marriage, the first being in or around 1898 ... according to family memories, to Francesca's nameless sister.

Mary was still thinking back to all those times her mother had chastised her and Angelina for being too friendly with the boys and trying to equate the grandparents she knew with the possibility of a distant skeleton lurking somewhere in the cupboard.

I could also see she was confused by these discrepancies with the family history that she grew up with, vis-a-vis the slightly different version of the story the existing documentation seemed to be throwing up. Assuming the 1930 census was correct about the date of Leonardo's first marriage—and bearing in mind the same census actually got their ages completely wrong—the only unknown seemed to be who Leonardo's first wife was, when she died and what she died of ... nobody had any real information relating to any of these questions other than vague family memories, made vaguer with the passage of time.

I could see only one explanation that would save Mary any more blushes and retain the integrity, as she saw it, of her grandparents ... and there was only one way to be absolutely certain. When I returned to Calabria, I determined to go to Casabona and check the documents in the *Anagrafe*, the department of the local *Comune* that houses all local records.

At the time of writing that is something still on my itinerary.

•

Mary's grandfather, Leonardo, worked in the construction trade. He was always the family comic, had a devil-may-care attitude and—surprise,

surprise—an eye for a pretty ankle. Perhaps this latter interest was the reason he seemed to have a predisposition to getting hit by cars and buses ... perhaps his wandering eye and a pair of pretty legs momentarily distracted him as he stepped off the sidewalk. It happened so often that family and friends apparently used to pray every day that he would return home unscathed.

The Aprigliano twins: Angelina and Mary.

His wife Francesca, on the other hand, was more of an authoritarian. She was known in the neighborhood for her fine pastries and cakes and around the house for her fastidious attitude to cleanliness ... she even used to clean the dog's snout with a washcloth after every meal. Nobody seemed to recall what she used the washcloth for next ... ?

Both came to America illiterate and it is likely that they died there illiterate but they had mastered the spoken language. This they passed on to their offspring and Vittoria, unlike her husband Vincenzo, also learned to read and write.

Mary remembered her father, Vincenzo, as being a quiet man who worked hard as a laborer on the subway but she came up with some other paperwork that showed a unique side to his character—he clearly had a predisposition to getting himself killed. Unusually, Vincenzo served in the forces in *both* Italy and the United States, the former as a conscript, the latter by choice.

One document showed that back in Calabria he was discharged after his two years conscription in April 1912, two years before he emigrated. Two other documents confirmed that towards the end of the Great War, in August 1918, he enlisted in the American army and the following April he was honorably discharged and received a payment of sixty dollars. In the Great War, of course, Italy and the United States were on the same side.

Vittoria was a housewife and mother and, apparently, a fun-loving person ... except when it came to her daughters and men-friends. Unlike her husband, she taught herself to read and write in English. She also worked as a seamstress ... Johnny, an irreverent twinkle in his eye, added that, behind her back, they used to joke that Vittoria played with mens' flies all day.

•

Katrina joined us as Johnny was recalling the day in 1952 when they got married—two couples, Louie and Angelina, Johnny and Mary—and the fact that this wedding was one of the first Italian weddings in Brooklyn *not* to be what was called a 'football' wedding, a term that referred to the party afterwards, the reception, and how the food was doled out to the guests.

Italian weddings were generally large affairs so the 'football' wedding was a cheap way of catering for a large number of guests. The evening before the wedding, family and friends would help make dozens of trays of sandwiches. On a long table, crammed with traditional Italian salamis, cold cuts and meatballs, cheeses, tomatoes, lettuce, cucumber, pickles, mayonnaise and mustard the sandwiches would come off the assembly line to be wrapped and stacked up on trays—different trays for different fillings.

Once the party was in full swing, guests would call out the type of sandwich they wanted, "Salami, cheese and pickle, over here," and someone would throw, football-fashion, the appropriate wrapped sandwich to the caller. Johnny remembered the mayhem as sandwiches shot through the air to the hungry guests ... but, he recalled, there was often another stash of better sandwiches and other goodies in a box underneath the table for particular preferred guests—family and close friends.

Angelina and Lou, Johnny and Mary.

But the wedding party for Louie, Angelina, Johnny and Mary was a more dignified sit-down affair with no children below a certain age. It was held in what was called the Willow Temple ... yes, a Catholic wedding reception in what was a Jewish Temple. The castle-like building, still stands on the corner of Willoughby and Nostrand Avenues; it started life as the private home of a German butcher and his family but then it was sold and turned into a Temple, a Temple with a large stylish hall, perfect for an Italian 'non-football' wedding party.

•

The relationship between these two couples seemed remarkably robust and I wondered how it had all started. Even though they didn't know each other at the time, Johnny remembered when Louie's mother Marianna passed away—his mother mused about how awful it was and talked about 'those poor boys'. Louie, the youngest of those 'poor boys', was nine at the time.

It was not for another couple of years that Johnny and Louie actually met and became friends. Louie was watching Johnny and his friends playing baseball in the street and Johnny invited him to join in—a simple gesture that initiated a life-long friendship.

Johnny's uncle got first one, then the other, a job at Fitzhugh, a company that made paper and cardboard boxes. Johnny started work there a few months before his eighteenth birthday in 1945 and therefore had to get so-called 'working papers'—a Department of Labor regulation that still prevails.

It was in the late fifties that they first talked about starting their own business along with another friend, their best man, Sonny ... and the Island Steel Rule Die Company was born. Soon afterwards Johnny was laid off Fitzhugh's and so he became ISRDC's one and only full-time employee. They ran the business together for sixteen years during which time Louie worked full-time as well.

In 1975, when Johnny got a job at Blum Folding Paper Box Company, they decided to dissolve the business. Johnny then worked the night-shift at Blums for sixteen years but, as I'd seen for myself, had always kept his hand in with the die-cutting and still does occasional work for a friend—making pages for wedding albums.

Johnny and Mary, raconteurs extraordinary.

Then Johnny got on to the nitty-gritty, how and when he and Louie came to fall for the Aprigliano twins ... who were more like sisters in that they were not identical twins. It was all Louie's fault, he was friendly with them first, though Johnny confessed to having eyed them from a distance a few times despite going out with another girl, Chubby. Louie wanted to ask Angelina out but didn't have enough money but they used to hang out in the ice-cream parlor together anyway. After Johnny had broken up with Chubby, Louie suggested they go and see the twins, who were fifteen years old at the time ... they did, and the rest is history.

Mary can't help a not-so-modest smile as Johnny remembers when she and her sister came to watch them play baseball and he started to lose his concentration and kept missing the ball.

As I'd just eaten a typical American breakfast, I asked Mary about what she liked to cook ... American or Italian? She nodded towards a sheepish Johnny and said, "Whatever he'll eat."

Johnny, it seemed, was a fussy eater, a fussy eater of the extreme kind who'd never cooked anything in his life ... never even cracked open an egg. When Katrina heard this admission, she suggested he add it to his bucket list. On the other hand, he reminded me of more than a few Calabrian men I knew.

Of the four people who celebrated their separate marriages in the Willow Temple in 1952, only Johnny and Mary survive ... they still feel the loss of their dear friends with whom they spend a lifetime together at work and play. For most of that time they shared this house ... here they raised their families, the Piezzos and their three children upstairs, the Fareses and their two downstairs. These two families still share this house—only the generation upstairs has changed.

•

I had enjoyed my short, unexpected rendezvous with Mary and Johnny immensely. Despite their recent losses they knew that life went on—their amazing sense of fun was infectious. Mary's breakfast was pretty good too and I envied Katrina and Lou having these two on their doorstep.

Life had been good to Mary and Johnny; I suspected that their Italian background was not as important to them as it was to, for example, Lou.

What they didn't get from their Italian inheritance, they made up for in how they reveled in their American heritage.

As I waved goodbye, I was pretty certain that I would not meet their like again.

POSTSCRIPT

It is late February 2013 and I have arrived at the *Comune*, the Town Hall, of Casabona to browse the large dusty ledgers that, from time immemorial, have recorded the births, marriages and deaths in this small Calabrian community.

My starting point is the birth of Vittoria Immacolata Curcio in 1899, I have a copy of the information from the record of her birth that she'd requested in 1963 and which I'd photographed when I was in Long Island in November. My goal is straightforward, I want to know the name of Vittoria's mother ... I want to confirm if her mother indeed was Francesca Scutifero, Francesca's sister or another family member?

I am shown many courtesies by Signor Vittorio Pisani, the keeper of the documents at the *Anagrafe* ... every single document that I need to see is in storage in another part of the building, a place without a desk and room only for one. I lose track of the times when Signor Pisani leaves me in his office to climb several flights of stairs in search of yet another ledger.

After Signor Pisani's first sortie into the garret upstairs, it is confirmed that Vittoria was indeed born in December 1899; now I need to know when her parents were married. We check the 1903 ledger—the date the family say (and the 1930 Census confirms) they were married—there is no record of such a union.

I ask Signor Pisani if we can check marriages around 1898 and 1899 and together we find a Leonardo Curcio who married in 1899. When Signor Pisani returns with the ledger, this too confirms that Leonardo married Francesca Scutifero in February 1899, perfect timing for Vittoria to have been born *within* wedlock that December. Signor Pisani points out that, unusually, this was a civil wedding, the couple were married by *il sindaco*, the mayor.

I remember noting that the 1930 Census got the couple's ages completely wrong; now it seems that the date of their marriage was wrong too. Perhaps it was an error as simple as the date when Leonardo emigrated getting mixed up with the date of his marriage ... for illiterate Leonardo completing the Census document would not have been easy. And, logically, did it really make sense that he married in 1903 and emigrated in the spring of the same year and didn't see his new wife and daughter for a further decade?

We are not finished ... I wonder if we could find out if Leonardo was married before and, sure enough, we find a Leonardo Curcio who was also married in 1894. Signor Pisano goes off in search of another ledger. When he returns it is confirmed that the same Leonardo Curcio had married Tommasina Vittoria Scutifero, the sister of Francesca, in 1894.

The last unanswered question was when did Tommasina Vittoria die? We find a Vittoria Scutifero who died in 1897 and Signor Pisania goes off in search of yet another ledger ... I get the impression he is waning and hopes this will be the last time he has to climb those stairs. When he returns he is carrying the ledger that confirms that Tommasina Vittoria died on 25 February 1897; it was two years later when Leonardo married her sister, the day after a two-year mourning period ended.

As I drive home to Santa Severina, I am picturing the moment when Mary reads this and the moment she knows that all her instincts were correct. I can already see the broad smile on her face ...

She will know for certain that her grandmother was not born out of wedlock, and that the reason it seemed a possibility was a combination of fading, faulty memories and an error in the 1930 Census information.

She will know the name of her grandmother's sister and when she married and when she died.

And she will know that her mother, Vittoria, was almost certainly named after her mother's sister, Tommasina Vittoria Scutifero.

And then, as an afterthought, I think of the person who unwittingly initiated this search ... of Lou Piezzo whose mother Angelina was Mary's twin sister, whose grandmother was his great-grandmother ... now he too knows the full story.

Food for thought

Katrina drove me to the station where I caught the train back to Penn in Manhattan, thence back to Jersey City and Wayne Street. On the way I stopped off at the parking lot, paid my dues to Mitch for looking after the small-house-mobile for the day, patted its extensive bonnet and told him I'd be taking it out for a while the following day, Saturday.

I had only been away for a little over a day but in that time I'd been privy to the stories of three different families and needed to try and organize them in my head, if not on paper.

That evening I was back at the Saigon Café to eat and to make up for my absence since Tuesday and there I met two regulars Maria Schwarzkopf and her husband, Samir. Inevitably, the conversation found its way round to Hurricane Sandy and its aftermath. I knew that many people in Jersey City had been effected by it to varying degrees and I knew that, apart from power cuts, the Wayne Street area had had a lucky escape. Maria and Samir, who lived only two blocks away hadn't been so fortunate ... their basement was flooded and some of the ground floor rooms had also suffered. But it was the smell that got to them ... so much so that Maria decided to leave and go upstate for a week or so. Samir remained behind to start the clean-up and to make sure their home wasn't looted.

The aftermath of Sandy left many people stunned ... rightly or wrongly, many felt they had experienced a Third World event right on the doorstep, they had lived through something they were used to watching on television as it happened to other people in less fortunate parts of the world. Whether that made them feel contrite remains to be seen but I couldn't help recall how it felt for Pat and Rosalie Scida, their 'survivors' remorse'.

After I said farewell to Maria and Samir and wished them well, I took up my position at the bar where, in the absence of Steve, Danny made sure my glass was always full ... and when he ran out of Pinot Noir, insisted that I try the Cabernet Sauvignon. The Pinot Noir had been a casualty of Sandy ... they had run out (not my fault, he assured me) and deliveries were likely to remain unpredictable, certainly till long after I'd gone. So, thinking ahead, Danny suggested that I get addicted to something else in the short term. To soothe the transition, Kim asked me to try her delicious coconut and rice pudding ... who was I to argue?

•

The next morning I realized there was a curious pattern to my breakfast habits since arriving in the States ... when I was staying with people like Tañia and Adam, Lou and Katrina, I actually had a breakfast. When I woke up in New York or New Jersey, I tended to do without. And that Saturday morning would have been no exception had I not woken early and had time to kill before heading to my next port of call, Fair Lawn in upstate New Jersey. I therefore decided to see what the area between Wayne Street and the small-house-mobile, the area close to Grove Street Path station, had to offer.

It was just after eight and it was mostly fast-food joints that were open to cater, it seemed, for those that were rushing to and from the Path. Fast-food is not my diet of choice—you will recall my difficulty in getting beyond the parking lot at the Burger King in Newark—but I had learned from that experience and so when I saw a McDonald's sign I thought that this was probably as good as it was going to get.

Unfortunately this particular McDonald's seemed to cater *only* for commuters on the go ... there was no seating, just a counter and an order line. I went in search of something else. Across the street I saw the Subway sign—Subway the eatery, as opposed to anything underground.

I had never eaten Subway food before, it was one of the few fast-food chains that I had never ventured into when traveling in the States—when you're on the interstate and hungry it is often difficult to ignore the Gas, Food, Lodging signs at almost every exit. And, as it happened, on a subway train the previous week I was crushed against a couple having an in-depth discussion on the fact that Subway had recently started to 'do' breakfasts ... at the time this meant nothing to me, nor did it seem particularly important in the grand scheme of things.

So, nothing ventured, nothing gained, I decided there and then that now was the time to rectify this omission, to give Subway the benefit of my business and see just what they had done with the Great American Breakfast. Of course, I realize that my particular Subway experience may have been unique, nevertheless it was my experience.

•

I entered a large, gloomy, featureless, refectory-like space with a counter at one end and a lone customer who looked as though she had seen better times. Behind the counter was a fresh, slim youth who was probably reveling in his first Saturday job; he could see I was new to this and waited patiently while I surveyed the photographs on the wall above and behind his head which were meant to whet my appetite with the range of colorful fare. It was the colors I had the problem with ... they didn't look real and I knew that whatever I chose, it would bear little resemblance to its photographic equivalent.

Also, I didn't want a so-called 'combo' because included was a large measure of something fizzy or, worse, of coffee that I had no doubt would be 'coffee' in name only. Instead I took a bottle of pure orange juice out of the cold cabinet in the knowledge that this would probably cost more than the food.

I opted for an egg with a bit of bacon in a muffin ... and watched as my flat white 'egg' was extracted from between two sheets of paper and placed with the bacon and the muffin in a microwave ... I looked at the description again and realized I'd inadvertently ordered an egg white.

My breakfast 'cooked' I went over to the long window and sat where I could see the world and feel less gloom-ridden. I opened my little surprise package and tucked in.

It was fast, it was food and it filled a space but it tasted of absolutely nothing, of nothing in the food chain that I could put a name to. The crisp, healthy image that they were trying to push with their 'eat fresh' slogan seemed a little jaded that morning ... maybe it was just a bad Subway day.

I thought back to my culinary experience in Newark and tried to compare and contrast, tried to decide which, in an emergency, I might risk for a second time. I just couldn't make up my mind.

The small-house-mobile beckoned; it was to time to go meet Carla.

•

Two things then happened that were to change not only the structure of that day but also of this book.

I was programming 'the voice' to tell her to take me to Hawthorne in New Jersey when I received a text message from Carla, the gist of which was that she wouldn't be able to see me that day after all. She suggested a list of alternative dates none of which worked for me and my only alternative didn't work for her.

More than a little crestfallen I headed back towards Wayne Street. I know it sounds stupid but, at the time, I was more preoccupied with what I was going to do with the Cadbury's Cream Eggs that I'd brought with me from England especially for Carla's English boyfriend Greg. Finally the penny dropped and I realized I'd just have to eat them myself.

On the way back to the apartment I popped into a small store in search of an essentially American delicacy called Rice-a-Roni. Now, Rice-a-Roni was not something normally part of my diet but since an American friend, Vicki, had decided it was a good present to bring *me* from America, I was not one to forget to repay the favor.

For those for whom Rice-a-Roni is not normally something on their culinary radar, let me explain. Rice-a-Roni is instant food originating in San Francisco ... a mixture of rice and macaroni, to which basically you add hot water or, as it says on the packet of the chicken-flavored version, you can also 'add chicken to make Rice-a-Roni a meal'.

My present from Vicki was, of course, a joke but one which gave us all a laugh when we ate together with her family at Le Puzelle (a local agriturismo in Santa Severina renowned for its cuisine) and I arranged with the chef to serve it to her as a starter. After a couple of mouthfuls she realized this wasn't normal Le Puzelle fare and guessed that I was up to no good. When her kids heard the magic words 'Rice-a-Roni', they devoured the lot ... they loved it.

So it was really for Vicki's kids that I wanted to get some Rice-a-Roni and, with time to kill that morning, I gave in to my embarrassment and bought a couple of packets.

Back at the apartment I checked my emails. I had two. The first was from Maria Cavaliere to flag up that she may have a problem with our Philadelphia rendezvous that Saturday but that she'd try to sort it out. The second turned out to be the antidote to both Carla's text and Maria's email.

The other email was from a complete stranger.

Carolina (Bonocore) Ventrella had read two of my books, *Stumbling through Italy* and *Scratching the Toe of Italy*, and went on to tell me a little about her Calabrian roots. Her email included what, in advertizing terms, would be called a 'teaser'—it caught my attention, I wanted to know more.

We exchanged a few more emails before I realized that I was going to pass close to Carolina's Chicago home the following Tuesday. My suggestion of a meeting was greeted first with enthusiasm and then with dismay when Tuesday turned out to be the only day she wouldn't be available. So close, yet so far.

But Carolina had already whetted my appetite with her family's unique story—a story I felt impelled to follow-up—but I had to resign myself to the reality that it would not be possible to do so face-to-face.

A further flurry of emails took both of us headlong into the realm of the virtual chapter—as Carolina was snapping family photos with her cell phone, I was distilling the salient points from her emails and asking more questions.

For much of that day, and every opportunity thereafter, I pursued electronically the history of the Bonocore family now living in the Chicago suburb of Roselle ... which would have fitted in neatly between the family I was to meet in Lyons and those I would visit in Kenosha, Wisconsin.

•

I had been poring over my iPad for most of the morning—mainly on the Ellis Island website trying to piece together the story of Carolina's family—and decided I needed a break and maybe some lunch. I walked to the parking lot, picked up the small-house-mobile and was heading towards the Newport Mall when I turned back on myself and headed instead for Grand Avenue and the Brownstone Diner and Pancake Factory.

I had suddenly remembered that, a few days earlier—in an idle moment on the flight back to Newark—I had done an internet search for the 'ten best breakfasts in Jersey City'. This is something I used to do before traveling to any American city but it didn't quite work the same for Jersey City as it did, say, for Las Vegas or Chicago ... perhaps there weren't ten places to have breakfast.

However, I did pick up a reference to the Brownstone Diner and Pancake Factory and had made a mental note of its location—a few blocks south of Wayne Street—and just hoped they didn't only serve breakfasts. If I'd thought of it earlier I might not have had the Subway experience; if I'd thought of it earlier I could have left the small-house-mobile in the parking lot. As it was, it was good to be driving again with the help of my visual memory and not 'the voice' and her monotonous instructions.

The view today from the New Jersey side of the Hudson river, a view once dominated by the twin towers of the World Trade Centre.

One gigantic, so-called 'breakfast sandwich' later, I knew I had found the perfect place to start the day ... and putting on the pounds. So I resolved that, when I returned (which I surely would), I'd always walk there and perhaps try to eat more modestly. I kept faith with only one of these modest goals.

I headed back to deposit the small-house-mobile at the parking lot ... the full-to-the-brim parking lot. Mitch shrugged his shoulders, there wasn't a single space, indeed there were cars scattered all around the lot, clearing blocking the exit of others ... but, he had an idea, I could leave the small-house-mobile double parked like some of the others as long as I left him the keys so that he could park it properly when a space became available. All I would have to do was make sure to return before he went home at seven ... I threw him the keys and left him to it.

But instead of going back to Wayne Street, I headed towards Jersey shore to walk off the breakfast sandwich and to take in the view for the first time across the Hudson to the Manhattan skyline. It was a cold afternoon, there were few people about ... maybe this was how it always was on this side of the Hudson, all the looking was being done from the Manhattan side. They don't know what they're missing.

I tried unsuccessfully to call Kay to tell her where I was and what I could see; I felt I was privy to something that was beyond description, a vista that I knew from so many second-hand images but one that, even in the gray crispness of that November afternoon, was both majestic and breathtaking. Although in the last hundred years the skyline has changed— become taller, denser, iconic—even in the early part of the twentieth century it was impressive and for the newly-arrived immigrant, surely breathtaking, even terrifying bearing in mind where they came from.

I think it was in that moment that I realized this was a place where I could spend time, that some day it would be good to spend more than just a few days on this—or the other—side of the Hudson. I understood too why it was that immigrants warmed to this place and, despite the degrading passage, the poverty, the wretched conditions that many initially had to endure, they decided this was a place where their lives could improve, where the only way was up.

I continued to walk south along the shore, the constant buzz of

Part of the New York skyline c1905 as arriving immigrants would have seen it.

The turn of the century and a family of Italian immigrants are ferried from their ship to their first landfall in the United States, the Immigrant Inspection Station at Ellis Island. It's hard not to wonder where their descendants live and what their lives are like today.

helicopters an ever-present backdrop. This is something I had noticed on both sides of the river, the number of helicopters plying the skies above the Hudson and Manhattan. I even thought I knew the reason why ... they were obviously the 'copters of rival news media feeding the latest Manhattan travel data back to mission control on the ground. All of which I discovered was complete nonsense as I continued my walk along the shore and came across a water-side heliport complete with signage offering one-hour trips over Manhattan ... at a price. I have to confess that I was tempted and to this day regret that I didn't go for it.

On a bit further, and I could see the shape of the Statue of Liberty rising above a myriad of uninspiring shore-side architecture to the south ... and seemingly in front of it the four towers of a lone building, a building I thought I recognized. I walked a bit further, a bit closer, just to confirm that the building I could see was in fact Ellis Island, the site of the Immigration Center that was the first stop for so many of the early Italian immigrants. It was, I thought, appropriate that I should see it from New Jersey as it is, after all, a part of New Jersey and not New York.

I thought back to a photo I had once seen of an Italian immigrant family standing on the deck of a boat looking beyond the camera at the place they had chosen to spend the rest of their lives, a skyline they could never have conceived of in their native Italy. I know of no way to find out who this family was, where they came from, where they were going or what happened to them. They were, in that moment, no more than the focus of a camera's shutter ... the man (or woman) behind the camera was only interested in them and their image for that split second ... they probably never spoke. It was possible the family had never before been the focus of a camera.

•

I headed back inland towards Wayne Street by a slightly different route and passed a sign outside a pub that was advertising Guinness, that rich, ebony, uniquely Irish, beverage that I adored—the result, so it is said, of an error made by Arthur Guinness when trying to brew something completely different. Nevertheless, uncharacteristically I walked passed ... and I got almost thirty yards before turning back.

As well as serving the ebony nectar, McConnells was a restaurant, close to the Irish pub environment that I had grown up with ... closer to the real thing, less contrived than some I'd been in. The lighting was just right, on the cusp of being gloomy the further away you were from the long bar with its backdrop of Irish whiskeys, enough distilled malted barley to satisfy any itinerant Irishman and his mate.

Even the barmaid was Irish ... a nice touch that, I thought ... I know it sounds obvious, but I'd not been in many so-called Irish pubs that actually employed any Irish staff. Even the woman sitting a couple of bar stools away was Irish and clearly a friend of the barmaid.

First of all I checked that they didn't also sell Murphys, another version of the black nectar from Cork rather than Dublin and my personal favorite ... ironically the best pint of Murphys I ever drank was in Portland, Oregon, and not Ireland. Sadly Murphys was not on the menu so Guinness it had to be. ... I knew I would cope.

The pouring of Guinness (and Murphys) is a true skill ... no, more an art than a skill. Down in their respective cellars, two neighboring pubs could have the same barrel of Murphys or Guinness, but how that tastes at the bar depends largely on how the barrel is kept and the pair of hands at the pump. Siobhan was my new best friend ... her pair of hands was well-trained and the Guinness was excellent.

I was already eyeing my first glass of Bushmills Irish whiskey when Kay called me back. I told her briefly about my cancelled visit to Carla's, how I'd then picked up the story of Carolina's family but that we wouldn't actually meet and why I'd felt impelled to call her from Jersey shore. I must have mentioned the two Cadbury's cream eggs still burning a hole in my pocket for I saw Siobhan—clearly eavesdropping to my half of the conversation—mouth nostalgically to her friend Orla the fact that she 'would die for a Cadbury's cream egg'.

Step forward Sir Galahad ... who just happened to have two Cadbury's cream eggs in his pocket; Siobhan's passion for these seemed more or less equal to mine for Bushmills so we did an unspoken deal—despite Siobhan's half-hearted protests, I insisted she have *both* the cream eggs and then Orla and I enjoyed our on-the-house glasses of whiskey. A fair exchange, I thought.

It was dark when I reemerged into the fresh air. I returned to my apartment for a brief break then headed back to the parking lot to relieve Mitch of the small-house-mobile's keys before he became too attached to them and to it. For the rest of the evening I took up temporary residence once more at the Saigon Café.

•

On Sunday morning I decided not to repeat the Subway experience nor had I time for the Brownstone Diner and Pancake Factory alternative and so headed straight for McDonald's—it may not have had any seating but the small-house-mobile did.

Between mouthfuls, I gave 'the voice' her instructions and she told me that my journey would take a little less than three hours which was more or less what I was anticipating. I was expected at midday so thought that leaving Jersey City at eight-forty-five would be perfect ... before I got to the interstate, I'd even have time for a short stop to fill up with gas for the drive back.

About twenty minutes into my journey, I did just that. I pulled off the road, stopped alongside a row of pumps, got out, then realized I had to press something inside the small-house-mobile to open the gas tank at the rear. But what? I got in and ran my fingers round everything in search of a switch; I got out again for a new perspective and kneeled down to look from the outside in. I was joined by the patient pump attendant but neither of us could find the illusive trigger. I checked to see if there was a manual, there wasn't. Another car pulled in behind, and another behind it.

I was just about to move the small-house-mobile away from the pump when the two-cars-back driver decided to come and investigate ... and within seconds the little cover to the gas tank popped open. I asked him where it was and he pointed to the inside of the door ... the second time I filled up, I wished I had taken more notice.

All gassed up, I continued on my journey north, expecting soon to be joining the interstate, that would quickly take me up to the Albany area and Schenectady ... this time, before I left Wayne Street, I had had a look on a map and had a better idea of exactly where I was going.

It was when the sun told me I was traveling south for a few miles that

I realized 'the voice', without so much as a by-your-leave, appeared to be taking me via the scenic route. I had no idea why or what, if anything, I could do about it. Apart from that little excursion southwards, I seemed to be generally heading in a northerly direction and although 'the voice's' estimated time of arrival had gone beyond twelve, I was still optimistic that I wouldn't be too late. Being late was one of the Italian characteristics I had not yet succumbed too.

Just before twelve I pulled over and called the Cariddi family to explain that I was behind schedule and hoped to be no more than another half hour (at least that's what 'the voice' was telling me at the time).

It was forty-five minutes later that I cruised along Brierwood Boulevard in search of a number.

Early in 2012 a student of English at Cosenza University, Klizia Mirante, asked for help finding a work placement in the UK. Two weeks later she left Santa Severina to work in a museum in Bath for five months.

When Klizia returned to Santa Severina I asked her if she had any family in America and she told me about relatives on her mother's side, the Cariddi family from Stróngoli. Klizia wasn't sure where they lived.

Klizia's mother, Isabella Scida, spoke with her relatives in Stróngoli, and in particular Filomena and Letterina LeRose; Klizia then got back to me with a contact number for Jennie Cariddi in Schenectady in upstate New York.

I called Jennie but could tell that she was a little unsure about this cold call from Santa Severina so I suggested that she talk it over with her husband, Leonardo, and said I would call back in a few days. I immediately emailed Klizia and asked her if one of her great-aunts could call Jennie to reassure her that I was who I said I was.

This she did and when I called back Jennie she had already spoken to Letterina and sounded much happier. We then exchanged emails and I arranged to visit her and her family in Schenectady.

Thank you Uncle Sam

I saw three young men hovering on the sidewalk, looking up and down the road expectantly, but it wasn't until I slid past them that I realized they were probably looking out for me ... they told me later that the small-house-mobile was not the sort of vehicle they were expecting me to be driving.

I retraced my steps and turned into the Cariddi family's driveway to be met by Jennie's sons, Michael, Leonard and Christopher, all still getting over the shock that—as they thought at the time—I had decided that the small-house-mobile was a suitable rental for one person. When Michael told me what that particular small-house-mobile was worth, I shuddered at the very thought.

As we were entering the house I was still apologizing profusely for my lateness and told them that, by way of the scenic route, it had taken me nearly four hours to get to Schenectady from Jersey City.

Inside I found myself apologizing to and shaking hands with many more people, including the woman I had come all this way to meet, the remarkable Jennie Cariddi, her husband Leonard and her older sister JoAnn. Also there was JoAnn's daughter Alice and her husband Louie, Leonard's partner Veronica, Michael's wife Cynthia, and Christopher's wife Kristie and their three-month-old son, Nico. I found out later, some had travelled even further than I had.

In addition, on the low table in the family room, neatly arranged so that I couldn't miss them, were copies of each of my other books about Italy. They had, Michael explained, just arrived the previous day and in the same breath apologized for not having read them all yet. Nevertheless, overnight he had managed to get through about a hundred pages of *Scratching the toe of Italy* ... a feat over and above the call of duty, I thought.

Jennie and her husband Leonardo Tamasi were first and second generation American respectively ... Leonard's family was originally from Carpinone, then in Abruzzo now in the new central Italian province of Molise, Jennie's from Stróngoli in Calabria, that uncompromising lump of rock close to the Ionian Sea that I can see across the valley of the river Neto from the balcony of our home.

Following my earlier visit to Pat Scida I already knew something about Jennie's family and how it was that the Cariddi family ended up in America.

Raffaele Cariddi came to America in 1909 and three years later he was joined by his brother Francesco. For over a year Francesco lived in a boarding house in Springfield, Massachusetts and worked on construction or in one of the many local fabric-printing mills. Francesco then returned to Stróngoli and married Antoinette Scida, the sister of Pat Scida's father, Pasquale, and then the couple returned to America and North Adams, Massachusetts where they settled.

While he was back in Stróngoli, Francesco is said to have waxed lyrical about his new life in America and to have told his father Vincenzo that if he worked hard he could eat meat every day. At the time in Calabria, such a notion was the stuff of fairy tales.

From the Ellis Island website it was clear that Antoinette decided to travel to America using the same surname as her husband, Cariddi, which, though the American way of doing things, was certainly unorthodox in Calabria. Curiously, someone altered the ship's manifest and overwrote 'Cariddi' with 'Scida' but there is no way of telling whether this was done in Naples or New York. Another anomaly was Antoinette's name ... for some reason she decided to shorten it to Antonia to travel to America which in subsequent documentation was mistakenly transcribed as both Andrina and even Annetta. It's as if, by becoming almost overnight Antonia

Cariddi, she had consciously Americanized her names before she ever set foot in the country. Once in America she reverted to Antoinette and was known as such for the rest of her life.

Back on American soil the Cariddis were met by Antoinette's brother Pasquale Scida, who lived in Brooklyn at the time, before they headed upstate to North Adams.

This much I knew but I also aware of something else ... I knew it was not so easy to assimilate a family's story when there was more than a couple of people there ... the large family gathering in Albuquerque was a case in point. Jennie had also worked this out and so we disappeared upstairs to one of the smaller bedrooms where she kept most of the family memorabilia.

A few paragraphs back I used the word 'remarkable' to describe Jennie Cariddi; that was not a slip of the pen. It was as if Jennie had been waiting for the last quarter of a century for someone like me to turn up on her doorstep and ask her about her family. The fact that when it did happen it was an aging, strangely handsome, Irishman was just a bonus. She had everything to hand, documents, photographs, newspaper cuttings and her diary. Jennie had already done most of the work.

By the time anyone really noticed our absence from the gathering downstairs, I had managed to assimilate the essence of her family's story after her parents, Francesco and Antoinette Cariddi arrived in North Adams in 1914.

Jennie asked me about Filomena back in Stróngoli and I then realized that she had assumed, from the time Letterina had called her to assure her that I was *bona fide*, that I had actually met and knew both Filomena and Letterina. Whereas the family member I actually knew was their niece back in Santa Severina, Isabella Scida, and her daughter Klizia Mirante. At the time I just wasn't sure what Letterina had said to Jennie so decided to focus on my friendship with Kilzia ... and to note how uncannily alike Jennie and Klizia were.

•

I wondered whether Francesco had always intended to come back to America after he returned to Stróngoli for it was not uncommon, particularly around the turn of the century, for Italian immigrants to earn quick money in America and then return to their home town and stay there.

This phenomenon of return immigration gave rise to the nickname 'birds of passage' or *i ritornati* being ascribed to many Italian immigrants. They were not the only immigrants to return to their homeland but, statistically, they were the most prolific. It has been estimated that about forty percent of those who emigrated between 1880 and 1920 returned to their native Italy—but, of course, many, like Francesco Cariddi and Bruno Cortese, emigrated again to America.

Despite the often menial existence in their home towns and the deprivations endured crossing the Atlantic, many Italians—and southern Italians in particular, as they were by far the majority of emigrants—felt the loss of family, friends and community deeply and wanted desperately to return home.

As if the journey were not bad enough, for many the conditions they experienced in America were not much better than in Calabria, Basilicata or Apulia. In lower Manhattan and Brooklyn the tenements were often squalid, infested and dark and the streets noisy, frenetic and chaotic. The chances of seeing the open sky, fields as far as the eye could see or folding mountains was slim ... the other side of the coin was that, if you worked hard, you could almost certainly better your lot in life. In Calabria there were friends and family, sky, fields and mountains but the prognosis was the same—a meagre, disease-ridden existence, punctuated with natural disasters, as far as the mind could wander.

At least those like Francesco and his brother Raffaele had moved on quickly from the city and settled in a part of New York State where the air and ambience was more reminiscent of their native Calabria ... albeit a little cooler in the summer.

So was Francesco Cariddi a 'bird of passage' or did he always intend to return to America? Did he come back to Stróngoli with the sole purpose of marrying Antoinette Scida, herself from a well-respected local family with a history of emigration?

Jennie didn't think so. She was sure that he always intended to return to America. He played it by the rules by respecting the requisite courting period before they were wed ... though exactly how long that was is anyone's guess. Two months later they were aboard the *Europa* and on their way to America with the blessing of Francesco's father Vincenzo who told him he should return to America where he would have a better life.

I asked about her parents' memories of the passage from Naples but like so many others they never talked about it other than to say that it was long and crowded ... little did they know, but the ship that Francesco and Antoinette travelled on, the *Europa*, had a steerage capacity of two thousand, four hundred but a mere four hundred and sixty travelled that August-September. It may have seemed crowded to them but it could have been much, much worse.

It is worth noting that up till now I had not talked to *any* family where those who had emigrated in the early part of the twentieth century handed down to their children or grandchildren any clear detail about what their passage to America was really like. Such reticence reminded me of my father who fought and was wounded in the Battle of the Somme in 1916 ... it took me many years of persistent probing and unswerving dedication to tease and coax the full story out of him. Perhaps, like my father, American immigrants simply didn't want to be reminded of a time in their lives best forgotten, a journey that was no more than a necessary evil, a means to an end.

•

Since the construction of the Hoosac Rail Tunnel in the latter part of the nineteenth century, the North Adams area boasted a significant Italian community. There was other work locally, most notably in the fabric dyeing and printing industry where Pat Scida's father worked but, around the same time as Europeans were killing each other *en masse* on the battlefields of France, many Americans were discovering that the motor car—and in particular the Model-T Ford—was becoming more affordable which in turn led to an increase in road construction and upgrading.

In north-western Massachusetts one of the old Native American trade routes, the Mohawk Trail, that crossed the Hoosac mountains following the Millers and Deerfield rivers, was reconstructed as a highway. The sixty-five mile route ran east-west between Orange and Williamstown and linked the communities in-between including, at the western end, North Adams.

Along with many other Italians, it was on this project that Francesco

Cariddi did his twelve hours a day for Uncle Sam when he returned to the States ... and Uncle Sam paid him well. And when the Mohawk Trail was completed he found work in one of North Adams' many cotton-fabric mills, the Arnold Print Works; his brother Raffaele worked in the nearby Windsor Print Works.

Their first home, while Francesco was working on the Mohawk Trail,

The Hairpin Turn on the Mohawk Trail c.1920. Today the road forms part of Massachusetts Route 2. North Adams can just be seen on the right of the photograph.

Inside the Arnold Print Works in North Adams where Francesco Cariddi worked.

was a rented, six-room apartment on the second floor of a twelve-tenement block in Holden Street just off Union Street.

This apartment block was owned by another Italian immigrant Giacamo Tomaselli from Caserta, north-east of Naples. Tomaselli, a mason by trade, had emigrated in 1906 and had clearly done well for himself.

It was here in Holden Street in 1915 that James was born, the first of twelve children which included two sets of twins—one of the second set died very young. Their last child, a daughter Frances, was born in 1935.

•

Many years later another inhabitant of the same Holden Street tenement, a boyhood friend of young Jimmy Cariddi, wrote about growing up in and around the street where they lived and played together.

The late Tony Tallarico described how the kids wheeled hoops that were taller than they were round the streets; how every hour, on the hour, in the run up to Christmas they watched the moving doll figures in the corner window of the Boston Store; how in the summer they followed the ice wagons just to gather up and suck any discarded slivers of ice; and how, when the carnival came to town, they made a bee-line for the wrestling tent to watch locals being goaded into trying to beat or last five or ten minutes with the resident wrestler.

He went to describe the tenements themselves thus:

"[There was] no central heating in those six room tenements. Every one had a kitchen range, with a water reservoir heated up by the fire in the box at the opposite end. The gas storage box hung from the ceiling. The gas was piped to an overhead lamp with a gas mantle. When the light suddenly went out it meant that the gas was all gone. You had to put in a quarter in a meter before you could get more gas.

"The closet was the toilet, which had an overhead box filled with water. You pulled a chain to let the water down to flush the toilet bowl. There were no bathtubs. My mother washed us in a small metal tub which she placed on the kitchen table.

"Joe Pizzi, who ran a woman's store on Main Street, had a big Buick. On Sundays he would take our family for a picnic to Sand Springs. It had a big swimming pool. It also had little individual bath rooms along the side of the pool. It was a popular spot. It wasn't until recently that I realized

Francesco Cariddi and Antoinette Scida with their firstborn, James.

why. Most of the immigrants in our area were hardworking laborers and what they needed most was that weekly bath. Sand Springs is where they got it.

"At that time we did not know we were living in a ghetto."

Ghetto or not, for Francesco and Antoinette and their growing family it was a stepping stone. According to Jennie, in those early days her father was driven by three aspirations: to become an American citizen, to own property, and to ensure that his children learned to speak, to read and to write in English. He was to accomplish all three.

•

This was the world Jimmy Cariddi was born into. And, just like his father, Jimmy was driven—he had an entrepreneurial zeal that first came to the fore when, at the age of nine, he started selling the *North Adams Transcript* on the streets of the town.

His embryonic 'business' flourished and every day, at five-thirty in the morning, Jimmy would be at the *Transcript* offices to pick up the first fifty papers hot off the press, then he'd run to Main Street to hawk them before running back for more. Every day he had his breakfast at Noel's Lunch and a donut at the Bakery, both satisfied customers, both gratis. Similarly with his other customers there were other perks for being the town's hard-working newsboy.

Eventually he bought himself a bike and could sell up to five hundred newspapers a day from his pitch on Main Street and as he dashed around the town. Even back then he involved his sister Anne—two years his junior—in the work by assigning her one of his routes, this was 1927 and for a girl to be doing a paper round was not common. And a bike for Anne was not a problem ... Jimmy now had three.

At first the money he raised was buried in a coffee tin in the back yard but by the time he was in the seventh grade (aged about thirteen) he had $405 in the bank.

By the time Jimmy become a young adult he had been involved in a long list of enterprises, each time something innovative led to something else more innovative until, in 1936, he set up the Cariddi Sales Company. Indeed the story of the Cariddi family in America is largely the story of

Top: 1925—twins JoAnn and Ralph with brother Joseph in the middle.
Bottom: 1934—Jennie is between her parents at the bottom; Jo-Ann is on the extreme
right; Jimmy is behind his mother.

James Vincent Cariddi and how he involved his family in his various businesses.

After he decided to move on from selling newspapers, Jimmy's next venture involved almost all the Cariddi family in the roasting and bagging of his garlic- and herring-flavored peanuts, pistachio and cashew nuts. He'd buy the nuts wholesale in 50-pound sacks and made up hundreds of little bags of flavored nuts then staple twelve to a long strip of card which he then sold to the local bars, clubs and stores at eighty cents a strip. The Mohawk Tasty Bits Company was born.

The year was 1934 and by coincidence, in December 1933, the Prohibition Act was repealed and people could at long last pop into a bar, have a beer legally and, of course, try a packet or two of Mohawk Tasty Bits.

Even young Jennie, thirteen years younger than Jimmy, helped with the enterprise and recalled how, after church on Sunday, she helped to assemble the cards under the watchful eye of Jimmy's foreman, brother Joseph. Everybody was involved and everyone was paid a nickel.

Jimmy's third venture also involved working with local bar and club owners but Jimmy had moved on from Tasty Bits and was now in the juke-box business.

In the wake of the end of Prohibition, legitimate bar entertainment— that wasn't of the 'speakeasy' variety—blossomed all over America. In 1934 and 1935 two companies, Wurlitzer and Rock-Ola, came up with the innovative idea of the so-called music- or juke-box where customers in bars and clubs could pay to hear the music they liked. And Jimmy Cariddi, ever on the lookout for a lucrative opportunity, was there at the beginning.

By the mid-thirties Jimmy owned and operated between forty and fifty machines, both Wurlitzers and Rock-Olas, throughout the city and neighboring towns in Massachusetts and even as far south as New York State.

Once again it was his brothers and sisters, Joe, Ralph, JoAnn, and even Jennie, who helped him—JoAnn and Ralph were responsible for making sure the music was up-to-date and for the collection of the money, Jennie it was who typed the labels for every new song and artist: hits then and classics now by Fred Astaire with *A Fine Romance* and *Let's Face the Music and Dance*, Bing Crosby with *Pennies from Heaven* and *The Touch of your Lips*, the Boswell Sisters with *I'm Gonna Sit Right Down and Write Myself a Letter* and Fats Waller with *Bye Bye Baby*.

The downside to the business was when they got calls in the middle of the night to tell them that a machine had stopped working and needed to be replaced or repaired. Still, at five cents a play it soon brought in plenty of dollars.

•

When Francesco, now known by everyone as Frank, started to work for the Arnold Print Works in the early twenties, the family had moved into a 'tied' house on Phoenix Street where they paid nine dollars a month in rent. It was in the back yard here that young Jimmy had hidden his stash in a coffee tin.

By the late twenties one of Frank's goals was well on the way to being

The Cariddi family in 1943.
Jennie is seated right; Jo-Ann is seated left; Jimmy is next to his mother.

realized ... all his children could speak English and those already in education were all doing well.

Then, in 1928, Frank fulfilled another of his goals when he bought his first house on West Main Street and, the day they moved, the youngest of those children, the infant Jennie, was pushed there in her baby carriage. The Cariddi family lived in one half of the two-story building and the other half was rented out. Shortly afterwards Frank bought another property right behind their West Main Street home and rented that out too.

Years later he went on to buy yet another property with four apartments which he also rented out and would have continued his foray into the real estate business had not his wife put her foot down and reined him back.

In the same year the Cariddis bought their West Main Street home, to the south of nearby Williamstown, a large, seventy-two-room mansion, Elm Tree House, was completed at Mount Hope Farm. It was to be the summer residence of Alta Rockefeller Prentice and her husband, Colonel Ezra Parmalee Prentice; Alta was the third daughter of the oil tycoon and philanthropist, John D. Rockefeller.

In the early thirties Frank Cariddi left Arnold Print Works to become a landscaper on the fourteen-hundred-acre Rockefeller estate.

•

Jennie and I were looking through a booklet of family memories of Jimmy and his exploits that the whole family - contributed to for his ninetieth birthday in 2005, when Michael appeared ... like everyone else, he'd wondered where we'd snuck off to.

While Michael photocopied each page of the booklet for me, Jenny and I tried to tie up one loose end ... I wondered had her parents ever returned to Italy. They had—twice—but before Jennie could elaborate on the details, she was summoned down to the kitchen to oversee the crucial final stages of the dinner she had prepared.

Like Sina Sculco, Jennie had mastered the art of cooking and engaging in intelligent conversation at the same time. Aided and abetted by her sister JoAnn, a sprightly eighty-nine, she told me about the two times her father and mother returned to Calabria in 1938 and again in 1951, on each occasion for three months.

On their first visit they took five-year-old Francis Patrick and toured much of Italy and of course visited family in their home town of Stróngoli. The sisters told me how, when Pat returned, he could no longer speak English ... instead Italian had become his language of choice.

By this time Frank was an American citizen but his wife wasn't and, on their return journey, she appeared on the passenger list of the *Conte di Savoia* as an 'alien'. By the time they went back to Italy in 1951, Antoinette, cajoled and helped by her many English-speaking children, *had* become an American citizen ... when the judge asked her a leading question regarding the Italian dictator Benito Mussolini, soon to be at war with America, she replied, "I am not concerned about him. This is my country, the United States of America!"

And on that second trip to Italy it was the young, twenty-three-year-old Jennie Cariddi who accompanied her parents. And this pretty, young American girl turned a few Italian heads and received several proposals of marriage in those three months. Jennie recalled how on one occasion she

The Cariddi family in 1952; yet another visit to Trabolds Studio for the family portrait. Jennie is seated left; JoAnn stands behind Jennie on the left; Jimmy is behind his mother.

went to a local bank with her father and the next day the young man who had served them turned up at the door to propose marriage. Her father said an emphatic "No!".

Jennie kept a diary and wrote about her cousin Nino (the son of Giuseppe, her mother's brother) whose engagement party (to Grazia) she attended in Stróngoli. Nino worked in the nearby city of Crotone where the Cariddi family stayed for a week at the Grand Hotel. Jennie remembered Crotone for its boardwalk, beach and shopping but mostly for the espresso bar by the hotel where the suave and handsome Nino worked and where she and her parents had their morning coffee and *brioche*. Her father had brought lots of American cigarettes with him and Nino was pleased to be given some.

The family then returned to Stróngoli before heading north to Genoa by train to catch their ship home to the States. Nino turned up at the station to say his farewells and present Jennie with a box of chocolates and to ask her if she had spoken of him to her mother. A puzzled Jennie said she hadn't.

The reasons behind this curious encounter became clear when, back in America, she received a letter from Nino in which he proposed marriage. He had it all planned and asked Jennie to have a suit made for him for the wedding ... he even chose the color. Apparently he had set his sights on Jennie and even broken off his engagement to Grazia. Jennie wrote back that she had no intention of marrying him.

In America of course to marry a cousin is frowned upon whereas in Calabria at the time it was not uncommon, particularly in small communities. When Jennie next returned to Calabria in 1992 with Leonard, the romantic Nino made himself scarce.

With a twinkle in her eye, Jennie went on to tell me about one of the fashion fads at the time, pedal pushers—pants from the waist to below the knee and just perfect for summer cycling and sports. And of course Jennie wore her pedal pushers in Stróngoli and Crotone—in Stróngoli the women giggled and in Crotone the men gawked.

On both trips the Cariddis traveled to and from Italy by boat and took a huge trunk with them filled with gifts and clothes for their relatives

... as was the way of things then, they were thrilled with anything and everything from America, especially jeans.

It was hard not to wonder what went through Frank and Antoinette's minds on those passages from their brave new world to their old, familiar childhood haunts and back again ... a far cry from that first crossing together in 1914 in the bowels of the *Europa*.

On Jennie's trip back aboard the *Atlantic* she recalled how the trunk was filled with lots of Italian goodies—especially cheeses such as *Parmigiano-Reggiano*, hams and olive oil. Also, the week before they departed, Frank went on a shopping spree—a wool top-coat and wide-brimmed fedora felt hat for himself, clothes for Antoinette, a woolen suit for Jennie and angora sweaters for all her sisters; he bought gifts for everyone as well as many fine Italian linens, tablecloths and bedspreads.

•

As we ate, the conversation returned to Jimmy and the growth of his business in the late thirties as he diversified and started buying in general merchandise such as shoe polishes, laces, stationery items, batteries, toothpaste and pharmaceuticals. This in turn expanded when he started to deal in larger items such as bicycles, fishing gear, toys and canoes until, in 1936, the Cariddi Sales Company was founded.

Initially this was based at the family's large West Main Street home but it soon out-grew its home-based origins and moved to downtown North Adams; product lines were added and more employees and sales people joined the family members already working for the company. The Cariddi Sales Company went on to serve every New England state and New York State as far as the Canadian border and as far south as Pennsylvania.

All the time Jimmy Cariddi was at the helm until, in 1943, he left it in the capable hands of JoAnn and Ralph while he went off to help the allied cause in the European theatre and saw action in the Normandy landings of June 1944.

Jennie produced a list of how family members had contributed to Jimmy's company over the years—it was an impressive mix of job descriptions and responsibilities.

Joseph was the Traffic Manager of Shipping Orders to Retail Stores.

Ralph was a 'Super Salesman' who opened up new territories by finding new customers in New England States and in New York State.

Pat was the Buyer for Toys and Sports Equipment.

JoAnn was the Secretary and Head Bookkeeper.

Jennie herself worked on Accounts Receivable and was a Secretary.

Jennie also recalled a saying of her mother's that served them all well over the years: *mescolare con persone puì meglie di voi e faccia la scuola ...* mingle with those who are better than you and learn from them. Jennie's own working career was the perfect example ... she started as a trainee in the credit department of Sears and was promoted to Credit Manager before she was 'poached' by her big brother.

Jimmy, courteous to a fault, later thanked the Manager of Sears for training his sister so well.

The Cariddi Sales Company still exists in State Road, North Adams, specializing in games, toys, arts and crafts and sporting equipment. It remains a family-run business and until his death in 2012 at the age of ninety-six, its founder, Jimmy Cariddi, still played a part. His daughters, Antoinette and Gail Ann, still run the business and for the latter this is now a family commitment that she juggles with being a Representative for Massachusetts State.

•

As was clear from her Italian experience, Jennie had many suitors but she met her husband-to-be, Leonard Tamasi, in not the most usual of circumstances. Sitting across from me, Leonard beamed knowingly as Jennie told the story.

In the second half of the fifties, just after Leonard had returned from Korea, he asked a friend who was dating one of Jennie's friends, to arrange a foursome ... he wanted to date Jennie. Jennie hadn't met Leonard and was at first skeptical about going on what, for her, was a blind date—not the sort of thing she would usually do and, besides, she had other arrangements.

But Jennie changed her plans and her mind and the three friends duly arrived to pick her up and were introduced to her parents before setting off to the dance at Crooked Lake. Leonard clearly made an impression for later Jennie father, Frank, was heard to remark that if she didn't marry him, she'd never marry ... and besides, he had the face of the Madonna. The rest, as they say, is romantic history.

•

Like all American-Calabrian meals I'd experienced on my travels this was the perfect blend of the two cultures ... fit for a king *and* his army. I couldn't help cast my mind back almost a century to that conversation Francesco Cariddi (as he was then) had with his father Vincenzo when he returned to Calabria in 1913 to court and marry Antoinette Scida. He told his father then that if he worked hard in America he could eat meat every day ... and his father said the Calabrian equivalent of 'go for it, my son'.

And he did, and the fruits of his labors were all around this table, first-, second- and third-generation Americans; Frank's dream of a better life

Frank and Antoinette Cariddi as the people of North Adams remember them.

for him, his wife and their family had borne such bounteous fruit. Jennie reckoned that from her parents, Frank and Antoinette Cariddi, had come a huge family of one hundred and sixty-three people, and rising—a family that every August, at a campsite in Greenfield, got together to remember and to party.

Francesco achieved all the goals that drove him back to America in 1914. The fact that he soon became 'Frank' was an important step ... as someone who did something not dissimilar over thirty years ago, I appreciated the psychological significance of this simple name change.

As he sat on his back porch in West Main Street looking at the large swathe of land behind the house that extended all the way up to a small hill, Frank surely relished in his own piece of America—while Francesco saw an opportunity to make it a small part of Calabria too.

First of all he stepped the land into five levels and soon there were pear, plum, apple and peach trees; blackberry bushes and tomato plants; green Italian beans, potatoes, cabbage and lettuce; eggplants, zucchini, squash, peppers, onions and garlic; basil, parsley, rosemary and oregano ... and, of course, a chicken coop. A wonderful vegetable garden and orchard, truly a Calabrian *ortocello*. Francesco built a small pavilion too where his growing family could enjoy wonderful summer picnics.

At the far end of the *ortocello* the land rose steeply to form a rocky bluff that overlooked North Adams. After the forties everyone knew Witts Ledge better as 'Coca Cola Ledge' after Coca Cola had its logo painted on the steep face of the Ledge—a huge natural billboard that could be seen for miles.

Frank watered his plants twice a day, at six in the morning and then again in early evening when the sun was weakest. As he watered each evening his brother Ralph (Raffaele) sat on the back porch and watched; Ralph was not a gardener, a quieter, thoughtful man who lived with his wife Jennie in one of his brother's apartments. They had no children of their own so Jennie was always at hand as the Cariddi family grew.

As summer began to wane the family was busy drying, bottling and canning the fruits of Frank's labor, putting in order the produce that would see them through the winter—still familiar sights and sounds in today's Calabria.

And as September reached out to October, Frank would go to Albany and fetch boxes of Californian grapes and soon the air was full of the tantalizing scent as the pressed grapes slowly, naturally, became wine. Jennie recalled how all the children were fascinated by this annual ritual ... and they liked eating the grapes too.

For me this too was a familiar story for every year at this time in Calabria, these same late-September aromas waft out of every *magazzino* and are carried by the wind through the narrow streets. Everyone is eager to know ... will this year's wine be as good as last?

But Frank didn't just tend his garden he would be seen out and about in North Adams—dressed immaculately, smoking his favorite Italian cigars, chatting to friends, sharing stories of then and now—a proud, personable citizen of the country he loved.

•

Here in Schenectady I was politely refusing any more of the Cariddi family's red wine ... I'd already had two small glasses and knew I had a long drive back to Jersey City.

Some of the Cariddi family sharing the hospitality of Jennie and Leonardo's home. Jennie is fourth from the left; JoAnn is third from the left.

Dinner over, people were heading home; I was gathering my things together to do the same when Leonard appeared with a bottle of wine and a glass for me. As I started to protest he politely raised his hand and said there was no point in me setting off for Jersey City now ... it made much more sense for me to have a couple of glasses of wine and a good night's sleep. Jennie and Michael (the only remaining family member) nodded in agreement so who was I to argue? I called Sherrie in Wayne Street and told her the change in plan.

•

Maybe it was the wine but somehow I inadvertently sparked off a well-rehearsed family disagreement with talk of the recent Presidential election ... it was clear that Leonard and Michael had voted for opposing camps and that their votes had cancelled each other out.

Jennie came to the rescue with more stories of family life in North Adams and one particular memory of her father after he retired. At the beginning of every month, regular as clockwork, he would sit on the back porch waiting for the mailman to arrive with his monthly pension check. And when the check did arrive he would smile broadly, hold it up in the air and say "Thank you Uncle Sam."

Frank Cariddi had worked hard all his life and the pension he received was a bonus; he was grateful for the opportunities this land had given him and, above all else, he was immensely proud to be an American citizen.

I couldn't help but wonder whether every immigrant capitalized on the opportunities that presented themselves when they came ashore at Ellis Island ... or were people like Bruno Cortese, Giuseppe Sculco, Pasquale Scida, Giuseppe Piezzo, Alessandro Tallarico and Francesco Cariddi just unique people? And in listing these six I realize that they are but one half of a family—were not women like Louise Fortino, Angelina Parisi, Maria Mazza, Marianna Tallarico and Antionetta Scida equally special? I was sure that before this trip was over there would be more names to add to both lists.

And not for the first time my thoughts returned to that unknown Italian family caught on camera as they stood, shell-shocked and expectant, on the ferry that brought them to Ellis Island. And still I wonder what happened to them.

The iconic Uncle Sam (the US's initials) poster first appeared as an army recruiting tool in the United States in 1917 when America entered World War I.
Three years earlier a similar poster of Lord Kitchener appeared in Great Britain as a similar call to arms.
Both were used again to recruit soldiers for World War II.

Frank Cariddi was never a member of the US forces but his son Jimmy was and saw action in the Normandy landings of June 1944.

•

The next morning over breakfast we talked about what it was like in the workplace to be an Italian-American.

This followed on from when, the previous evening, I had asked Michael what it was that brought immigrants to Schenectady for, like North Adams, there had been a significant settlement of Italians in the area. The answer was simple ... two words ... General Electric. Until then I had no idea that Thomas Edison was in any way connected with the city ... actor Mickey Rourke yes, but not Thomas Edison.

General Electric was formed in 1892 with the merger of the then Edison General Electric Company of Schenectady and the Thomson-Houston Electric Company of Lynn near Boston. At the time General Electric was by far the largest employer in the area and where many Italian immigrants worked.

In the early sixties Leonard himself worked for their US Navy Atomic Training Base in West Milton, New York ... but this was a far cry from what it had been like for immigrants in the twenties and thirties.

Leonard recalled some of his father's stories about how Italians were discriminated against when it came to bettering themselves—at one time it was General Electric policy to advertise managerial positions with the rider that no Italian need apply.

Even getting a job as part of the workforce was not straightforward and involved a hurdle or two. First of all you had to get past one of the 'Toni's, themselves always Italian, and the self-appointed Mr Fixits when it came to working for General Electric. Paying 'Toni' a hundred dollars was the sure way to get inside the gates and hopefully have a secure a job for life.

This was Italian exploiting Italian and I wondered to what extent there was discrimination from non-Italians which brought us on to the more abusive names Italian-Americans were called ... something that Lou Piezzo had encountered once when he was called 'wop'. Leonardo had a list to hand of the others he remembered being directed towards him and his friends ... greaseball, dago, guinea and ginzo. These last two I'd never come across before ... the first, guinea, being a reference to the dark complexion of some southern Italians and its similarity to the so-called Guinea Negro while ginzo is a term relating specifically to Italian-Americans, often of Sicilian descent.

Our etymological wanderings were not quite completed for Leonardo, aware that I had arrived without a hat and it was a bit fresh outside, found the perfect headgear for me—a green Jameson Irish Whiskey baseball cap. The etymological element was when I pointed out how Irish 'whiskey' was spelled, with an 'e', the American way; Scottish whisky is e-less. As it happened Leonard had a bottle of Scotch in his cupboard and so did a routine check that it was indeed so.

Impressed with our new-found vocabularies, Leonard and I embraced before Jennie and I did the same. I felt I was saying goodbye to a woman I'd known half a lifetime, instead of less than a day. Jennie gave me a gift for Filomena back in Stróngoli and, just I was heading out the door, reminded me that, should I like to use the title of her diary for my book, I was welcome to do so.

I decided there and then 'Thank you Uncle Sam', it would be.

Goodbye dear friend; hello Mazda

I didn't immediately tell the small-house-mobile to take me home ... I thought it was time I leaned a more enquiring mind into how 'the voice' worked and just why it had brought me here via the scenic route. If, indeed, that's what it had been doing.

I turned out onto the main road and pulled over and started to tap on-screen buttons until I found what I was looking for ... someone, the last hirer presumably, had programed the GPS to avoided roads where a toll was paid. In other words to avoid the interstate highways. It seemed incomprehensible that someone had paid to rent the small-house-mobile, the most expensive car on the lot, and then not want to pay the tolls.

Anyway, I had spent too long behind the wheel of the small-house-mobile the previous day and was looking forward to a fast, direct journey back to Jersey City for which I was prepared to pay anything.

Re-programed, 'the voice' did my bidding and in a little over two-and-a-half hours the small-house-mobile was back in its temporary home and under the watchful eye of Mitch and I was back on Wayne Street.

There were two important emails awaiting me on my iPad. One was another message from Maria Cavaliere in Reading, Pennsylvania who was wondering if we might meet on Sunday instead of Saturday. Although I had hoped to go to the birthday party of Gino and Sina Sculco's granddaughter, I was prepared to change days rather than not see Maria.

The second was an email from Tommaso Fonte with whose family I would be spending Thanksgiving in Kenosha, Wisconsin. This was in response to two emails I'd sent him.

The first was following up a inquiry from my friend Vicki Kelly from Roccabernarda—she with the passion for Rice-a-Roni—about a distant relative of her father-in-law whom she believed also lived in Kenosha; she wondered if Tommaso Fonte might know the Piro family there.

And following my discovery that Elvira Arabia, the sister-in-law of Ralph Sculco, also lived in Kenosha, I wondered did Tommaso know her too. At the time I had no idea how large or small Kenosha was and if it was the sort of place where Italian-American families might mix, even those from Santa Severina and Roccabernarda.

Tommaso's email was the perfect antidote to Maria's for he knew both families and had already arranged that we'd visit Ippolito Piro on the day I arrived and that he was trying to get in touch with Elvira too.

Monday was the evening I knew that the Saigon Café was closed but I was adequately prepared for this minor catastrophe and had, if you recall, already checked out a nearby Thai restaurant on my very first evening in Jersey City. The Sawadee was open and, though I missed the special ambience of the Saigon Café, I enjoyed my meal but didn't linger as I had some packing to do in preparation for my eight-thirty flight the next morning from Newark to Chicago Midway.

For the first time, I set the alarm on my new toy, the iPhone.

•

I woke a quarter of an hour before the alarm went off … or rather a quarter of an hour before it *didn't* go off. I've always had a habit of waking up just before the alarm … though I'd like to bet that if I didn't set an alarm, that habit would not come to my rescue.

I told 'the voice' to whisk me and the small-house-mobile back home … it's off-airport home, that is. That twenty-minute drive was to be our last adventure together and perhaps it was that I just wanted to prolong the parting but somehow I managed to misinterpret two instructions and in so doing add another ten minutes to the journey. And, for the second time

I came close to writing off the small-house-mobile when I found myself partially up the ramp to the interstate ... the ramp down which traffic was *exiting* the freeway. As I turned sharply down another ramp to the right I wondered just what those other drivers were thinking when they saw that lone pair of headlights heading momentarily in their direction.

I had envisaged a parting that would give me time to take a photo of the small-house-mobile, maybe even get somebody to take us together, but sadly the opportunity to tap its extensive hood and bid it a fond farewell slid by as the driver of the shuttle bus to the airport urged me to get a move on as he was just about to set off.

This was my second departure from Newark in just over a week so it was all the more perplexing to have had a smooth, seamless passage through passport control and security the first time and an everlasting one the second time, and both at more or less the same time of day.

The problem seemed to be focused on the one person in charge who seemed not only agitated and downright rude to some people, but blissfully unaware that there was even a problem. He strode up and down the lines, ignoring the entreaties of people who believed they were on time for the flights but now were facing the possibility of missing them.

A young Asian couple behind me were on a flight that departed before mine, so I insisted they go on ahead. Safely air-side myself, I saw a young frenetic man, running and weaving round those with time to shop, and still carrying the shoes he'd taken off at security ... he cut a swathe through bewildered crowds as, trying desperately to stay upright in his socks, he sought the relief of his gate and his flight.

On board my Southwest flight I once again discovered that I could use my iPad online ... I was still trying to decide whether I would book accommodation that night in or near Chicago or take a chance on one of the many roadside inns well flagged up on American freeways. I decided to go for the latter option as I wasn't sure how long I would be at my first port of call in the suburb of Lyons.

I was deliberately leaving things flexible as, for me, Chicago has always been a special American city, a place I have been drawn to a number of times. I just wasn't sure if I would have time to go downtown or whether I would just have to circumnavigate the city on my way out towards

Wisconsin for my mid-morning rendezvous with Tommaso Fonte the next day.

At Midway I picked up the shuttle bus that took me to my rental base, a distance of no more than a couple of hundred yards which I could easily have walked. The young driver was trying to pack as much information into his two-minute drive as possible in the forlorn hope his charges would think he had offered them a service that was worthy of a tip.

At the rental office there was no one at hand who hailed from Calabria so there were no perks. I left with more or less what I had booked ... when the guy in charge saw that I was expecting a car in the 'economy' range he shrugged his shoulders, told me they didn't have any of those, pointed to a couple of rows of cars (models from the next range up) and suggested I picked one I liked. I went for a white Mazda.

I didn't actually leave immediately as I had to ring Pepe Fragale, the woman I was here to see and tell her I was on my way and also get used to a GPS system that, with this car, was a sit-on-the-dashboard 'extra' not, as had been the case with the small-house-mobile, built in to the dashboard. The first thing I did was check that it was not programed to avoid toll-roads ... I wasn't expecting any such roads on the first part of my journey but I was later in the day and the following morning.

Next I typed in my destination address on South Rose Avenue only to be told it didn't exist. I tried again; the same. I took the GPS to the kiosk and told the guy there that it didn't seem to work. He then tried it and confirmed that there seemed to be a problem. He took it across to where the cars were serviced and told me somebody would bring me a new one.

A few minutes later, another guy turned up with the same GPS and the good news that I would go to the ball for he had solved the problem. For some reason the GPS did not like the prefix 'South' ... it didn't distinguish between South Rose Avenue and North Rose Avenue, these were designations, it seemed, that only the locals who lived there used.

Alone at last with Mazda and my new 'voice', the same 'voice' that had been in the small-house-mobile, I set off due west across Cicero Avenue towards Lyons. I'd noticed the name 'Cicero' earlier on a road-sign between the airport and the rental base and was still trying to unearth something from the recesses of my memory that made it familiar. Then the penny dropped—this part of Chicago was Cicero, the place where Bruno Cortese once lived and worked in 1906 and from where, from the early twenties, Al Capone ran his bootlegging empire. Until that moment I hadn't realized that Midway Airport was on Cicero Avenue, Chicago.

In the late summer of 2012 Pepe Fragale and her eleven-year-old grandson Lorenzo spent a month in Pepe's home town of Santa Severina. Pepe and Lorenzo had traveled from Lyons, a suburb of Chicago.

My friend Carlo told me about her visit the day after she returned to America; she had had a last drink at his bar the evening before, the one evening when we were not there.

Carlo gave me the number of her nephew Gustavo Tigano at Cosenza University. I had met Gustavo before but never realized he had American connections; Gustavo gave me his aunt's Chicago number.

The first time I called Pepe something went wrong with the connection; I checked the number with Gustavo and tried again a couple of weeks later.

This time I got through and arranged to visit her at her Lyons home on the western outskirts of Chicago on the Tuesday before Thanksgiving on my way to Kenosha in Wisconsin.

The woman who emigrated alone

Without mishap, wrong turns or recalculating, Mazda and 'the voice' got me safely to Rose Avenue where I found that the number I had been given didn't appear to exist in Rose Avenue itself. I did a couple of passes along the road to confirm that the number I was looking for was definitely AWOL. I turned back onto Plainfield Road and the junction with 43rd Street and saw a house, fronting on to 43rd Street but somehow also sandwiched in between Rose Avenue and the service road behind.

A young man came out of the house just as I pulled up outside behind a car which displayed a 'For Sale' sign. Anthony Fragale welcomed me to Lyons, a suburb of Chicago.

We went inside and Anthony introduced me to his mother Pepe, a diminutive woman in her late seventies with a broad and engaging smile. Pepe welcomed me to their home and we sat round the table in the kitchen.

I told them the story of the GPS not recognizing the address because it included the word 'south' and they realized that perhaps that was why couriers sometimes found it hard to locate them as these days most use satellite navigation of some sort.

We went on to talk about Pepe's visit to Santa Severina in the summer and how our paths had failed to cross despite the fact that we'd both

Pietro Gerardi, Pepe's father, is on the right standing next to his brother Umberto; another brother, Francesco, is on the chair. They are with their mother Rosa Salerno.

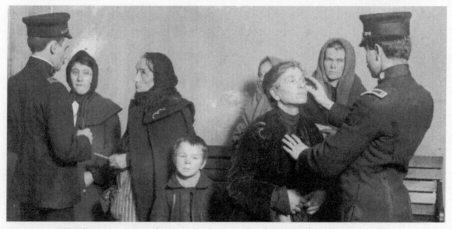

Immigrant women having their eyes checked at Ellis Island, c1905.

been up and down to the town's square umpteen times that hot August ... and even though I knew her nephew Gustavo, had I seen them together I would just have assumed she was his mother.

Once again, although Pepe—her Italian name is Guiseppina—herself only emigrated in 1958, there was a history of emigration in the family going back almost a hundred years.

In 1913, at the age of seventeen, Pepe's father, Pietro Gerardi, arrived in New York aboard the *Principe di Piemonte*; earlier that same month another young man from Santa Severina, a twenty-two year-old joiner called Francesco Marasco also turned up in New York.

Three years later Pietro came back to Santa Severina and never returned to the States—he was one of the many Italian *ritornati*. Back home in Santa Severina, he courted and married Francesco Marasco's sister Marietta (Maria) Marasco.

Maria and Francesco were two of Gaetana Tallarico's six children, four girls and two boys. In 1921, Gaetana, at the age of fifty-six and now a widow, herself emigrated to the States with two of her daughters, Annina and Robina, and they were met by Gaetana's son, Francesco, who now lived in the Cicero area of Chicago. Coincidentally it was the same year that Al Capone also moved to Chicago to work alongside his mentor, the infamous gangster Johnny Torrio.

Gaetana's entry to the States was not straightforward. Her age was a disadvantage and the medical examination, such as it was, threw up two apparent problems—senility and double immature cataracts. Had not her son been there to meet her, it is likely that she would have been sent back to Calabria; perhaps the fact that she was accompanied by her two daughters was a bonus—she could be seen to have a built-in support network that wouldn't be a burden on the state.

Anthony told me that the attraction of the Cicero area for Italian and other, largely east-European, immigrants was not dissimilar to the work opportunities offered by General Electric at Schenectady. From 1905 Western Electric started operating from their massive Hawthorne Plant at the intersection of South Cicero Avenue and West Cermak Road (22nd Street). Within a few years all Western Electric's manufacturing was centered on this one site which, it is said, resembled a small town complete with its own hospital, fire brigade and laundry. Today all that is left of this huge enterprise is a tower that stands alongside the railway as a lone reminder of another age.

•

So it was into this family background that Pepe Gerardi was born ... her father had lived in America for three years, her grandmother had emigrated there and she had uncles and aunts on her mother's side of the family still there. It is not surprising therefore that in the late fifties the young Pepe, now in her early twenties, decided that her time had come.

Her father Pietro, now in his sixties, knew his young daughter well. He could see she had no interest in school and knew that opportunities in Calabria without education were limited. (Pepe's sisters were more studious and most later became teachers.) Pietro wrote to his brother-in-law Frank Marasco in Cicero and asked if Pepe could come and stay and take advantage of what America had to offer.

Of course Pepe had family in the States but nevertheless it was a huge

Left: Pepe's parents, Pietro Gerardi and Marietta Marasco.
Right: Marietta's mother, Gaetana Tallarico, with her grandchildren—Pepe (left), sisters Antoinetta and Gina, brother Nicola and baby Rosalba.

step for a young woman of twenty-four to take by herself. She was not going to America with a husband or a brother or a father; nor was following at the heels of close family members. Rather she was taking an enormous leap into the unknown, more akin to what many of her male ancestors and their *paesani* had done half a century earlier.

Diminutive and unassuming she might seem, sitting across the table from me ... but I knew I was in the company of a quite remarkable woman.

And so it was, in October 1958, that Pepe Gerardi said *arrivederci* to Santa Severina and set off to join her relatives in the United States. At Rome she caught TWA flight 835 to New York's Idlewild Airport (today's JFK) via Paris. At New York she transferred to Chicago.

•

Pepe's uncle Frank had become an American citizen back in 1936 and he and his wife Maria still lived on West 28th Street in Cicero and it was there that Pepe began her new American life. It was, she recalls, almost like being at home for her uncle's family were so kind and supportive.

She knew too that this would set her mother's mind at rest for there were stories of other young immigrants having been taken advantage of by their so-called relatives in America—perhaps the extent of this problem depended on how close those relatives actually were as, sometimes, Calabrian familial connections have an undefinable elasticity.

Pepe soon found work at Copenheimer Tailors on Pulaski Road and then moved on to two other local tailors AG Meyer and Nemcheck before working in a number of clothes shops.

In the early sixties Pepe went to a wedding in Kenosha, Wisconsin—to where, coincidentally, I was traveling the following morning—and here she met a man who tried to set her up romantically with another young Calabrian who, it turned out, was already engaged. He, in turn, passed Pepe's photo on to his brother, Frank Fragale, and Pepe and Frank began communicating with each other by post and, through the letters and photos they exchanged, they fell in love.

In March 1963 Pepe returned to Calabria and married the man she'd never met and never spoken to, even on the phone.

This story was, it seemed to me, almost a mirror image of all the other stories I'd heard about immigrants returning to Calabria to claim their younger bride ... in researching this book I had come across many such cross-Atlantic liaisons. The difference with Pepe and Frank was that it was Pepe who returned to Calabria to claim her husband and Frank who was planning to follow her back to America.

The priest who married them also noted this unusual aspect of their relationship when he remarked that it was more usual for the wife to follow the husband and not the other way round; he also couldn't resist mentioning the age difference—Pepe was the older by six years.

•

Frank Fragale and his parents, Antonio and Caterina, all hailed from San Giovanni in Fiore in the foothills of the Sila mountains and just over twenty miles from Santa Severina. When I asked what Caterina's surname was I was told 'Fragale' which of course it was for those used to living in America but in her home town of San Giovanni in Fiore she was, and always would be, Caterina Biafiore.

When English author Norman Douglas passed through San Giovanni around the time Antonio and Caterina were youngsters, he noted in his travelogue *Old Calabria* that "... the chief objects of interest in San Giovanni are the women" and that in times past "it was dangerous to approach these attractive and mirthful creatures, [as] they were jealously guarded by brothers and husbands". But in recent years things had changed and, Douglas went on to observe that, "the brothers and husbands, thank God, are now in America, and you can be as friendly with [the women] as ever you please ...".

Despite the attraction of the womenfolk, Douglas went on to paint an unpleasant picture of the town: "accumulated filth ... ineffably squalid ... sordid ... unhealthy ...". It is little wonder that so many people left. That said, neither Antonio nor Caterina did leave, though many of both their extended families emigrated.

This difference in how Calabrian and American women named themselves post-marriage—where the wife took the husband's name in America but retained her maiden name in Calabria—explained the many blank looks I got when I told people in Santa Severina that I was going to visit Pepe Fragale. Everyone here knows her only by her maiden name of

Guiseppina (Pepe) Gerardi. More than half a century after she became Pepe Fragale in the States, she *always* remains Pepe Gerardi in Santa Severina.

Similarly, I did not know until we met that Pepe was indeed a 'Gerardi', a name not unknown to me for the house we live in is owned by another 'Gerardi', Silvana Gerardi. 'Our' Gerardi family treat my wife and I as part of their extended family and we are frequently the only non-family members always invited to what would normally be family occasions. So, in Santa Severina we are also part 'Gerardi'.

It is not unusual, even in a small place like Santa Severina—with less than two-and-a-half thousand inhabitants—for there to be two or more families with the same surname that do not to have any obvious familial connection. Nevertheless, when asked, people will usually play safe and say something like "*Si, siamo parenti ... tanti anni fa, però*", yes, we're family, but many years ago. It's a half-hearted admission that nobody actually knows—or considers it important—and a bit like the 'cousin' syndrome I have already alluded to when people call each other cousins when at best, they're third- or fourth-cousins, at worst, probably not even related but simply long-standing friends or neighbors.

Not that it's a problem, it's just a quirk of the way things work. Sometimes you can know two or three individuals for months, years even, before realizing they are siblings—this was the case recently with two local men whom I knew independently for years before finding out they were brothers—while there are others you assume are related in some way and they aren't, they just share a surname.

Occasionally a family with the same surname as another will be adamant that they are *not* related in any way, even back in the mists of time. This is often an indication that one family believes itself to be better than the other and does not want to be seen to be associated with it. Sometimes small-town rivalries can be very confusing and it is best not to dwell on them for long.

Nevertheless I was more than a little curious to know if 'our' Gerardi family was related to Pepe's and, if so, in what way. The answer was a guarded 'yes' but the exact relationship between grandparents and great-grandparents could not be pin-pointed with any accuracy. To all intents and purposes the mists of time reigned supreme and there were now at least two separate Gerardi families in Santa Severina.

•

As Pepe started to serve another magnificent Calabrian-American lunch, we returned to the time when she and Frank married, when Frank was in the army ... the Italian army serving his two-year's conscription which was compulsory at the time.

After the marriage and honeymoon, Pepe, now pregnant, returned to the States where, early the following year, she was joined by her mother, Maria, who helped look after her and her first-born, Anthony.

There was never any question that Maria would return to Calabria once everyone was back on their feet ... though apparently she soon became addicted to American television soaps, even if she could not understand a 'lick' of English.

By this time Pepe had not only mastered English but had also become an American citizen which she knew would make it easier for her husband to join her. But Frank, still based in Cotronei (between Santa Severina and San Giovanni) doing his stint in the Italian forces, was desperately missing

Anthony Fragale (right) and his cousin Pepe Tigano on their Vespas.

his wife and had not yet met his son. Soon it all became too much and, in early 1964, he applied for and got an early discharge on the proviso that, if he returned to Italy within twelve years, he would have to complete his service.

Within a matter of days Frank Fragale joined his American wife and son in Cicero.

Frank soon found work through his cousin Vince Marazzo in a factory in Cicero that worked in stainless steel. He then moved on to Elkay Manufacturing which at the time specialized in stainless-steel products for the home; Frank worked at Elkay until he retired thirty-seven years later.

He never became an American citizen and reckoned that unless he was thinking of running for President—which he wasn't—it wasn't such a big deal. That said, he became American in all sorts of other ways, from turkey at Thanksgiving and Christmas to burgers and fries at McDonald's. Of course, when it came to soccer and other sports, Pepe and Frank remained Italian to the core.

As the Fragale family grew, lurking somewhere in the background, there was always the small problem of Frank's relationship with the Italian military and, through them, the government. Finally, having remained in the States for twelve years, his status was normalized and at long last he was free to return to Italy.

Now that Frank could travel, the Fragale family did have one brief flirtation with the idea of returning to Calabria for good.

It was Frank's idea originally but it was Pepe and their three children—Anthony, Dino and Cathy—who crossed the Atlantic to test the Calabrian waters. This was the end of the seventies and Anthony, a teenager at the time, recalled that he found it difficult at school in Santa Severina as, unexpectedly, the academic level was higher in Calabria than in the States. Difficult though it was, he did well and when the family eventually returned to America he went up a grade at school thanks to his Calabrian experience.

In Calabria Antonio (as he now was) also had another extra-curricular interest in the form of Santa Severina's first Vespa Club. There were about fourteen or fifteen members, he recalls, who regularly headed into the countryside on their scooters to picnic on wine, cheese and *sopressata* (Calabrian salami).

Anthony Fragale and his mother Pepe at home in Lyons, a suburb of Chicago.

Fun though the experiment was, and despite the draw of family, friends and scooters in Calabria, the Fragale family realized their home was now in America. Antonio parked up his Vespa one last time and became Anthony again and a year to the day after they arrived in Santa Severina, Pepe and her children returned to America to join Frank back in Cicero.

Family visits both ways continued over the years but, like so many others before and after, the growing Fragale family was firmly embedded in the United States and so it remained.

•

When Anthony spoke of his father it was with a faltering voice. The man he and his mother adored, the man whom he described as "an Italian Clint Eastwood—rugged, handsome and righteous—the salt of the earth" passed in 2011.

Despite their loss, Pepe still found the energy in August the following year to take her eleven-year-old grandson for his first visit to Santa Severina, to show her daughter Cathy's young son Lorenzo where *she* was born and to introduce him to his many uncles, aunts and cousins who spoke a different language.

Within a fortnight, Lorenzo was independent enough to walk up to the town's square to meet with and talk to his growing band of friends, much as his mother and his uncles Antonio and Dino had done back in 1979. I must surely have seen him there—though I didn't know it at the time—and assumed that, as is normal in the town at that time of year, he was the child of a Santa Severinese returning home for the summer from 'up north'.

Pepe told me how, back home in America, Lorenzo has not stopped talking about his holiday in the Calabrian sun and that, though he is American through and through, he can't wait to return to his other home in Santa Severina.

Perhaps one summer soon he'll be back in Calabria and he'll start another Vespa Club and he and his friends—and their cell phones—will head off into the countryside to picnic on wine, cheese and *sopressata*.

•

As I was preparing to leave Pepe and Anthony I thought back to that mental list I'd made a few days earlier in Schenectady, the list of 'unique' and 'special' people. I knew there was at least one more name to add to it, Pepe (Gerardi) Fragale. And what made Pepe even more unique was that she was the only one that I had actually met.

Before I left Lyons, Anthony gave me detailed directions on how to get to the interstate and round Chicago and on my way north to Wisconsin.

As I pulled away from the house, I realized that I was no longer confident I could cope without the help of 'the voice'. I never thought I'd ever admit that I had become used to being told where to go, used to 'the voice' and her reassuring ways, used to relying on her expertise instead of a picture in my head.

What was the world coming to?

On the road again

I followed Antonio's directions to the interstate ... until, that is, 'the voice' contradicted them. I decided to go with 'the voice' who, though she may not have his local knowledge, had been reasonably faithful thus far and was probably taking her knowledge of traffic conditions into consideration.

I had also made an executive decision to circumnavigate Chicago and head out northwards towards Wisconsin and resist the temptation to visit old haunts ... and one bar in particular near The Loop on South Wabash. Because of this initial uncertainty I had not booked any accommodation for that night, deciding instead to take my chances with one of the many inns normally flagged up just before interstate highway exits. It was something I'd never done before but always had had a secret urge to give it a try.

It was getting dark, not because of the time of day but because of the persistent heavy rain. The interstate was ablaze with car headlights and I had just passed an exit which in the old days would have said Gas, Food, Lodging but these days was more up front about what enticements were on offer within a few hundred yards of the exit.

I decided the next such exit was mine. I was, I reasoned, heading for a quiet, inexpensive and impersonal bedroom and something to eat ... something to fill a space rather than to relish.

I filtered off right at the Grand Avenue exit where I could also see a sign for La Quinta, a chain of inns that I knew by name only. I turned right again and found myself in a semi-circle of enticements for the weary traveller—mostly places to eat but also a couple of inns. I turned into the La Quinta car park and checked the prices on my iPhone before going inside ... I just wanted to be certain there wasn't a huge burst of inflation as soon as I got to the reception desk.

I needn't have worried, the young man at the reception desk had been groomed to be personable and he certainly was that ... when he saw my home address he even told me that it was his goal in life to retire to Italy; by my reckoning he had about forty years or more to wait. He also noted my advancing years and gave me the generous 'senior' discount and I ended up paying less than the web page had given me to understand.

I had the wi-fi code for the iPad, a surprisingly comfy bedroom and a selection of places to eat on my doorstep; I was content with my lot.

Before I stepped out into the drizzle, my iPad had already told me there were five places to eat within walking distance. I decided to check out a chain I'd never heard of, Outback, which, I discovered, was 'an Australian themed steakhouse restaurant' offering 'a casual atmosphere suggestive of the Australian outback'. Never having been to Australia, I thought this would be a good place to start.

Like all such American chain restaurants, the staff were personable and polite to a fault ... it was as if they'd been waiting all day for me to arrive and, now that I had, they were going to pamper me and spoil me rotten. Maria, my waitress, personified this ethos and I soon felt special among a sea of younger-than-me eaters having fun together.

A table or two away, one couple caught my eye. They were ordinary in the sense that, like almost everyone else, they were in their twenties and were enjoying their evening of mock-Australian fare. They were also extraordinary for they were two of the largest people I had ever seen—I seriously wondered how they'd got in the door. Still, they seemed happy enough, nevertheless they unwittingly shifted my focus on the menu away from my fruitless search for kangaroo steak and on to the fish choice where I opted for the grilled mahi.

I know people always say you should drink white wine with fish but

I come from a different school of thought ... if the red wine list includes Californian Pinot Noir, then order it and enjoy the moment. If it's good enough for a James Bond villain, it's good enough for me.

The decor was that contrived mock-authenticity that such places exude with flare ... there is no embarrassment and no pretence that it actually resembles whatever the theme is trying to convey.

It wasn't the best 'chain' meal I'd ever had, nor was it the worst. I found the fish a bit bland but that was more than made up for by the excellent wine and my on-going curiosity about the couple across the aisle who had started their meal before I got there and were still working their way through the puddings when I left. At least they had found each other and shared an interest in health issues.

I left having learned nothing about Australia ... or its outback.

Back at La Quinta I emailed Tommaso Fonte to confirm that I would see him at ten in the morning as arranged. I told him I was just around the corner, still in Illinois but a stone's throw from Wisconsin and Kenosha.

I also received another email from Maria in Reading, Pennsylvania to say that we would not be able to meet as planned that weekend ... family travel complications following Thanksgiving now ruled out both the Saturday and the Sunday. I was very disappointed but at least on the Sunday I would be able to go to the birthday party of Anna Sculco's daughter.

While I was in America, Carolina (Bonocore) Ventrella had contacted me via email after reading two of my other books and we subsequently exchanged a number of emails about her Calabrian roots.

From these exchanges it was clear that her parents' story—and how they came to leave their home in Marano Marchesato near Cosenza—was more than just fascinating, it was unique.

Carolina lived and worked in Roselle, a suburb of Chicago and a part of Illinois that I had passed close to after I left the Fragale family in Lyons en route to Wisconsin.

Although I already knew it would not be possible for us to meet—even following my trip to Wisconsin—I felt it would be worth finding out more about Carolina's Calabrian roots and recording them alongside the other stories in this book.

The internet made this virtual chapter possible ... perhaps Carolina and I will meet another time.

The man with the scar on his forehead

I asked Carolina if her grandfather (on her father's side) had a scar on his forehead. She emailed me back to say that she thought he had but that she would need to check with her mother. She also wondered how I knew.

The answer was simple: the Ellis Island website not only recorded Enrico Marchese's passage from Marano Marchesato to America aboard the *Madonna* in March 1920 but also his 'marks of identification'. Enrico Marchese had a scar on his forehead.

Of course when her grandfather was around Carolina was too young to remember such details but her mother, Carmela Morelli—whose family were from nearby Marano Principato—remembered it well and understood the scar was result of an accident when he'd been in the military. Carolina wondered if that was why he always wore a hat in all the family photos.

Until that moment Carolina had not realized that Enrico Marchese had ever emigrated and was even more surprised when it turned out that he had been to America before March 1920 ... and after.

However, she did know that on her mother's side there had been some comings and goings as far back as 1907 when Carmela's father Gaetano came to Chicago where his older brother Raffaele already lived and worked; three years later another brother Eugenio joined them.

Both Raffaele and Gaetano returned to Marano but Eugenio stayed and eventually moved to Kenosha in Wisconsin. Family memories suggest that Gaetano got himself into a bit of romantic trouble in the States and decided that the time was right to return to Calabria where he later married Angelina Savaglio.

His older brother, Raffaele, also returned to Calabria and thereafter the two never got on .... whether or not Gaetano's American problems somehow rubbed off on Raffaele nobody knows but thereafter the two were brothers in name only.

It seems too that Gaetano brought his philandering ways back with him and was known to be a bit of a womanizer. It is said that he even gave some of Angelina's prized possessions, such as linens and jewelry, to other women in his life. He and Angelina had one child, Carolina's mother Carmela; her father, Gaetano, died when she was four.

Small, close-knit communities such as Marano Marchesato can breed

Carolina's mother, Carmela Morelli, and Carmela's mother Angelina Savaglio.

petty rivalries that sometimes blossom into full-blown vendettas ... more often of the 'not-speaking' kind as opposed to something more violent. The root cause is almost always something to do with land and its ownership.

Carmela was due to inherit a piece of Morelli land when she was older but it never happened. Her uncle Raffaele, who had already given her mother the cold shoulder after his brother died, then persuaded Angelina to sell him the land at a knock-down price. It seemed to the family that whatever grudge he had against his younger brother was taken out on his widow and her daughter.

So Carolina knew the story of her mother's side of the family and their American connections ... indeed when her parents emigrated in the 1960s her uncle Eugene (Eugenio that was) still lived in Kenosha. What was a surprise to her was that the man with the scar on his forehead, her grandfather (on her father's side), Enrico Marchese had also emigrated ... but the story was infinitely more intriguing and complex.

•

We still haven't got to the crux of the story that Carolina first enticed me with for the main protagonist, the man with the scar on his forehead, Enrico Marchese, was clearly a unique character. I discovered that he emigrated in March 1920 and that on the *Madonna*'s manifest he declared that he had lived in America between 1905 and 1914. This set me off on a mission to map Enrico's chronology of emigration-immigration, a complex trail that occupied many of my idle moments for several days until I finally got the better of his movements between 1909 and 1924.

Over these fifteen years Enrico Marchese emigrated to Chicago *four* times: March 1909, March 1920, October 1920 and June 1924.

In itself his cycle of goings and comings was curious. Having spent five years in America he returned to Italy the very year when many others were keen to go in the opposite direction.

In June 1914 the assassination in Sarajevo, Serbia of Archduke Franz Ferdinand of Austria, triggered military alliances that within a month resulted in a European conflict of global dimensions. Although Italy did not enter the conflict until 1915, many saw the writing on the wall and headed west. Enrico, on the other hand, arrived back to Italy in time to be conscripted into the military and to acquire that scar on his forehead.

And then in 1920 he returned to America twice. That year the *Madonna* plied seven times between Marseilles and New York via Naples and on two occasions Enrico Marchese was on board. The reason why he was going backwards and forwards remains a mystery and of course he must have returned to Calabria again some time between 1920 and 1924.

In October 1920 and again in 1924 he even gave his place of residence as Chicago and not Calabria; on the same manifests he declared that he was married and that his wife, Concetta Trombino—though he gave her the surname 'Marchese' on one occasion—lived in his home town of Rende, not far from Marano.

The only thing that is known for certain is that not long after Enrico returned to Calabria for the last time he embarked on an extra-marital relationship with another married woman called Carolina Covelli and one of the results of this liaison was Carolina Ventrella's father Emilio.

•

For Enrico and Carolina, both married to others, to embark on such a relationship and to have children was, for the time, a singularly brave, some would say reckless, act. They must have known that social and religious pressures locally would have made life more than uncomfortable so, I reasoned, their relationship must have been special.

The *Prinzess Irene* aboard which one of the Caroline Covellis travelled to America.

I then thought about Carolina Covelli, about whom the Carolina Ventrella's family knew very little, and wondered whether it was possible that she had something to do with Enrico's predilection for scurrying backwards and forwards across the Atlantic. Could it be, I surmised, that these two had met in America, that Carolina Covelli was also an emigrant who, like Enrico, had returned to her Calabrian roots?

The Ellis Island website beckoned.

The answer was both simple and complex. Carolina Covelli arrived in America in December 1913 ... twice.

According to the records, a Carolina Covelli arrived in New York, bound for Chicago, on both December 18 *and* December 19 on two different ships, the *Prinzess Irene* (which left Naples on December 5) and the *America* (which left Naples on December 6).

Both Carolina Covellis were twenty-four, came from the same town where their next of kin was their father Gaspare; both were going to stay with a brother named Luigi at the same address on Forquer Street (today's Arthington Street) in Chicago.

Forquer Street ran parallel to Taylor Street the erstwhile hub of Chicago's own 'Little Italy' and is the street where Enrico Marchese also lived for a time; on his two visits to Chicago in 1920 he stayed with his cousin Eugenio on Aberdeen Street which ran between Taylor and Forquer.

All of this suggests that it is possible that Enrico and Carolina's paths crossed between late 1913 and 1914 when they both lived on the same Chicago street or it could be that they met later in 1920 when Enrico returned to Chicago and lived in nearby Aberdeen Street.

At some time, of course, Carolina herself returned to Calabria where she married and later gave birth to the two illegitimate sons she parented with Enrico.

None of this explains why there were two young women with the same name and seemingly the same family on two different ships at more or less the same time. The only obvious difference between the two was that one was a couple of inches taller that the other. This puzzle kept me awake many a night and I never resolved it satisfactorily ... all I could do was speculate.

First of all I checked and rechecked every piece of information on the Ellis Island website and could find nothing that changed any of the facts outlined above.

I immediately ruled out the notion that Gaspare and his wife had twin daughters and liked the name Carolina so much that they gave them both the same name. That said, stranger things have happened, for I did come across one immigrant family who called their firstborn, Primo, their second child was Secondo, their third Terzo, their fourth Quarto ... and so on.

The only explanation I could come up with was that one Carolina was indeed the genuine article: a twenty-four year-old woman leaving Marano Marchesato and heading for a new life with her brother in Chicago's Little Italy. The other Carolina Covelli was therefore using the real one's identity and documentation in order to enter America. The fact that both women left Naples on consecutive days is unlikely to be mere coincidence.

There is some circumstantial evidence to support this theory. As was normal for a single woman, the Carolina Covelli who arrived aboard the *Prinzess Irene* travelled with other (unrelated) people from her home town; unusually, the one on the *America* appeared to travel alone. Indeed on the page of the *America*'s manifest which records her passage and where there are thirty people listed, there is only one other from Calabria and thirteen are not even Italian.

The fact that one of the women ostensibly came from Marano and the other from Marchesato also suggests a degree of collusion. But which one was the impostor and whether or not she conceived her subterfuge independently or as part of some low-key people trafficking business will probably never be known. Perhaps they were both impostors and the real Carolina Covelli never actually emigrated.

What *is* certain is that it was not uncommon for women—and men— who had previously been deported, to try to return to America as someone else with, for example, the help of a friend or relative in the local town hall—there is just such a story on page 307.

Most of the above was not initially part of the story Carolina Ventrella told me but it is an indication that her grandparents, Enrico Marchese and Carolina Covelli, led unusually colorful lives even before they initiated a scandal closer to home.

•

Emilio and Giuseppe were illegitimate and both born of the same couple—Carolina Covelli and Enrico Marchese. At the time both Carolina and Enrico were already married to others and how and why they chose to become lovers and have children together is a story that their descendants have never fully understood. It is possible they met in America and began their liaison there; even if this is not the case, they almost certainly knew each other before they went there.

Whatever the reasons, some time in 1927 Emilio was conceived and their parents Carolina and Enrico chose to live openly with the resulting stigma that typified the age.

In the late twenties and early thirties divorce was almost unheard of—some would argue that, almost a century later, things haven't changed much in Italy—and 'living in sin' was not the best way to make friends and influence people. It seems that Carolina's family were better off than Enrico's and they illustrated their disapproval of the situation by disinheriting her.

The local *comune* (town hall) made its contribution to the scandal by their own scandalous behavior when they denied both boys their father's surname, Marchese, and instead 'allocated' them surnames of their choosing. Emilio, the elder, became Emilio Bonocore; Giuseppe was Giuseppe Pianese. Bonocore was in fact a common surname locally while Pianese was a name more usual in and around Naples.

Both boys grew up with a stigma that was not of their making—the local, ostensibly Christian, community was generally not inclined to make life easy for them. But things got worse before they got better ... with both boys in their early teens, their mother died and they were more or less left to fend for themselves. Even other family members, used to shunning the brothers, came to the house and took their mother's hope chest and its bounty of blankets and sheets and everything else to start a home.

Out of this story there emerged a typical Calabrian superstitious fiction—reminiscent of *il malocchio*, the evil eye, that Luigi Cubello told me about—whereby those who took the chest were thereafter plagued by the 'ghost' of Carolina Covelli and its nocturnal knocking sounds until they decided to return the chest. A guilty conscience, I'd call it.

Concetta Trombino, Enrico's wife, had always shunned both boys and continued to do so even after their mother died.

The occasion is the christening of Carolina (Bonocore) Ventrella.
The girl with two birthdays is sitting on her godmother's knee; the shorter boy on the left is Carolina's older brother Antonio.
Her parents, Carmela Morelli and Emilio Bonocore are top left and the man with the hat on the extreme right is Enrico Marchese ... the man with the scar on his forehead.

•

The brothers' lives took them along different paths; it was wartime and Emilio went north to do a brief stint in the army and stayed on in Pavia to take up an apprenticeship in tailoring. And as a tailor in post-war Pavia he made good money before returning to Calabria in the fifties.

In the meantime his younger brother Giuseppe had found himself a wife and, being a bit short of money, asked Emilio to lend him enough to buy some land to cultivate. But within a few years the tables were turned—Emilio was not doing so well as a tailor in his native Marano and Giuseppe had established himself as a seller of fruit and vegetables in and around the town.

It is not known if Giuseppe ever paid Emilio back the money he'd borrowed or even if Emilio ever asked for it … whichever, it was never an issue between the brothers. Emilio too was now married and he and Carmela Morelli had two children, Carolina and Antonio but, increasingly, the Bonocore family was finding it difficult to make ends meet in Marano.

When Carolina was born the family had yet another run-in with the eccentricities of the local *comune* in Marano Marchesato. She was born on a Sunday but the *Anagrafe* office at the *comune* (where all births marriages and deaths are recorded) was closed that day. On the Monday her father went to register the birth but the *comune* official insisted that, as the *Anagrafe* office had been closed on the Sunday, little Carolina's birth would be officially registered as being on the Monday.

Each year Carolina and her family celebrated her two birthdays—her real one and, a day later, her 'official' one, the one on all her documentation.

As we have seen, the family of her mother, Carmela Morelli from nearby Marano Principato, had a history of emigration to the United States dating back to 1907 when Carmela's father Gaetano Morelli went to Chicago, only to become one of the many Italian *ritornati* when he resettled in Calabria.

It is therefore likely that, as with other families I met, talk of emigrating and life 'over there' was a normal part of Carmela's upbringing. As is now clear, it was also a part of Emilio's heritage though whether he actually knew this remains uncertain. Until I began to do a bit of digging on the Ellis Island site, neither Carolina Ventrella nor her extended family in

Calabria were aware that their grandfather, Emilio's father, was both a serial emigrant and a serial *ritornato*.

So, when things became difficult economically for the Bonocore family, it was not such a huge mental leap for Carmela and Emilio to themselves talk of emigrating in the hope that they might secure a better future for their children. The fact that their deliberations should have focused on Chicago is as indication that perhaps Emilio was indeed aware of his father's connections with the city, True, Carmela's father had also lived there and her uncle Eugene (Eugenio) had remained in America when his brothers returned to Calabria. But Eugene now lived in Wisconsin.

The family's plans came to fruition in late 1963 when Emilio left for Chicago. Ironically he was sponsored by Carmela's cousin, Luigi Morelli, the son of uncle Raffaele who had given Carmela's mother such a hard time over thirty years earlier. Emilio's mission was to find gainful employment and an apartment before the rest of the family could join him in America.

The Bonocore family in 1963 and 1964 ...
the last photo in Calabria and the first in Chicago.

Carolina recalls how, even at three and a half, she felt her father was leaving forever and even tried to hide his luggage but it was too heavy to move. She felt abandoned but needn't have worried ... a little over six months later she, her brother Antonio and their mother Carmela were themselves packed and ready to leave their native Calabria.

For little Carolina this parting was a traumatic experience. She wept uncontrollably as did her grandfather Enrico Marchese as he stood on the platform at Cosenza station waving farewell to his son's family. She didn't know it at the time but the man standing on the platform had already experienced those same emotions on four separate occasions.

Carolina never saw her grandfather again.

Emilio had found accommodation on Taylor Street in 'Little Italy' and soon found employment with Brittany Limited, an upscale tailors and clothiers on Michigan Avenue, the so-called 'Magnificent Mile'.

Carolina is sure her father never knew that the home he had found for his family was just a block away from the street where his own father Enrico had lived forty years earlier.

•

In the early sixties, two brothers with a complex common inheritance found themselves at opposite ends of the economic spectrum in their native Calabria. But Emilio, a thoughtful, literate man, knew he had a skill that, though it might not pay dividends in Marano Marchesato, was much sought after in the stylish, swinging sixties in Chicago; and he went for it.

Emilio knew too that in making such a momentous decision he was also putting behind him 'the slings and arrows of outrageous fortune' that had dogged his young life through no fault of his own. In every sense he was making a new start.

In Chicago the Bonocore family prospered. Within two years there was a new addition to the family, Carolina's sister, Maria (Mary), born not long after the family spread their wings and moved away from Little Italy.

In 1980 Emilio became an American citizen; Carmela never did. Both learned to speak English but were never fluent—Emilio had a hearing problem and worked with other Italians so it was Carmela who assimilated the language better even though she retains her Calabrian accent. In the mid-eighties, Emilio and Carmela returned together to Marano Marchesato to visit family; Emilio and his brother Giuseppe shared some home-made wine and childhood memories together for the last time.

Unlike her siblings, Carolina Ventrella, now a Chicago-based accountant and part-time wine connoisseur, has a passion for her Calabrian roots. Her passion is so strong that sometimes I sense she misses her Calabrian homeland so much that it hurts—it's as if, every so often, her childhood memory of that day on the platform at Cosenza station replays in her mind's eye.

Of course missing Calabria so much doesn't make her blind to the reality that she is now American and that her family is also American. She knows too that her mother, who still lives in Chicago, is the exception and, despite having lived and worked in the city for most of her life, remains an old-world Calabrian, caught in a time warp of a life lived in another place.

Marano Marchesato, summer 2010: Michael Ventrella (Carolina's son), Carolina (Bonocore) Ventrella, Lina (Pianese) Ferrara (the widow of Emilio's brother Giuseppe) and Carmela (Bonocore) Morelli (Carolina's mother).

So Carolina maintains a close on-going relationship with the parts of her parents' families who are not still locked in the mind-set of stigmas, scandals and vendettas and every few years she returns to Calabria to visit them; to recharge.

•

Not long after we first exchanged emails, Carolina sent me a poem she'd written. Its sentiments speak for themselves.

Italia—Land of Sunflowers

It has been such a long time since I felt the warmth of your sun on my face; such a long time since my tears touched you, the land of my birthplace.

I will celebrate my 50th birthday very soon; how I would have loved to celebrate under the Calabrian stars and moon.

No matter how far I shall be, you will forever own my heart; no matter the years and the distance we have been apart.

Remember me the small ragazza taking the train from Calabria to Rome; yes, I knew I was saying goodbye to my home.

Fleeting memories of the ocean, mountains and clear blue sky; throwing kisses to the wind and saying the final long distance goodbye.

Years have passed and the memories of you are scattered in my heart so bright; like the rays of sunlight on a field of sunflowers—you can feel the warmth and the light.

It is in my heart forever and shall always be a part of me no-one can take away; because in my heart I know that in the journey called life I will return there someday.

Ciao Italia for awhile longer. I will see you again and you will embrace me and make me feel whole; and fill that emptiness that touches down in the deepest part of my soul.

•

The next time Carolina comes this way, I look forward to finally meeting her, to sharing a glass or two of Calabrian red wine and to thanking her in person for sharing the story of the man who had a scar on his forehead.

My friend Vicki from Roccabernarda emailed me not long after I arrived in America. She knew I was visiting Tommaso Fonte (indeed she had been instrumental is setting this up) and wondered if he might know the Piro family in Kenosha.

Vicki's husband was a Piro and the family had unsuccessfully tried to visit them in Kenosha a few years earlier.

Tommaso got back to me to say that he did indeed know the Piro family and that he had arranged for us to call in on them the day before Thanksgiving (which I would be spending with Tommaso and his family).

Other than the connection with Vicki's husband, Pasqualino, and his wonderful parents, Salvatore and Caterina, I knew nothing about this branch of the Piro family.

We went from heaven to hell

With the help of 'the voice', I arrived in Kenosha on schedule. Tommaso Fonte was doing a bit of husbandry outdoors as he awaited my arrival. The greetings over, I went inside to meet his wife Lucia) Lucy and deposited my worldly goods safely upstairs in the guest room—home for two nights— before we set off together to visit the Piro family.

Apart from the fact that they hailed from Roccabernarda—a small hilltop town about seven or eight miles south and west of Santa Severina— and had some distant connection with the family I knew of the same name in Roccabernarda, I knew absolutely nothing about this Piro family. En route I gleaned from Tommaso—who asked me to call him Tom—that he thought that they had emigrated in the sixties; Tom was also coaching me on how I should pronounce the first name of the head of the family, Ippolito Piro.

On reflection, it's not quite true that I knew nothing ... the family was, after all, Calabrian-American and so I was pretty sure I knew what, given the time of day, was going to happen next.

We were greeted by one of Ippolito's sons, Angelo, though in fact Tom introduced him as Johnny which is what he had always called him. Inside I was introduced to Ippolito, his wife Domenica and Angelo's brother, Ralph.

The Piro family and friends in the late 1930s.
The woman on the left with the babe in arms is Anastasia Vaccaro, Ippolito's mother.
Ippolito himself is the oldest boy on the left.
Top right is Domenica Rosa, whom Ippolito later married.

My hunch about what was going to happen next was confirmed when we all sat around a large, partially laid, table ... a table which, it was clear, meant business. The Italians have a way of distinguishing between a table which is the object itself, a piece of furniture, *il tavolo,* and a table which is being (or has been) prepared with eating in mind, *la tavola.* What we were sitting round was *una tavola.*

But it wasn't yet time to eat ... I was still explaining why I was here and the sorts of things I was interesting in finding out, something I hadn't had to do before as I'd normally had some contact before leaving Calabria.

So we started at the beginning.

It came as no surprise to me that, though Ippolito had emigrated in 1965, a generation back other family members had sampled the waters so to speak. But this wasn't the same old story, this had a new element in the person of Ippolito's forceful mother, Anastasia.

In 1905 eighteen-year-old Francesco Vaccaro left Roccabernarda and headed for the States. His final destination was Kenosha where he worked in the bed-making business.

In 1913 Francesco Piro, then nineteen and also from Roccabernarda, emigrated and he too ended up in Kenosha where his cousin Raffaele lived and worked.

It is likely that the families knew each other for, like Santa Severina, Roccabernarda is a small town, the sort of place where everybody knows everybody else. So it was not surprising that some time around 1920 Francesco Piro became a lodger in the Vaccaro household in Kenosha.

By this time Francesco Vaccaro was married and had Americanized his name ... not to Frank as would have been normal, but to Guy. A curious choice in that it is not even a regular American name, though it is a word he probably heard over and over again.

In the late twenties Francesco Piro returned to Calabria to court and marry Anastasia Vaccaro, the sister of his landlord 'Guy' Vaccaro, so it is likely that this union was arranged between the two families in Roccabernarda. They married in 1927.

In his head it was likely that Francesco was expecting to return to America, to Kenosha and his clerical job at the Simmons bed factory where, seemingly, he oversaw the sharpening of pencils. He had lived in

America for almost half his life and had even joined up when the US army needed interpreters during the First World War. He assuredly felt more American that Calabrian.

But Anastasia was not impressed by tales of this brave new world that Francesco talked about with such fervor and put her foot down. This turn of events must have taken Francesco by surprise for, though Anastasia had never been to the States, in addition to her brother 'Guy' there were several other members of Roccabernarda's Vaccaro family living and working in the Kenosha area. Anastasia would not budge and any thoughts Francesco had of starting a family there were soon put on the back burner. Try as he might, this lady was not for turning, there was no way she was going to America, no way she was going to leave her parents and family. So Francesco had to reconcile himself to the reality that this branch of the Piro family, including young Ippolito, would be born and bred in Roccabernarda.

Francesco had earned sufficient American money to buy land in and around the town where he grew olives, oranges, figs. pears and, of course, grape vines and was therefore better off than many of his *paesani*. Nevertheless, Francesco retained a strong affinity with the United States and would talk about America to his children in a way that demonstrated his love for it, his pride at being an American citizen and the sadness he felt for not having ever returned.

Perhaps he still hung on to a spark of hope that one day he might indeed go back—after all, he'd served in the military and he could pass his citizenship on to his children. So when it came to the next global conflict, not surprisingly he felt an allegiance to America rather than the Italy of Mussolini; he always thought that Italy had made the wrong choice and sided with the wrong axis.

For Ippolito's father this must have been a bewildering experience ... he had to reconcile himself to a change of plans and exchange the life he pictured himself having in Kenosha for the more mundane rural life in Roccabernarda.

So it is hardly surprising that some of these fond memories of the American dream rubbed off on his eldest son, Ippolito, and that eventually it also became Ippolito's dream to follow in his father's footsteps and go to America.

It was in 1965 that he and Domenica decided to take the plunge and head across the Atlantic ... after all, like his father, Ippolito was an American citizen and it seemed ungracious not to capitalize on that piece of good fortune.

•

As lunch-time approached, Angelo went up and down the stairs checking on what was happening in the kitchen downstairs. His mother was not able to negotiate the stairs any more so he had taken on the role of head chef but all the time he was trying to balance these chores with his deep interest in the family's history.

But before we went any further, for my piece of mind I needed to 'see' the exact relationship between the Salvatore Piro (the father-in-law of my friend Vicki) I knew back in Roccabernarda and Ippolito sitting next to me in Kenosha.

It turned out to be more straightforward (and more direct) than I had expected: Ippoloto's father Francesco Piro was first cousins with Salvatore Piro's grandfather, also called Francesco Piro.

That little riddle sorted, we talked about the family's life before 1965, before they came to Kenosha.

Ippolito and Domenica had known each other all their lives ... I was shown a photo of them taken in the early forties when Ippolito was about nine and Domenica four. At opposite corners of the picture then but, by 1957, husband and wife.

By the early sixties they had two children, Francesco and Anastasia, and Ippolito was working away from home. It was a time when southerners could find work in the north of Italy and it was to the area around Milan that Ippolito and others from Roccabernarda found work constructing new highway bridges.

It was steady work and paid well and every week Ippolito would send checks to Domenica back in Roccabernarda. Domenica wasn't sure what to do with them, didn't realize she could convert them into real cash so, week by week, the pile of uncashed checks grew larger in the drawer where she stored them.

Clearly Domenica was a resourceful woman, she was raising their two children on the money she could earn from their own livestock and home-grown vegetables ... Angelo said he would show me later how this was something that the family had never forgotten.

So when Ippolito returned from Milan, he discovered they had more money than expected ... perhaps it was this new-found wealth that made it possible to consider emigrating to America, a place he had grown to love through his father's second-hand stories, a place where he was a citizen.

In 1963 their third child Rosa was born and two years later Ippolito was heading by ship to the States. Domenica remained in Roccabernarda where she worked on a farm and in 1967 with their three children, she too flew to America to join Ippolito in Kenosha.

Until a few weeks earlier, I had never heard of Kenosha so I wondered what brought so many Italians here and, in particular, so many people from one small Italian town, Roccabernarda. Of course the answer was simple—work brought them there, the community they established kept them there. But unlike Cicero and Schenectady there was no one single large employer, rather a number of industrial plants, including car manufacturers, in the south eastern corner of Wisconsin between Chicago and Milwaukee. The tradition of Roccabernardese gravitating to Kenosha was one that Francesco tapped into in 1913 and one that his son took advantage of over fifty years later. That said, for the two years before

Life on the farm where Domenica plucked geese and chickens. With her are three of the Piro children, Rosa, Frank and Anastasia.

Domenica and the children joined him, Ippolito worked and live in nearby Racine.

Ippolito looked back on their first six years in America with little enthusiasm.

"They were", he said, "hell".

"We left heaven for hell." he repeated, as if to emphasize the point.

One of the problems was that they had no close relatives in the area. Although Ippolito's sister, Maria Piro, came to America around the same time with her husband Tommaso Bonofiglio, they only stayed a short time. Like Ippolito, Maria had citizenship but Tommaso didn't take to the eight-hour-day working conditions and was adamant about returning to Calabria. For Anastasia, this was a devastating outcome and with Ippolito working hard and long each day, she felt particularly isolated.

At first they lived above a garage on a farm and there were many times when the 'dream' that Francesco had talked about so eloquently seemed a distant and tarnished reality. For the first few years Ippolito walked five miles to his work at Belle City every day before finding work closer to home with American Brass in Kenosha. It was working here that he renewed his acquaintance with his *paesano* from Roccabernarda, Tomasso Fonte.

Anastasia worked on the farm and plucked geese and chickens day in, day out. She recalled how almost every day she thought they had made a terrible mistake and wondered why they'd exchanged the Calabrian countryside and their friends and family for this. But she hung on in there willing things to improve and, despite the hardships, she still believed they would and that, in the long run, it was the best choice for their family.

Ippolito and Domenica were the first people I'd met who were quite so forthright about how hard it had been in the early days. Others perhaps reflected on their first months and years by selecting the good parts whereas the Piro family vividly recalled how difficult it had been for them.

Gradually they began to understand that the American Dream came at a price, it was not just something that happened when you set foot in the country. You had to work at it, you had to absorb a new culture and you had to assimilate a new language ... none of which is easy when you don't have the support of other family and friends round the corner.

But things did get better and in 1970 they were able to buy a house in Kenosha, the same house where we were all sitting expectantly as Angelo worked his magic in the kitchen and then appeared with something else to add to *la tavola*.

Gradually Ippolito and Domenica began to realize that they were better off in the States than they would have been back in Calabria ... they could see the fruits of their labor all around them, in their home and their family. Sitting with them and two of their children was a humbling experience. I could see their determination they had shown still etched on their work-worn faces—it was clear that there had been times when their life in America took them to the edge but that their resolve had pulled them back and helped them move forward.

It was time to change the focus and there's no better way of doing that than sitting round a Calabrian-American *tavola*, now being brought to fruition by the energetic Angelo. For the first time on such an occasion I did not have the specter of drinking and driving hanging over me. Tom was my driver of choice and I was free to enjoy the Piro family's wonderful red wine.

Ippolito asked me about the *vendemmia* (the grape harvest) in Calabria and wondered whether I had experienced that late-September ritual. I was able to explain that not only had I experienced it but also played my part every year as one of Aurelio Gerardi's team of helpers and that after the work was done we all—husbands, wives, children, helpers—sat round the table and ate *al fresco* and drank what was left of the previous year's efforts. Sadly, the post-eating music and dancing that used to be a feature of this occasion when Ippolito was a lad is the exception rather than the rule.

I told him about the sounds and smells of Santa Severina—the sound of wheels on cobbles as the three-wheeled *apè* and tractors carefully negotiate their cargos through the narrow streets and the intoxicating aroma of the fermenting must seeping out from under every door of every *magazzino* (garage, storehouse) in the town. For Ippolito it clearly brought back fond memories and Angelo promised that, after we'd eaten, we'd pop downstairs and take a look at the Piro *magazzino* and its American bounty.

Even Tom Fonte was taken aback by the feast that began to fill every square inch of the table; I recalled that Tom had only mentioned my visit to Ippolito and Domenica a few days earlier ... thank goodness they didn't have time to arrange anything special!

This being a Calabrian tavola, there were several courses including cheese ravioli, *sopressata*, *capocollo*, olives and pasta with meatballs followed by donuts, homemade chocolate cake and *pitta ccu passuli,* that winter pastry made with raisins, walnuts and honey, a bit like baklava, that cropped up in my conversation with the Sculco family a week earlier.

Angelo called it *pitta ccu odia* but it was the same dish and of course local Calabrian dialects being what they are it is not surprising to find many different names for what is essentially the same thing—it is also called *pitta 'nchuisa* in Roccabernarda.

I was grateful that at long last somebody had unwittingly given me the opportunity to write something about the iniquitous *pitta ccu passuli*, that dear, dear friend of Calabrian dentists ... indeed I had been long-convinced that some people's recipe for said dessert was concocted by the dental fraternity as a way of making money.

Pitta ccu passuli is one of those Calabrian dishes, like *pasta al forno*, where there are as many recipes and 'secret' ingredients and 'special' techniques as there are Calabrian families. Around Christmas many households make oodles of the stuff and, of course, share it with their friends ... friends such as us. The end result can lie anywhere on the spectrum between deliciously succulent, aromatic and moist to 'would-have-made-the-perfect-door-stop'. Unfortunately, whether it be by design or by chance, much of it seems to gravitate towards the door-stop end of the spectrum.

Having road-tested countless incarnations of *pitta ccu passuli* over the years, I have only eaten three which I can honestly say I enjoyed. Their creators will remain anonymous but they know who they are; one of them made it for the first time in her life last Christmas and it was absolutely wonderful—I just hope it wasn't an accident. I raved about it so much that I'm sure to find out next year.

And now the Piro family had given me the opportunity of adding a fourth name to the list ... definitely not of the door-stop variety.

With such a feast I suppose it was inevitable that the conversation should return to leaner times when things were not so good. Anastasia recalled that for her the change was gradual, a part of her wanted to return to Calabria but as time passed she realized that life in America was better than it was for her family back in Roccabernarda. She swapped stories with them and realized that her Calabria counterparts didn't have the same access to the things that she now took for granted, like an in-house telephone and sometimes even postage stamps. Even in a rural community like Roccabernarda a commodity as basic as milk could be a hassle to

The Piro family's American *magazzino* and its bounty.

find on a daily basis—in America every store sold milk. Ironically the ingredients for a traditional Calabria dish such as *pitta ccu passuli* were probably more accessible in an American grocery store than back home.

As Anastasia began to see and understand the greater picture, America increasingly became the better option for her and her growing family. Even though she missed her Calabrian family, now she and Ippolito had to consider their own family and how growing up in America would best benefit them.

Angelo was on a roll ... no sooner had he finished his duties as master chef and head waiter than he morphed into keeper of the family archive and began to share some of the family's photographic history with me. That said, somewhere between head waiter and archivist he became, for just a few moments, master of ceremonies and presented me with a Thanksgiving present which took me completely by surprise. Actually it was 'presents' ... a musical Christmas tie and a beautiful, warm winter scarf.

After the chief archivist had completed his duties he became, in an instant, a tour guide and, as promised, we descended first into the kitchen and then beyond into the holy of holies, the Calabrian *magazzino*. Here there were shelves packed with all the preserved fruits and vegetables that you would expect to find in any self-respecting *magazzino* in Roccabernarda, Strongoli or Santa Severina ... *passata*, zucchini, ancient sweet peppers (the long variety), figs, peaches and olives and, of course, grapes. And what better way to preserve grapes is there than as red wine, demijohn after demijohn of rich red wine? Not everyone in Calabria has vines, still fewer in America, but they can still have their own private *vendemmia* by buying in the grapes with which to make the wine at home, just as if they'd grown them themselves. It's what most Calabrian families did—and do—in America; it's what many landless Calabrian families have to do in Calabria.

And here in the States families like the Piros have developed their American variant of the antipasto condiment *giardiniara*, in Calabria generally pickled celery, zucchini, carrots and cauliflower. The north American version comes in two guises, a hot version with peppers and a milder version without and often preserved in oil rather than vinegar.

I stared in awe at this veritable Aladdin's Cave, the variety of preserved

Ippolito Piro and Domenica Rosa holding a very special photo of their childhood memories in Roccabernarda.

Ippolito and Domenica at the Piro *tavola* with Ralph (left), a presenter at a local cable television station, and Angelo who works in the medical sector.

foods and the manner of their display akin to the Calabrian manifestation I had become used to. Through another door we emerged out into the open and did a quick circumnavigation of the house and its small but bounteous garden. By the front fence we stopped to pay our respects to one particular tomato plant, a plant that shouldn't have been there, a plant that had self-seeded and grown strong that season as it forced its way up through a crack in the concrete. That summer this plant had excelled itself by producing more tomatoes than any other ... also, Angelo assured me, tastier tomatoes than any other.

Its struggle to survive and flourish in a hostile environment made me reflect on the Piro family itself and the story I had heard that day.

Ippolito and Domenica had not had it easy but they kept focused and showed some true grit to resist the temptation to call it a day and head back to Calabria like Ippolito's sister Maria and brother-in-law Tommaso had done so long ago. Their resolve was etched on their faces and the fruits of their persistence and perseverance radiated from every nook and cranny of the American home they created for their family.

And like others who made this journey they have returned to their roots in Roccabernarda on a number of occasions and each time they did so, though they were understandably drawn to the place where they grew up, they returned to their home in America.

I felt honored to have met Ippolito Piro and Domenica Rosa and to have eaten at their bounteous *tavola*.

My American friend Vicki Kelly from Roccabernarda it was who first mentioned Tommaso Fonte to me. Tommaso, a native of Roccabernarda, lives in Kenosha, Wisconsin and had contacted Vicki once when he was visiting family in Calabria.

Vicki called Tommaso on my behalf and told him about my planned visit to the States and then passed on his number to me. He was, she said, expecting a call.

I called Tommaso late one evening from here in Calabria, seven hours earlier in Kenosha, and we had a long chat as a result of which Tommaso invited me not only to drop by but to stay over a couple of nights and spend Thanksgiving with the Fonte family.

It was an invitation I couldn't refuse.

The man who emigrated three times

Tom and I returned to his home scarcely able to move. We had been the recipients of uncompromising Calabrian-American hospitality and the extraordinary cooking skills of Angelo Piro. In my case sampling and resampling the wine didn't help.

It was late afternoon and Tom wanted to play on his computer ... and to share some of the fruits of his online sleuthing about events in and around his native Roccabernarda. It was in this sub-culture of Roccabernarda-on-YouTube that he first came across Minnesota-born Vicki Kelly—in an interview she gave about a project she had been involved with through the English language school she runs in the town.

Naturally I had to watch the Vicki-video before we moved on to some others and it was then that I realized I knew more people in Roccabernarda than I thought. I saw my own doctor, Rocca De Rito (whom I call The Good Doctor) his brother and others that I recognized before we came to the Giant Mushroom video.

Roccabernarda is not far from the foothills of the Sila mountains, a place renowned for its wonderful *porcini* mushrooms. Here, some time in 2012, a group of mushroom hunters from Roccabernarda found a massive mushroom that weighed in at around fifteen kilos (thirty-three pounds). Not unnaturally, in these multi-media days, instead of eating it they paraded it in the town's square and filmed it to show it off to the online world.

Throughout the clip the mushroom remained static but the people coming to have a look changed by the minute. I saw a man hovering in the background waiting for an opportunity to work his way to the front to scrutinize this prize mushroom—it was a face I recognized, it was Salvatore Piro, Vicki's father-in-law. Earlier that same day we had been talking about Salvatore at the Piro home, trying to establish how he fitted in to the Piro family tree.

Tommaso, ever eager to put a name to another face in Roccabernarda, asked me if I was sure it was Salvatore. I was ... he and I had had a close friendship from the moment we met, a friendship that neither of us can explain and that is forever frustrated by our lack of the other's language. Strange it was to be sitting in Wisconsin watching dear Salvatore examining a mushroom.

Having exhausted the clips of Roccabernarda, Tom called his brother Marcello and his wife Maria on Skype. Though until then I knew neither by name, I recognized both ... we had, I surmised, often sat in the same waiting room as we awaited our turn to see The Good Doctor. It was indeed a small world.

Mention of The Good Doctor, Rocco De Rito—who has his clinic in Roccabernarda—brought the conversation round to the relationship between Rocco and Tom. Just before leaving Calabria I had bumped into Rocco in Santa Severina and told him about my impending trip and that I would be meeting up with Tom Fonte in Kenosha ... until that moment I did not realize the two were related. Also, it has to be said, in Santa Severina I had become a little cynical about so-called Calabrian familial relationships as they often proved to be no more than vague connections rather than an incontestable direct line. Tom completed the story Rocco began back in Santa Severina ... Rocco De Rito's grandmother was a Fonte and a first cousin of Tom's grandfather Leonardo; Rocco and Tommaso were third cousins.

Since we were making connections, I reminded Tommaso about Elvira Arabia and asked if he had had a chance to speak with her. He told me that he had but that, this being Thanksgiving, she wasn't sure if she'd have the time to meet. Undaunted, he called her there and then.

The first and last time I spoke to Elvira was a year earlier in Santa

Severina and now here I was talking to her in her home town, having also met her brother-in-law, Ralph Sculco the week before down in New Jersey.

Of course I knew this holiday weekend was not the best time for a relative strange to drop in so I was glad to have the opportunity for a brief chat. It was then that I realized that Elvira had not planned to emigrate at all. Her sister Franca had married Ralph Sculco and Elvira was visiting America as a tourist when she met her husband-to-be Eugene. Elvira had emigrated, not by design, but by accident.

It was an interesting story and I would have liked to have had more time to explore it. I also chatted with her husband Eugene and somehow, even over the phone, I warmed to him and knew we would have enjoyed each other's company.

But it was not to be. That evening Elvira's Thanksgiving guests would begin to arrive and there was a lot to prepare for the following's Thanksgiving celebrations and the morning after I would be heading back early to catch my flight at Chicago Midway.

I was picking up that Tom had a penchant for using the phone and, by switching it to speaker phone, involving everyone in the conversation ... so I was not surprised when I found myself speaking to another Kenosha-based family member, Betty (Fonte)Johnson.

Like Tom, she was the granddaughter of Leonardo Fonte and Vittoria Bonofiglio, their son Antonio was Tommaso's father and another son, Francesco, was Betty's father; they were cousins.

None of this I knew while I was speaking to her and even afterwards I was still trying to get my head round the various strands of the family that had become Fonte households in and around Kenosha.

•

As what would normally have been dinner time approached, Tom, Lucia (Lucy) and I decided instead to talk about how it was he ended up here in Kenosha; after our indulgences at the Piro home, food was the last thing on our minds.

Driving to the Piro home earlier I'd gleaned that Tom had come to America some time in the fifties, almost a decade before Ippolito Piro. I was therefore expecting that in Tom I might have found my first family without a history of immigration. It was not so, it more complicated, for his father, Antonio Fonte, had emigrated three times—in 1920 at the age of nineteen, in 1929 at the age of twenty-eight and in 1956 in his mid-fifties. On this third and final occasion he was accompanied by two of his sons Tom (Tommaso at the time) and Francesco.

When he emigrated for the first time in 1920 Antonio went to live in Kenosha where his brother and sponsor, Francesco (Betty Johnson's father), was already living and working. Francesco had emigrated in 1913 and was met by *his* sponsor, his cousin Antonio, who had already lived in Kenosha for two years.

At first it all sounded confusing for there were two 'Fonte' families living in Kenosha at the time and they both had a Francesco and an Antonio—there was 'old' Francesco, father of cousin Antonio and there were the brothers, Francesco and Antonio Fonte, the latter the focus of my interest and the father of my host Tom.

Their disentangled emigration history goes like this: 'old' Francesco had

Tom's father Antonio Fonte (left) and his brother Francesco (Tom's uncle and Betty Fonte Johnson's father).

emigrated in 1902 at the age of forty with three *paesani* (friends from the same town) but then returned to Italy; his son Antonio subsequently emigrated in 1911. 'Old' Francesco was the brother of Leonardo Fonte and it was two of Leonardo's sons, Francesco and Antonio, who emigrated in 1913 and 1920 respectively.

All three went back to Roccabernarda at least once and all three returned to the States in better style than their first steerage-class journey.

•

Cousin Antonio was the first to return and did so shortly after the First World War. Like his cousin Francesco, his contribution to the allied cause at that time fast-tracked him to his citizenship. Antonio came back to the States in late 1919 less than a year before his cousin Antonio (Francesco's younger brother) emigrated for the first time. It is likely therefore that the older Antonio's tales of life on the other side of the Atlantic had an influence on his younger cousin's decision to follow him there the next year.

Interestingly, when cousin Antonio returned to America he sailed direct to Boston (from Naples) on the White Star Line's *Canopic* and then on to Chicago and Kenosha. He was an American citizen and was traveling in the style to which he had become accustomed. Although the *Canopic* had served as an immigrant vessel from Italy to Ellis Island earlier the same year it was, at this time, more of a trans-Atlantic liner than immigrant ship.

There was rivalry in the trans-Atlantic passage of immigrants and in the Mediterranean this was mainly between Cunard and White Star. Cunard had the faster ships so White Star began to include modest inducements to would-be steerage passengers who were by far the majority. Instead of Cunard's open-berthed dormitories for everyone, White Star introduced divided steerage into two parts—one for single men in one part of the ship and single women, married couples and families in another, in more private two-, four- and six-berth cabins. As mentioned elsewhere there had been Reports which showed that single women in particular were sometimes vulnerable to both other male passengers and crew.

Because most people at the time traveled to America via New York and the Ellis Island Immigration Center, it is often forgotten that some used other routes and probably the most popular of these was to Boston, a city which, since the late nineteenth century, played host to an ever-increasing Italian population, most of whom gravitated to what was called Boston's North End.

Nobody knows why cousin Antonio chose this particular route for his second passage to the States for there was no advantage in terms of journey time once in America ... indeed the opposite would have been the case. The ship's manifest shows that he had booked his passage from Naples straight through to Chicago and presumably completed the Boston-Chicago leg by train.

•

To recap, the other Antonio, Tom's father, arrived for the first time in 1920 and was sponsored by his older brother Francesco. After having seen that his younger brother was settled in Kenosha, Francesco returned to Calabria in the early twenties for a brief period and then came back to the States in April 1924. By 1926 his brother Antonio had also become an American citizen and, as Francesco had done, he worked at Vincent-

Waiting for food during the Great Depression at the end of the twenties.

McCall Company where they made mattresses, box springs, aluminum chairs and other garden furniture. Francesco had moved on and for a time in the late twenties ran a small grocery and meat store where it seems that cousin Antonio, a butcher by that time, may also have worked. The store eventually became known as Fonte Foods.

In 1927 it was Antonio's turn to do as his brother and cousin had done and he too turned up again in Roccabernarda for a couple of years but by the spring of 1929 he was reunited with his brother and cousin back in Kenosha.

In all these comings and goings, from cousin Antonio in 1911 to Antonio, Tom's father, in 1929, there were generally others from Roccabernarda on the same vessel and, to a man, they were heading for Kenosha in Wisconsin. I recognized some of the surnames from my visit to the Piro household ... Rosa and Pulera in particular. They were all friends and all, one way or other, *parenti*—family.

It was beginning to look more and more likely that the Piro and Fonte families were related in some way but that their common heritage somehow had got lost in the mists of time.

Tom didn't know why these three young Fontes each came back to their native Calabria and then returned to the States. They were all American citizens so it can be assumed that they always intended to return to Kenosha; and all three returned single so, unlike others, marriage was clearly not the motive ... or, if it was, their hopes and expectations were thwarted.

•

Antonio couldn't have timed his return to the States worse if he'd tried. He got back to Kenosha in April 1929, four months before the first signs of recession and six months before the Wall Street Crash and the beginning of the Great Depression. He lived with his brother Francesco, who was still in the grocery and meat business. He tried his hand working in the confectionery trade before he was back on the boat to Italy and Roccabernarda and here it was he met and wooed the love of his life, his mother's niece, Silvia Bonofiglio.

Antonio and Silvia settled into life in Roccabernarda and raised their family of five—Leonardo, Vittoria, Francesco, Tommaso and Marcello. Both Antonio and Silvia had inherited some land on the outskirts of the town in an area called Cacabarba and as luck would have it they were adjacent to each other and made a perfect orchard. With the money he'd earned in the States Antonio bought some more land near the Convent of San Francesco where there were grape vines and olive trees. So, despite the rigors of wartime austerity, the Fonte family became quite a self-sufficient unit; a meagre living it was but better than many other folk in the town.

Like Ippolito Piro, Tommaso (as he was then) grew up in a household where talk of emigration and settling in America was commonplace; it was part of the Fonte family's normality.

His father talked about the cold weather, the size of cities like Chicago and New York and their amazingly tall buildings. Tom recalled him speaking about his time in the United States with so much enthusiasm ... enthusiasm tinged with a touch of melancholy as he came to realize he ought to have returned to America when he and Silvia first married and raised his family there.

Tommaso's mother and father, Silvia Bonofiglio and Antonio Fonte.

So, like Francesco Piro, Antonio Fonte had the urge to return and as his family grew up—the youngest, Marcello, was born in 1949—he and Silvia conceived a grand plan whereby Antonio and his sons Tommaso and Francesco would fly to the States and, once settled, the rest of the Fonte family—wife Silvia, daughter Vittoria and sons Leonardo and Marcello—would follow.

The year was 1956 and Antonio Fonte, now in his mid-fifties, was emigrating to America for the third time—September 1920, April 1929 and March 1956. And once again he was sponsored by his brother Francesco.

•

Tom was seventeen when he first set foot on American soil. Before catching the TWA flight from Rome to New York, the furthest he's ever been was to Santa Severina, less than ten miles from Roccabernarda.

He still remembers the reunion with zio Francesco (uncle Frank), zia Bettina (aunt Betty) and their family in Kenosha and the excitement of those first days and weeks. He was amazed at the number and size of the cars ... of course he'd seen cars before in Calabria but never actually been in one. And then there was television ... in Roccabernarda non-existent, in America already a normal part of people's lives.

But there was a bittersweet side to all of these new experiences for he missed his mother and his siblings and hoped they would be able to join them soon. Back in Roccabernarda the rest of the family experienced the same sense of loss and separation but were looking forward to being reunited in Kenosha, sooner rather than later.

But things didn't turn out as planned and, because of his age, Antonio found it difficult to get permanent work. On the other hand, Tommaso and Francesco *did* find work at the same Vincent-McCall bed-making business as his father—ironically because the works' foreman knew uncle Francesco and still remembered Antonio from when he worked there in the twenties.

So, without permanent employment, Antonio kept putting off fixing a definite date for Silvia and the rest of the family to join them; the time never seemed to be quite right. In the end it never happened and Antonio's third emigration ended after only two years when he realized he could be more use to his family back in Calabria.

In 1958 Antonio Fonte returned to Roccabernarda; he never went back to America.

In Kenosha Francesco (now Frank) and Tom remained in good hands and for a while became part of uncle Frank's and aunt Betty's extended family. Speaking of this time Tom became wistful. He knew that he and his brother Francesco made the right decision to stay in America; nevertheless there was pain in that decision. They both missed their parents and particularly their gentle, kind-hearted mother and Tom in particular, being the younger by four years, was very homesick in the beginning. He admitted that he had been tempted to return with his father in 1958 but decided to stay on and soon became reconciled to his new life in Kenosha.

Brother Frank got married but later divorced and left Kenosha and settled in the Bronx area of New York. He remarried there before moving to Florida ... he and his second wife, Filomena, felt Florida was a better place to bring up their kids, Franco and Orlando.

In the end Tom's mother never made it to the States, even to visit; nor has his sister. His brother Leonard came in 1977 and Marcello in 2000 and again in 2011. Tom returned to Roccabernarda four times, in 1978, 1994, 2002 and 2007. He believes he has one more visit in him.

•

For no apparent reason we went off at a tangent—leaving Tom still coming to terms with life in America—and started instead to compare and contrast our memories of television and movies in the fifties and sixties. We soon realized we had watched and enjoyed the same shows and films at more or less the same time ... Tom was also learning a new language as he watched and marveled.

We also discovered that we recalled the titles and names of actors as if it were yesterday ... *I Married Joan*, *The Cisco Kid*, *Circus Boy*, *The Phil Silvers Show*, *Hopalong Cassidy*, *The Prisoner of Zenda* and lots more. We also had the same interest in what would now be called trivia but for us it really wasn't trivia, it was how we catalogued and recalled an impressionable time in our lives. Today we are bombarded with images and probably forget most; back then it was a novel experience and one which people of our generation cherished.

•

It was in 1960, at the same time as Fred and Wilma of *The Flintstones* fame first graced American television, that Tom moved on from Vincent-McCall and went to work for Leblanc.

Leblanc is a musical instruments manufacturer owned by an Italian-American and a Frenchman, Vito Pascucci and Léon Leblanc. Towards the end of the Second World War the two met and befriended each other in France where the Leblanc company already existed; Vito and Léon struck up a deal to open up an American branch in Kenosha. Originally Vito worked from the basement of a house but the company grew rapidly and at one time employed over three hundred people. For a couple of years one of these was Tom Fonte who assembled the keys and body for saxophones and clarinets.

He moved on from Leblanc to Fonte Foods, a store founded by his uncle Frank (Francesco) Fonte, Betty's Johnson's father and Tom's uncle; he was working there at the time Kennedy was assassinated. Like others I had met, Tom recalled Kennedy with affection, he was, it seemed, beloved my most of the Italian-American community and at the time many homes had a photo of him on its wall. Perhaps this was because he was, for many who emigrated at this time, their 'first' president and also the first not associated with the Second World War like his predecessor Eisenhower. Also, I'd noted—and this was once more confirmed by Tom—the love for Kennedy seemed to be almost as strong as the dislike for Nixon.

At this time, with Frank in New York and his father back in Calabria, Tom was on his own ... though not quite for he now shared a house with three Calabrian friends, one of whom owned the house. At that time Tom reckons that the population of Kenosha was about eight to nine percent Italian, and of these about eighty percent were Calabrian, mostly from the Cosenza area. Of his three Calabrian friends, one returned to Italy and the other two married and moved elsewhere.

After Fonte Foods, Tom worked the graveyard shift (eleven to seven overnight) for a short time for a company, J.I. Case, that made tractors and other farm machinery before moving to his last port of call, American Brass. He started working there on September 9, 1965 and married Lucy six weeks later; they didn't have time for a honeymoon.

Tom worked for American Brass until he retired in 1999, the same time

Tom and Lucy Fonte on their wedding day in October 1965.

The door of the Roccabernarda home Tom left in 1956.
Lucy and Tom standing on the front porch of their home in Kenosha, Wisconsin.

that Tom and Lucy moved from their first house to the home where they now live.

We took time off from rattling through Tom's potted history to put together a few things to nibble and pick at, *stuzzichini* they'd be called in Calabria. And, of course, we washed it down with some fine red wine.

As we leafed through the family album Tom was in a more reflective mood. We looked at photos of his early life in far-off Roccabernarda and, a few pages on, other images of his family and working life here in Kenosha where, in a matter of hours, he and his family would celebrate another American Thanksgiving as American citizens.

He told me that he never truly felt American until after he was married—everything changed when Sylvia was born in 1966. Sylvia and her two sisters, MaryAnn and Vittoria (Vicki), were American children, born and bred. They might travel to Calabria, they might feel a special relationship with Calabria but they will always be American, just as their children, Jimmy, Tommy and Patrick are American.

As his American family grew Tom reflected less on life back in Roccabernarda and by the time he retired he and his family were a typical American unit—they spoke and thought American, they lived American, they were American. Also, as is the way of things, none of the children married Italian-Americans so for the next generation, Tommy, Jimmy and Patrick, their Calabrian heritage has been diluted, it has its place alongside their other heritage, that of their fathers and they will grow up with stories of family in Ireland, Greece and Germany.

But Tom's retirement coincided with the age of the computer and with it the ability to make contact with people and places thousands of miles away ... places like Roccabernarda.

As I'd already witnessed for myself, today Tom Fonte has an umbilical cord between his home in Kenosha and his family and friends in Roccabernarda. It's called the internet ... and through the internet Tom Fonte has become Roccabernarda's unofficial ambassador in Kenosha.

As if on cue, Tom suggested we call Vicki in Roccabernarda and surprise her with Thanksgiving greetings from Kenosha ... I suggested we wait till after midnight when it would be seven in the morning in Roccabernarda and Vicki might just be up and about to get the children ready for school.

We killed time by looking at some more Tales from Roccabernarda on the computer and even re-ran the Giant Mushroom story. As the minute hand approached midnight, Tom had an even better idea ... why don't we call Kay too? Thanksgiving wouldn't mean much to her but it would be a cunning plan, wouldn't it? Well, yes and no ... Kay was in the UK and where the time was only six hours ahead and it was my considered opinion that Kay would not really appreciate an early-morning call, even from me. Tom conceded that I might have a point.

So there was only to be one Thanksgiving surprise—for an unsuspecting Vicki from far-off Wisconsin, only a few hundred miles from her home turf in Minneapolis. The nervous laughter of surprise or the incredulous hysteria of shock, call it what you will, she coped admirably with her early-morning call from Kenosha from two tired pensioners ... and probably put it down to the fact that we'd drunk too much. Which. of course, we hadn't.

My first Thanksgiving in America had dawned and already it was time for bed.

Thanksgiving

The day of Thanksgiving was, as predicted by the weather pundits, wonderfully spring-like: warm and sunny, and a clear blue sky. Definitely not the norm ... Tom and Lucy recalled many more Thanksgivings when the order of the day was shoveling snow from the driveway so that they could visit family.

Having talked Tom out of calling Kay the night before, I knew I could put it off no longer and we caught up with her that morning, mid-afternoon in London. Unlike Vicki, the notion that it might be a special day didn't really mean much but it was good to talk with her and for her to hear that I was in safe hands.

The Fonte family's Thanksgiving meal was to be at the home of Tom and Lucy's daughter MaryAnn, husband Jim and children Jimmy and Tommy. There we would be joined by eldest daughter Sylvia, husband Dennis and son Patrick and youngest daughter Vicki with husband Brian. A family gathering which this year would include a total stranger ... albeit one who hailed from Calabria and had tenuous connections with Roccabernarda.

•

I wanted to come bearing a gift of some sort for our hosts MaryAnn and Jim but Tom attempted to talk me out of it. I won the day and, while Lucy got on with some cooking for later, we set off in the car in search of shops that were open ... which turned out to be most of those that sold the sort of thing that would make a good last-minute gift, including the local hypermarket. Here I bought a large basket of fruit and a bottle of Sicilian wine, the nearest I could find to something from Calabria.

After we returned Sylvia, Dennis and Patrick popped in en route to MaryAnn's home from the airport having just flown in from Maryland where they'd spent the first part of the Thanksgiving holiday with Dennis's family. An hour later Jim and Dennis set off for MaryAnn's and not long after Sylvia and I followed with a car-load of goodies, most of it made by Lucy, and my fruit basket ... somehow I forgot the wine. Tom and Lucy would follow a little later.

I really had no idea what to expect ... all my Thanksgiving preconceptions had been picked up from American movies which invariably honed in on all the things that can go wrong with this annual family gathering— the unpredictable weather, traveling nightmares, culinary disasters and household rivalries. Or, the other side of the same coin, they depicted a sugar-coated world where, because of Thanksgiving, everyone would be friends again and all the bad people would be won over.

None of the above happened.

●

Sylvia and I arrived at MaryAnn and Jim's house and started to unload the car; apart from Tom and Lucy, everyone else was there—their three daughters plus husbands and the three grandchildren, all boys.

A sort of division of labor was in evidence as the boys and some of the men were taking in the first of three annual Thanksgiving Day (also referred to as Turkey Day as turkey is a mainstay of the meal) football games between the Houston Texans and the Detroit Lions, while the women were sorting out the kitchen. I hovered as my main interest was in what was going on in the kitchen but Jim and MaryAnn made sure I hovered with a never-empty glass of red wine in my hand.

In an adjoining room a long table was being set for dinner.

Because, yet again, I had found my way to Kenosha by letting 'the voice' do all the hard work, I had no real sense of where I actually was, apart from somewhere between Chicago and Milwaukee, but nearer the latter and close to Lake Michigan. My impression of the approach to the town was that it was incredibly flat and, apart from the shopping precinct I'd been to earlier in the day, I had no sense of a center, of perhaps an older town somewhere by the lake.

I tried to fill this gap in my knowledge and asked MaryAnn about how, for example, Kenosha differed from what at the time I thought was the state capital Milwaukee. Her answer took me by surprise and nearly caused me to spill my wine.

"Milwaukee is just like Kenosha, only taller," she said with a straight face. (Later Tom put me straight on Milwaukee ... it may be the state's largest city but Madison is the state capital and Kenosha is the state's fourth largest city)

It was over two weeks since I had arrived in the States but this was only the second time I truly felt that I was 'off-duty' and I was enjoying my time immensely with this family who were incredibly warm and hospitable. In one sense I felt that I was an intruder at what, up until now, was exclusively a family gathering but I also felt that I was genuinely welcome as opposed to being tolerated.

As the time to eat approached, the men seemed less interested in the football (their team was probably losing) and began taking a greater interest in what was going on in the kitchen—a little picking here, a little tasting there. Dennis seemed in charge of cutting up the turkeys ... there were two, cooked in different ways, one in the oven, one grilled.

The meal was to be a sort of buffet with everything laid out around the kitchen where people could select what they wanted and come back for more ... and more. As far as I could see there was no sign of pasta or pizza ... this was truly an American occasion.

Sylvia said a few words of thanks as all the adults stood round the table and then everyone headed into the kitchen to pile up their plates.

It was an incredibly relaxed meal—the buffet arrangement meant that there was more space on the table, people were not passing plates round or serving each other, they chose what they wanted to eat without any pressure of having to try this or that. You could eat as much or as little as you wanted. It was truly a family meal without formality, with neither tension or pretension. And, of course, this being essentially an *Italian*-American family, the turkeys and all their attendant trimmings— the stuffing, the dressing, the potatoes, the cranberry relish, green beans and the potato, squash and sausage casserole that I'd watched Lucy make that morning—were all just to die for. And afterwards there was pumpkin pie and MaryAnn's 'monster pie', so-called because it had different fruit sections baked into one pie and reminded her of Frankenstein.

Jim, astutely observing my predilection for red wine, left the table for a few moments and returned with something special, a bottle of local Cranbernet. Being so far north it never struck me that Wisconsin would be a wine-making area. But Door County (near the state's upper eastern peninsula) has an ideal micro-climate for growing both grapes and cranberries and it is the blend of these that produces the aptly named Cranbernet. Exquisite.

•

The Fonte, McGreal, Roiniotis and Sharkey families. Left to right, front row: Tommy, Sylvia, Patrick, Vicki, Jimmy, Jim; back row: Brian, Tom, MaryAnn, Dennis and Lucy.

So none of my preconceptions came to pass. My first Thanksgiving was just a normal American family partying and taking pleasure in each other's company. Next year they'll do it again—without an extra adult mouth to feed—and down the line there will be other young mouths to feed and a new generation beyond that.

I have no way of knowing whether this was a typical Thanksgiving or whether it had some indiscernible Calabrian-American undertones ... my guess is that every culture brings its own little twist to the tale and that all these improvisations have become each family's normality.

From all the families I had met it had become clear that this uniquely American festival was immensely important to them; a way of truly participating in something Americans have done for generations; a way of acknowledging and demonstrating their claim to be part of the American tribe.

Each immigrant family will surely remember their first Thanksgiving, that special day when they sat round the table and tucked into a turkey rather than what was the normal daily fare of their homeland. The more turkey they ate, the more they felt themselves to be American ... the more turkey they ate ...

•

Back at Tom and Lucy's there were no late-evening calls to London, Roccabernarda or anywhere else. Bed beckoned as I had an early start the following morning to catch my flight from Chicago Midway back to Newark. I would drop the Mazda off at Midway and pick up another car in Newark ... I wondered would Charlie be there this time with another of his very special offers?

Winding down

'The voice' got me back to the airport without incident though not without sentiment. As I circumnavigated Chicago's downtown area with its iconic skyscrapers looming large, I reflected on times spent here—particularly in the cocktail lounge of the Hancock Tower—and couldn't quite believe I was this close without allowing myself the time to take a closer look.

But I had other things on my mind. I was thinking back to Thanksgiving with the Fonte family and to the concept of this uniquely American celebration. (Canadians also celebrate Thanksgiving, though at a different time and with a different emphasis). A few days earlier somebody told me that Thanksgiving was his favorite festival because of its secular nature and it was this notion that did not tie in with my then understanding of the celebration's origins.

On the flight back to Newark I was able to do a little research on the internet to confirm what I knew—that Thanksgiving had its roots in the 1621 harvest feast shared by the Plymouth colonists from England and Wampanoag Indians native to America and again in 1863 when, during the Civil War, President Abraham Lincoln proclaimed a national Thanksgiving Day to be held each November.

But I also found a substantial tranche of opinion that, while recognizing that Lincoln used God-fearing language—"No human counsel hath devised nor hath any mortal hand worked out these great things. They are the gracious gifts of the most high God, who, while dealing with us in anger for our sins, hath nevertheless remembered mercy", sees this as little more than the normal language of the time. There was definitely a another school of thought that saw Thanksgiving as a unique festival in that its central tenet—of being grateful—was something that Christians and non-Christians, believers and non-believers could, and did, embrace.

I couldn't help but wonder how my friends at the Saigon Café had spent the day.

•

Back in Newark, I caught the shuttle bus to the rental base, the same place where I'd left the small-house-mobile a few days earlier. My Calabrian friend Charlie was nowhere to be seen—I wasn't sure if I was disappointed or relieved—so I knew that there would be no upgrade, apart from the one I was expecting as, yet again, they didn't have any cars in the 'economy' range. My new car was also white, a Ford. Before leaving I checked whether or not there would be an additional charge for leaving the car back at JFK instead of Newark. There wouldn't be.

And the first thing I did when I sat in the driver's seat was to check that nobody had set the GPS to avoid all toll roads.

Once again 'the voice' did her stuff and within half an hour I had dropped my luggage back at base on Wayne Street before taking my nondescript Ford to its overnight resting place, my usual parking lot. Mitch wasn't there.

No prizes for guessing my next port of call ... the Saigon Café where I knew I would be dining for the next three nights. It was good to be back and, after I had eaten another excellent meal, I took up residency once more at the bar to chat to Steve.

Of course I was on a mission and asked him about his Thanksgiving as I was curious to know how these Vietnamese immigrants spent the day. I can't say I was surprised to discover that his family and friends had had almost exactly the same meal in the privacy of their closed restaurant as I had had in Wisconsin. Normally they ate Vietnamese but on that particular day it was turkey and the trimmings like everybody else; no more than a normal American Thanksgiving.

•

The following day, Saturday, was to have been the day when I would have driven to Reading, Pennsylvania to visit Maria Cavaliere so I had to come up with an alternative to spend the time before Sunday's birthday party and the beginning of the long trek back to Calabria the following day.

I had saved one pilgrimage for just such an eventuality though, in truth, I had expected to make this particular trip on my last full day, the Sunday ... I wanted to visit both Ellis Island and the Statue of Liberty.

But I hadn't allowed for on the ravages of Hurricane Sandy.

The hurricane did no real damage to the structure of either but it did severely damage the infrastructure of both. Ironically Sandy hit the day after the interior of the Statue of Liberty had been re-opened following a year-long renovation—I remembered trying to book a visit to the top a month earlier but was told to try again after November 1. Now, because of severe flooding to the basements of both and damage to the security-screening facility by the ferry terminal at Battery Park on the southern tip of Manhattan, both were closed to the public indefinitely.

I had actually been to Ellis Island in the late nineties, in pre-digital camera days, and the photos I took apparently went AWOL around the time we moved to Calabria. My reason for returning was not only to replace those photos but, in the light of what I now knew from talking to Calabrian families and having become a frequent visitor to the Ellis Island archive online, I knew i would experience this place from quite a different perspective. I also wanted to revisit the island's circular, stainless-steel American Immigrant Wall of Honor on which are etched some 650,000 names of immigrants to America ... I hoped to find and photograph some of the names in this book.

Undaunted, I had conceived an alternative plan. The iconic Staten Island Ferry links lower Manhattan and the New York district of Staten Island and passes close to the Statue of Liberty. I guessed that if I took the ferry across to Staten Island I could possibly get a glimpse of Ellis Island as well.

So, on a bitterly cold Saturday morning, I wrapped up well—ruing the

The Statue of Liberty, the iconic gateway to New York, to America.

The erstwhile Ellis Island Immigration Center, for so many the real gateway to America.

fact that I hadn't brought a longer coat, still I had Angelo's scarf—and walked first to the Brownstone Diner and Pancake Factory for another breakfast sandwich. I reasoned that on such a cold day I would need the extra calories.

Full up, I then headed for the parking lot to pay Mitch and to explain to him that I was the owner of the mysterious white Ford that had been there overnight. I told him I'd probably be leaving it there all day and taking it out on Sunday morning.

Next I caught the Path—which continued to operate a reduced service with some stations, including World Trade Center, still closed—from Grove Street, under the Hudson to Christopher Street. Here I changed to the subway to head south to Battery Park ... only to find that Battery Park station was also closed and that all trains now terminated at Rector Street, about a ten-minute walk from the Staten Island Ferry terminal.

Everyone else who exited at Rector seemed to have the same destination in mind so I just followed the crowd and soon found myself on familiar territory at Battery Park.

•

The Staten Island Ferry is an institution with a history that dates back to the eighteenth century. Originally privately-owned, it was taken over by the City of New York following an accident in 1901. Today the distinctive orange ferries still ply the same waters—all that has changed is the ferries themselves and the fare. Back in 1897 it cost just five cents; in 1972 the fare doubled to ten cents; in 1975 it went up to twenty-five cents and in 1990 that doubled to fifty cents. Then, in 1997, the fare for foot passengers was eliminated altogether ... that's why I waited all this time to make the trip.

One other episode in its long history is worthy to mention—the role the Staten Island ferries played on and following the 2001 9/11 attacks on the nearby World Trade Center. On the day itself the ferries transported tens of thousands of people away from lower Manhattan to the safety of Staten Island. This was no easy task as the ferries had to be docked in almost zero visibility caused by the clouds of smoke and debris from the Twin Towers. In the days that followed, the ferries were used to transport emergency equipment and personnel to and from the area. Military personnel and equipment, including tanks, were also ferried between lower Manhattan and Governor's Island ... those tanks were the last vehicles to be carried on the Staten Island Ferry as cars were prohibited thereafter.

I joined the line waiting for the eleven-thirty ferry, trying to edge my way to pole-position as I guessed I might not be the only person who might want to be on the Statue of Liberty-side of the boat. Then again, unlike me, perhaps most of my fellow travelers *did* actually want to go to Staten Island. I was only going there so that I could come back again.

I needn't have worried, the wind on the Statue of Liberty-side was cold, gusty and razor-sharp and most people preferred to look out for landmarks from the relative warmth of indoors. I, on the other hand, braved it all in search of a photo and had even tightened the wrist-strap on my camera so that it couldn't pass over my hand.

I was standing along the rail by a pillar with the aim of using the pillar to support my arm so that I could take less shaky photographs; on the other side of the pillar a young woman was standing, her long scarf thrown up towards me by the gusting wind. Several times I re-positioned myself after being momentarily distracted by this inconsiderate piece of clothing. For the umpteenth time I removed it from around my head and face and looked

Approaching lower Manhattan on the Staten Island Ferry.
The Barge Office was waterside, roughly in front of the taller building on the right.

round to see if there was another rail-side space that I could adjourn to. At that moment this wayward accessory once again flapped round the pillar and brushed against my eyes ... only this time it also removed my glasses and they started their descent towards the depths of New York Bay.

Without thinking I let go of the camera and thrust out my right hand and caught them just below rail-height ... with the camera still dangling from the wrist of the same hand thanks to that tightened wrist-strap. I can't think which would have been worse, to lose the camera or the glasses.

It was at this precise moment that the woman with the scarf chose to move off to annoy someone else further up the boat.

Unlike the ships that arrived here from the east with immigrants, the Staten Island Ferry's passage was more or less north-south. My view of the Statue of Liberty and Ellis Island was therefore one of passing by; for the immigrant it would have been more dramatic as both gradually loomed larger as their ship approached its final destination and anchored between the Island and Manhattan.

The scene back then would have been much busier with half a dozen or more ships anchored here awaiting their turn to discharge their passengers via the fleet of ferry boats that took them from ship to Island. And all around there was the normal hustle and bustle of the busy harbors on both sides of the bay, in lower Manhattan and New Jersey. And of course there were all the regular ferries, such as that to and from Staten Island,, Brooklyn and Jersey City, scurrying backwards and forwards though a sea of ships and boats.

For me that November morning it was enough to have had those few fleeting moments to acknowledge this place and its part in the stories that families had shared with me. I had paid my respects and on this particular journey I could do no more; I realized that I would have to come back and spend a longer time here, sooner rather than later.

•

At Staten Island everyone had to leave the ferry; those, like me, who wanted to head straight back to Manhattan, scurried out of the arrivals area and into the fresh air before heading back into the terminal building to join the throng for the next ferry—the same one from which we had all just disembarked. I was surprised just how many people had done the same ... made the trip just to return to Manhattan *and* to say they'd been on the Staten Island ferry.

But, for me, there was a bonus for the Staten Island terminal that I was heading back towards stands more or less on the site of the old Barge Office which acted as New York's Immigration Center for two short periods: from 1890 to 1891 when the original reception center at nearby Castle Clinton closed and before Ellis Island opened; and again from 1897 to 1900 when a fire destroyed the purpose-built center on Ellis Island. (Unfortunately the Ellis Island buildings had been built of attractive but combustible Georgian pine.)

So, for millions of immigrants it was instead this part of lower Manhattan that was their first view of the United States, a bustling, frenetic lower Manhattan with its skirt of tall masts and its backdrop of skyscrapers and, for the Italian immigrants a bonus—the sanctuary of what became known as Little Italy just a few blocks to the north.

Back on Manhattan I strolled round the Battery Park area. There was no obvious evidence of the damage that Hurricane Sandy had done ... it

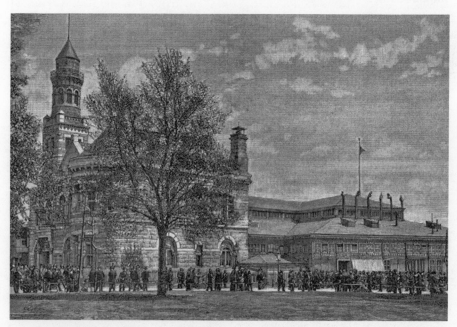

The Barge Office, New York's Immigration Center for two periods in the 1890s.

was more a sense that something momentous had happened, it was as if this part of Manhattan had been struck by a stun gun and was still in a state of disbelieving shock. The hawkers were still there selling everything from baseball caps to helicopter trips but there was so much you couldn't do—you couldn't visit Ellis Island and the Statue of Liberty or the South Street Seaport Museum or Castle Clinton or arrive at and leave from the South Ferry subway station.

Of course the circular sandstone fort known as Castle Clinton was on my radar because, from 1855 to 1890, it was New York's first immigration center ... the place where the several waves of Irish immigrants landed and were processed. I was able to walk around the outside, take a few photos and imagine what this place would have been like a hundred and fifty years ago, teeming with emaciated, haggard humanity, a mixture of fear and hope deep in their eyes.

I thought back to a fictional account of life for many of these immigrants around the slum streets and alleyways of the area known as Five Points (the convergence of five streets), close to today's Chinatown. This was the setting for Martin Scorcese's *Gangs of New York* and although the essence of the story was a work of fiction, this was a place of squalor and violence—this was also the place where many of those people who left their forty shades of famine, deprivation and degradation in Ireland ended up. For the majority, *their* gateway from one version of hell to another was Castle Clinton.

•

Still trying to work out why Scorcese had mis-cast Cameron Diaz in the role of Jenny in his movie, I walked back to the subway at Rector Street, changed once more at Christopher Street and returned to New Jersey on the Path. I was tired and I had a devious plan.

I collected the car from the lot and drove to the Newport Mall; this time I managed to get there without frightening any more Jersey City cops.

My first port of call was to check out the times at the multiplex cinema ... thinking about *Gangs of New York* had given me the idea of taking in a movie, a year or more before I'd see it in Calabria. I checked out what was on and narrowed it down to two, *Lincoln* and *Flight* ... my final decision was based on which one I thought Kay was least likely to want to watch and therefore went for *Flight*.

I had almost an hour and a half to kill before it started so headed for the restaurant zone to check out the delights being offered. I decided to try an Indian dish which was pretty good and it filled a space. Then I started to look for a birthday present for a five-year-old girl whom I'd never met ... a bit like looking for a needle in a haystack. When I asked one shop assistant for advice she looked at me as if I'd just flown in from Mars. Eventually, having spend ten minutes walking round Macy's studying the size of children's feet, I bought a pair of *Hello Kitty* slippers that I guessed would fit a five-year-old. Exhausted I sought the relief of a comfy seat in the dark.

Despite all the fresh air and the pressure of present hunting, I didn't fall asleep during the movie (which surely says something about it) though I do recall wondering whether, bearing in mind that I was just about to embark on three flights myself, I'd made the right choice.

It was when I got back to Wayne Street that I first missed it ... Angelo's lovely scarf. I assumed I had left it in the car and decided to check before I went to the Saigon Café later. But before I went back out, I asked Sherrie

Gino Sculco and Sina Audia with their daughter Anna and her family.

if she'd like to join me there for my last meal the following evening, it was she, after all, who had told me about it in the first place. It was a date.

En route I checked the car but there was no scarf ... I must have dropped it in the cinema, worse still in the mall or in the parking lot.

•

Next morning I naturally breakfasted with my new best friends at the Brownstone Diner and Pancake Factory before picking up the car.

I programed 'the voice' and told her to take me to Harrington Park in upstate New Jersey. Once again I miscalculated the time it would take and would have arrived almost an hour before the festivities were due to begin. I remembered seeing what seemed like a large liquor store about four or five miles back and, to kill time, drove back to it to see if they had any Calabrian wine. I actually found some and also some other confections that I thought might appeal to a five-year-old girl.

For the second time in less than an hour, and at one o'clock precisely, I arrived at my destination to be greeted in the driveway by a beaming Gino Sculco.

Finally I met Gino and Sina's other daughter Anna—the one that everyone back in Santa Severina seemed to recall because she looked like her father. I also met Anna's husband David, their two sons Joseph and Jonathan and, when she could be torn away from her friends, the birthday girl herself, Sara Rose.

Sara Rose, took a few seconds to acknowledge my birthday greetings before returning to the mayhem that only five-year old girls and their friends can make.

Gina looked at the space put aside for such mayhem and, shook her head and shrugged her shoulders. "It wasn't like this with my children." she said.

Her daughter Anna overheard her and countered, "Yes, mom, but times have changed."

This brief encounter made me think back to the young couple from Santa Severina, Gino Sculco and Sina Audia, who came here in 1967 and who raised their family in New Jersey. Their kids were raised the Calabrian way and were the stronger for it, but as adults themselves they had absorbed

Mission Control on Wayne Street, Jersey City.

other influences, other ways of doing things, other boundaries for their own children growing up in a different environment. These different boundaries, were not, it seemed to me, *instead* of what they themselves had experienced as children, rather *as well as*.

I thought back to the first birthday party we were invited to in Calabria ... it was for Alessia, at the time a couple of years older that Sara Rose and, as it happened, also a distant relative of hers. And yes, they were very different occasions given the cultural differences ... but then that's what happens, that's what living in a different culture is all about—you retain the best of the old and absorb what you like about the new.

As a 'foreigner' living in Calabria I know that this part of Italy is a place with which I feel a special connection but, as I've already made clear, I also feel an affinity with many aspects of American culture. And then again I always insist that I am Irish.

More people arrived, more children, more friends and more family, including Sara Rose's other set of grandparents. In the extended kitchen-cum-diner a table was being laid while in both the adjoining room and the sun-room—where there was table soccer—the children got on with being children. The adults were hovering around the table expectantly.

We ate Italian, pure and simple. Neither turkey left-overs nor cold stuffing, just straightforward Italian fare, clearly the speciality of this house.

Unfortunately I couldn't take part in the table soccer tournament that got underway after we'd eaten ... three generations of Sculcos and extended family, wrists, hands and voices working overtime, excitedly sensing victory, desperate to avoid defeat.

I had to leave before Sara Rose received her presents and the cake was cut for two reasons—I had to start packing and I'd also arranged to have an early evening dinner with Sherrie at the Saigon Café. But before setting off I was allowed to interrupt the table soccer momentarily to take a photo of this branch of the Sculco family.

The table soccer championships back in full swing, Gino and Sina saw me to my car and we embraced one last time ... I felt certain we'd meet again soon in the square in Santa Severina.

•

Basing myself in Jersey City had been a spur-of-the-moment decision—not unconnected with economics—and, as I drove back there for the last time, I knew I had made a good choice. My Wayne Street base had worked well and the proximity of a gem such as the Saigon Café and the family who ran it was but the icing on the cake.

It was an evening for two emotional farewells ... first with Steve, Karen, Kim and Danny and then, back on Wayne Street, with Sherrie, who I knew would be up and out to college before I woke.

Steve gave me one parting piece of advice about my drive to JFK the following day ... he advised me to allow at least two hours for the journey, even if it was less than twenty-five miles.

POSTSCRIPT

It is August 2013. It is hot and Santa Severina is bursting to the seams with *ritornati*, those who have come back to the town of their birth for a few days, a few weeks, even a few months. Most are from the north of Italy, a few from further afield.

I go into Pino's bar and there, ordering a drink, I recognize a couple of faces I had seen only once before—Gino Sculco's son Gino and his fiancée Jennifer. They are buying some drinks for Anna and Rose's children sitting together round the corner, inside rather than out.

The five kids, with the youngest, Sara Rose, clearly in charge, want some straws but don't know the Italian word; I help them out as they try to get their tongues round *le cannuccie*.

Gino, Jennifer and I step outside to join the rest of the Sculco family sitting together in the square—only Rose's husband Jose and Anna's husband David are missing.

For Gino Sculco and Sina Audia it is the first time they have been together with their extended family in the town where it all began.

Homeward bound

Because my flight from Rome to Crotone was at nine on the Tuesday evening I had chosen to fly from JFK to Venice and from Venice on to Rome. This meant that I had five or six hours to kill in Venice rather than in Rome Airport—enough time to take the bus into the city and do a bit of sightseeing.

My flight departed from JFK at seven-fifty in the evening so, keeping in mind Steve's advice, I had decided to leave New Jersey just after lunch.

I woke earlier than usual and, feeling restless, decided to get up and walk to you-know-where for one last breakfast sandwich and then on to the Newport Mall to buy that cap I'd tried on at least a dozen times in the previous couple of weeks. All that procrastination had been worthwhile ... there was a special offer that day and I bought two.

I went to the cinema to ask about my scarf and, just my luck, got Mr Unhelpful who went through the motions of looking but I could tell he wasn't really bothered. I couldn't help but think that it he'd looked a bit harder he would have found it.

I returned to Wayne Street to finish packing.

As I'd had a late breakfast, I decided to have a late lunch at JFK so, around midday, I took one last walk to the parking lot to pick up my car and say goodbye to Mitch. I took a photo of him too, only to discover later that he had his eyes closed at the time.

Back at Wayne Street I parked illegally for the time it took me to climb four flights of stairs twice and bring first one, then the other, case down to the car.

I set up the GPS on the dashboard and plugged it in. I checked its preset 'favorites' that would take me straight 'home' to the rental base at JFK—from my experience with earlier rentals I'd discovered that companies preset their GPS's memory with their base, their 'home', at all major airports. However, in the case of this particular GPS I soon discovered that this apparently meant their rental base at all airports in the known universe *except* one of the largest, New York's JFK.

Thinking I must have made a mistake, I tried again. Definitely *all* major airports in and around New York *except* JFK ... the rental company had either forgotten to program this particular GPS with their JFK base or, worse still, they didn't have a base at JFK despite having told me I could drop the car off there.

I searched through my rental paperwork and found the number of the base at Newark Airport where I'd picked up the car. I called them. The reason for the omission was reasonably straightforward ... they had only recently opened an off-airport base at JFK, so recently in fact they hadn't had time to program all their GPSs with its address. Not a problem, I thought, just let me have the address and I can program it

Silence ... then, "Just a moment ..."

Longer silence ... then, "We're trying to locate it ..."

Still more silence ... then, "We've found it ..."

I typed the address into the GPS's memory and selected 'drive'.

Steve was right, it took me almost two hours from door to door and half of that was the time it took me to cross Manhattan from the exit of the Holland Tunnel to the time I passed the end of Clinton Street and crossed Williamsburg Bridge on the opposite side.

•

On the SkyTrain from the rental drop-off I saw that Alitalia flights departed from Terminal One and exited there. I went to the Alitalia check-in and showed them my e-ticket. I was told that, even though the ticket clearly said Alitalia and I had booked it through the Alitalia website, I was actually flying on an Alitalia flight operated by Delta and that was Terminal Three.

Back to the Skytrain.

How difficult would it have been, I wondered, to add to the list of airlines and their departure terminals 'Alitalia/Delta'.

I checked-in my larger suitcase, had my late lunch and did some last-minute shopping ... in a terminal that looked and felt jaded; it reminded me of London Heathrow's Terminal Two before they started ripping it apart.

It was time to wander over to Gate, B22. I was a bit early but was having difficulty finding it. I was following all the right signs but there didn't seem to be a Gate B22. I saw a group of people hovering expectantly by a door in a back wall and among them recognized the man who'd been in front of me at the bag-drop check-in. There was a uniformed woman at the front seemingly in charge and intermittently calling together all passengers for Gate B22. I asked someone what was going on and was told that we were waiting for the bus to Terminal Four. B22, it seemed, was actually in Terminal Four and the way to Terminal Four was via the back door of Terminal Three and a bus ride.

Not sure why I expected more of New York's JFK Airport.

On the ten-minute journey in the dark en route to Terminal Four, I wondered how many people were likely to miss their flight by not allowing enough time for this extra little complication. I was lucky in that I had left myself plenty of time but I had only hit upon the Gate 22 people by accident. I wasn't looking for the back door, I was looking for a Gate with a couple of airline staff and a window with an aircraft waiting on the other side.

•

We landed at Venice Marco Polo on schedule and, after checking that my bags would go straight through to Crotone, I caught the bus into the city.

Some years ago Neff, my nephew and occasional traveling companion, got married on a beautiful Venetian bridge over a canal in the busy Piazza San Marco. After the ceremony he and his wife stepped onto a gondola for a short, romantic glide along the still waters under a clear blue sky and an occasional flurry of wispy clouds.

The sky was false, the clouds were on a loop, the gondola was electric and the Piazza San Marco was in a shopping mall in the Venetian Hotel in Las Vegas ... the only thing that was real was the water, albeit a bit cleaner than you might expect in Venice. Until I stepped off the bus in the Piazzale Roma, that Las Vegas wedding was the closest I'd ever been to Venice.

Venice seemed to be one of those places that divided people: most loved it; many hated it. For me after about a couple of hours wandering the streets of the Rialto, the jury was still out.

I knew I had a built-in this-place-may-not-be-what-it's-cracked-up-to-be button for tourist hotspots; I started with skepticism and waited to be convinced.

That's why I was ambivalent about the Grand Canyon but loved Death Valley; couldn't wait to get out of Alberobello in Apuglia and could have stayed longer in nearby Ostuni.

Apart from killing time, my reasons for coming into Venice that morning were twofold: initially I just wanted to get a feel for the place to see if it was somewhere Kay and I might visit together at some future date; but now I also wanted to see why my iPhone wouldn't work despite the fact that I had already inserted it's Italian SIM. For the latter, I needed to find the store of my Italian provider, Wind ... normally, in even the smallest of towns, this is a relatively easy task, the stores of cellphone providers are everywhere. In some Italian towns there are even two or three stores for the same provider which explains why Italy has one of the highest per capita concentrations of cell phones in the world. I was anticipating a veritable glut of Wind stores in Venice.

It didn't take me long to find the Grand Canal, it ran alongside Piazzale Roma. I crossed the canal and explored the narrow streets beyond on the off-chance that I might stumble upon a Wind store. The lack of any kind of store told me I was in the wrong part of town. I headed back to where I'd seen water taxis and asked at a nearby kiosk where the shopping hub of Venice was located. I was told the Rialto area of the city. I saw that one of the water taxis went there so bought a day ticket, in case I wanted to get off somewhere else.

The Rialto was a maze of streets that twisted and turned, crossed and re-crossed minor canals and would have been altogether thoroughly confusing had it not been for the surfeit of signs pointing the way to touristy hotspots. Occasionally I came across an Italian predilection that I have written about elsewhere, the scourge of the missing sign, the junction, where there is clearly a choice of which way to turn and where the sign you have been following doesn't exist.

I soon realized that 'Wind store' was not going to figure on any of the signposts, so started asking people for directions. In total I must have asked about seven or eight people, shopkeepers mostly but also some locals out for a stroll in the rain. Yes, it was now raining.

Each time I followed their directions to the letter until my head was dizzy with going up and down the same streets, passing the same shops, crossing the same bridges in opposite directions. Confused, cold, wet, tired and hungry, I gave up on my Wind quest and followed the signs back to where I'd got off the water taxi. I had already decided that eating near the Piazzale Roma was going to be infinitely less costly than anywhere in or around the Rialto.

I enjoyed a wonderfully warming bowl of minestrone soup and crisp fresh bread before catching my bus back to the airport. I was already on the bus when I realized I'd been in Venice and not taken a single photograph ... perhaps next time, I thought.

•

Three hours later I was in Rome Airport waiting for my late-evening connection to Crotone where I knew my friend Giuliano would be waiting.

On board uncharacteristically I slept all the way to Crotone and only just came round and got my bearings just as the plane was parking up outside the small terminal.

At that moment America, New Jersey, Jersey City and Wayne Street all seemed light years away but they were people and places there I would never forget and hoped to see again.

As I descended the aircraft steps and stepped once more on to Calabrian soil, I wiped away a tear. I was more than a little pleased to be back in this place.

POSTSCRIPT

It is late May and Kay and I are en route back to Calabria from Croatia and are spending a day in Venice before catching the early-morning flight back to Lamezia Terme.

We decide to walk to the Rialto rather than go by water taxi. We are nearly there and turn a corner into a small piazza on the corner of which is a large Wind store—the object of my fruitless quest six months previously. As it happened the Wind stores I eventually found in Crotone were no help whatsoever with my problem ... it was an Apple solution that eventually got my Wind SIM working.

As we walk out of the square I recognize a couple of the shops ... this was where I had had enough of my labyrinthine wanderings in the persistent drizzle and had given up my search. I had been no more than twenty-five meters from the store.

Looking back

When I left Calabria in early November to visit Calabrian families in the United States, I had no idea what was going to happen, what—if anything—I might learn, whether or not it was even a worthwhile project to talk to families and individuals about the past and to try and bring their stories up to date.

The stories people shared with me are, I realize, only a snapshot of the million and one stories out there that I did not hear.

I did however meet some extraordinary people and heard about many others who came before them and made possible the achievements of the current generations. Even those who emigrated in the fifties and sixties had other, older family members who had already tested the waters, sometimes more than once. Indeed, every single family or individual I met had at least one ancestor who emigrated and, of these, all but one entered the United States through the Ellis Island Immigration Center, even if they themselves didn't emigrate until much later.

I was also privy to a few stories that I decided not to attribute to any specific family, either because I was asked not to or I thought it inappropriate. That said, there is anonymity in the pages of this chapter and so I have included some of these here to illustrate or highlight some of the text.

•

Every Italian individual or family who emigrated, did so for a complex mixture of reasons, reasons which at this distance in time are difficult to assess in specific terms though generally most were driven to leave through economic deprivations in their home country.

Those who left Calabria were poor beyond our imaginations; they generally lived in small towns in the countryside with, as it seemed at the time, little prospect of things getting better. Around them in the larger towns and cities they could see that, for some at least, things were edging forward, for a few people there were prospects.

The rural peasant had eked out the same existence for generations, living off the land and its natural bounty and working other people's land for next to nothing. And day in, day out, year in, year out, life had and would continue in this way—they would marry, have children, who would marry and have children ...

Then, in the late nineteenth century, another option presented itself ... there was an opportunity to break the never-ending cycle of a menial Calabrian existence. But for individuals or families to break the mould there were huge sacrifices—to leave Calabria for America meant leaving behind family, friends and a familiar pattern of life.

The ongoing economic and political instability of the time—particularly in the years either side of the First World War (1914-1918)—only served to make southern Italians feel more put upon than they normally did and, increasingly, such huge sacrifices seemed more feasible.

Intermingled with all of the above there was another scourge that befell many Calabrians, particularly those who had to try and make a living on low-lying areas between mountains and sea ... the scourge of malaria.

On his *Old Calabria* travels, English author Norman Douglas described the conditions as he observed them in the first decade of the twentieth century. It was not a pretty picture and even loftier hill-top towns were not exempt.

Douglas tells how, in 1908, forty menfolk of one such town south of Catanzaro had no option but to seek work in Crotone and all returned infected save the two who had "made liberal use of quinine as a prophylactic".

His conclusion is straight to the point, albeit possibly somewhat extreme, "Malaria is the key to a correct understanding of the [Calabrian] landscape, it explains the inhabitants, their mode of life, their habits, their history."

•

I have long tried to understand why it was that the members of one family emigrated and their neighbors didn't; what it was that made two families, or two brothers, or two cousins, or two friends with seemingly the same background of social turmoil and endemic poverty and the same prospects and who heard the same stories about life in America, choose a different route through life. The only hypothesis I can come up with is an individual's perceived capacity to break out of that 'familiar pattern of life' and take a giant leap into the unknown.

I refer here to those who emigrated in the early twentieth century and not those who left Calabria in the fifties and sixties for whom moving images of America and the American way of life, coupled with family stories and experiences of life there, were more commonplace. *Their* 'leap' was less into the unknown though, as I saw and heard for myself many times, that in no way dilutes their resolve and courage in deciding to leave their homeland.

Also, post-war, many Calabrians had become more used to seeking employment elsewhere, most notably in Germany where they found work in the burgeoning car industry. Indeed to this day I have a number of Calabrians friends in their eighties who still receive a regular pension payment from, among others, Volkswagen.

Whoever they were, whatever their circumstances, whenever they left, wherever they went, the enormity of the choice these people made can never be underestimated.

There were of course a few individuals, like Peter Chiarella's father Raffaele in *Calabrian Tales*, who felt that emigration was the only answer to a specific problem ... in his case to the constant shame that had beset his family; arguably Raffaele Chiarella and his mother fled rather than emigrated.

Similarly in 1906, at the age of eighteen, young Bruno Cortese's first emigration was prompted by the unwanted attentions of a woman whose family had set their sights on marriage; Bruno had escaped rather than emigrated.

Even in the sixties for the Cubello family the economic realities of life in Calabria was less of an incentive than the hope that, if they emigrated to America, it might help alleviate Giuseppe Cubello's debilitating medical condition; the Cubello family had emigrated to preserve the family unit.

And of course Elvira Arabia only went to the States as a tourist ... emigration was the last thing on her mind until she met Eugene DeBartolo; Elvira had emigrated, not by design, but by accident.

Of course every story is an individual story, there may be similar patterns and convenient generalizations but there are always individual stories that break the mould, that defy categorization.

•

Italian immigrants disembarking from the *Prinzess Irene*, c1911.

The reasons why Gaetano Gaudio and Angelina Bruno emigrated is such a unique tale.

Gaetano's father and mother, Marcello and Antonella, were a typical Calabrian couple who married young—because their families had arranged it so—in the early 1890s and who then scraped a living off the land, went to mass every Sunday, respected the local landowner to his face by calling him Don Francesco and cursed him behind his back ... and generally conducted their lives as others did.

In quick succession they had three sons, Antonio, Francesco and Gaetano. In 1910, with their parents' blessing, the two oldest boys decided to emigrate to America where they had a distant 'uncle' on their mother's side who promised to help get them on their feet. The youngest boy, Gaetano, remained in Calabria to help his parents as his mother Antonella was not in good health. Almost two years later, when Gaetano was in his late-teens, his mother died.

At first Marcello thought seriously about leaving Calabria and taking Gaetano with him to join his two brothers in Brooklyn but instead, after an appropriate period of mourning, he re-married.

Marcello's second wife, Angelina Bruno, was almost twenty years younger than he was but they seemed happy enough and both families had clearly accepted their unorthodox union ... a union, like so many others at the time, forged through necessity. Gaetano now had a step-mother, albeit one who was only a few years older than he was.

A year later Angelina had a son, Vincenzo, but a few months after he was born tragedy struck yet again and her husband Marcello died. In the space of four years, Gaetano had lost both parents, his step-mother was a widow and his infant half-brother had no father.

Gaetano did the only decent thing ... he married his step-mother, Angelina, and together with their 'son', Vincenzo, they left Calabria and joined Gaetano's brothers in America.

Angelina and Gaetano went on to have seven American children; the wife of one their sons told me their story.

•

In 1912 eighteen-year-old Marialuigia D'Amato too had a personal reason for leaving her home town of Scandale—she was pregnant and the child's father, Domenico Franco, had sloped off across the Atlantic to

Pennsylvania. Determined and courageous to a fault, Marialuigia followed him to America to read him his rights and she took her fourteen-year-old brother, Angelo, along with her.

But it is Angelo's story that turned out to be the more intriguing for he decided to stay on in America after Marialuigia had found her man, married him and taken him back to Scandale with her on a ball and chain.

Angelo was now eighteen and living and working among Brooklyn's Calabrian community off Park Avenue when, one fateful evening, he and his friends got into a brawl with some Sicilian lads. The skirmish became more heated and finally came to a gruesome end when Angelo bit off the ear lobe of his opponent.

The adversaries retreated to their respective enclaves but word soon got round the Calabrian neighborhood that the Sicilians were out for revenge. They were looking for Angelo.

Angelo was fortunate for he had some good, loyal and inventive friends who didn't exactly stand by him but did the next best thing—they shipped him off to Canada. Somebody had heard that there was work and prospects in the booming gold-mining town of Kirkland Lake, known also as the Mile of Gold, in Ontario ... so Angelo was duly packed into an

Would-be emigrants arriving at the Emigration Office in Naples prior to departure.

empty whiskey barrel and said barrel and its human contents were shipped northwards to Kirkland Lake.

Angelo lived out the rest of his long life in this small, remote town. He gave up biting off ear-lobes and instead became a respected member of the local community where he married a Canadian woman and opened a hotel.

Nobody knows what became of the barrel.

•

Whatever the reasons for emigrating, people usually did so with family members or with a group of friends from the same town or village; in addition to being in general good health, they had to have a sponsor on the other side, an address and enough dollars (over the years the amount varied).

The surviving ships' manifests (up to 1924), that give today's generation the nuts and bolts of individual lives at the point of embarkation (normally Naples for Calabrians), don't tell the whole story.

Every person who emigrated left behind a trail of sorrow, grief and misgiving, right back to the place of their birth. Although, for a few, there were friends and family who were able to come to Naples to shout out one final *arrivederci*, most of the emotion of the occasion was confined to the family home.

In a lifetime most Calabrians would never have ventured much further than a dozen miles from their home town and here they were, courageous, desperate people, preparing to leave everything they knew, not just as far as Naples, but for an unimaginable distance beyond Naples to a new life in a new land.

As the day dawned they folded, rolled and stuffed clothes; filled cases, knapsacks and bags; hugged, held and reassured loved ones; said goodbye, promised to write and shed tears; felt hesitant, overwhelmed and resolute; waved, were apprehensive and knew fear; heard the rumble of the cart on the cobbles, saw faces glued to windows and cast a last glance down a familiar street.

A day when each emigrant and the family he or she left behind shared the same outpouring of raw emotion ... wondering would they ever see each other again.

•

From the ships' manifests that listed everyone who entered the United States through Ellis Island, it is clear that most of those who emigrated from southern Italy had no skill other than their ability to work; neither could they read or write.

That said, a few did have skills—from the families I talked to alone there were, dressmakers, cobblers, and tailors and some of these could also read and write—but in terms of how these separate stories unfolded, the skills or lack thereof with which they emigrated didn't seem to make any difference—first generation Pat Scida was the son of an illiterate farm laborer and retired as a senior vice-president of Morgan Stanley.

Literate or skilled, most of those who arrived in the United States between 1900 and 1924, had to pass through Ellis Island, *l'Isola delle Lacrime*, the Island of Tears, as many Italian immigrants dubbed it. Tough, invasive and harrowing as Ellis Island's regime was—the more so after a long and debilitating crossing—it was infinitely better than what preceded it. Both the Barge Office and Castle Clinton were notoriously mismanaged

Mulberry Street, the hub of Little Italy around 1905 ... I wonder if any were from Calabria?

and dens of corruption—as well as all the usual status and health checks, immigrants often had to run the gauntlet of all sorts of low life including con men, thieves and pickpockets ... as if the streets of New York were not bad enough.

•

For obvious reasons people tended to gravitate to areas where their *paesani*—people from their home town or surrounding area—lived. This could be anything from several tenement blocks to half a dozen streets in Brooklyn or a largish community in Kenosha. There was safety, familiarity and cooperation in numbers.

There were—and to some extent still are—clusters of Calabrians in particular areas which made me wonder if Calabrian immigrants were more Calabrian and less Italian than others? And, if so, was this a self-inflicted segregation or was it a reflection of how other Italians perceived Calabrians? It remains the case today that there are many Italians who view Calabria as a backward region of their country, inhabited by lazy individuals who don't pay taxes. Perhaps all the hard-working Calabrians emigrated?

Generally Boston Italians lived in what was called the North End but, according to Stephen Puleo (in his book *The Boston Italians*), Calabrians tended to mix instead with other non-Italian immigrants and peopled Boston's South End.

Similarly, while there must surely have been some Calabrians who gravitated to the area of New York around Mulberry Street and Mott Street that became known as Little Italy, I never came across a single one.

Then again, perhaps this is not surprising for at the time Mott Street was home mostly to Sicilian families, many of whom—rightly or wrongly—had a reputation for being 'connected'. It was here that one of New York's notorious gangsters, Ignazio Lupo, opened the largest of several wholesale grocery stores through which he preyed on other Italians.

It was the connotations of the word 'connected' that finally persuaded me that I should look for an alternative to the original title of this book, *Calabrian Connections*.

Nicholas Ciotola's book, *Italians in Albuquerque*, illustrates the same tale in reverse by telling the story of the city's Italian immigrants who mostly came from Lucca in northern Tuscany. The book focuses on a few prominent families and of course they were, by far, the Italian community in the city. That said, there was a Calabrian cobbler living there too, name of Bruno Cortese, but then Bruno settled there because his wife was ill with tuberculosis—originally he lived in Cicero near Chicago and Elkhart in Indiana, both of which had Calabrian enclaves.

•

If the evidence of Boston is anything to go by, the early Calabrian immigrants kept themselves apart from other Italians—kept themselves apart or were not welcome, either is possible—so it hardly surprising that, initially at least, most families were quite conservative when it came to marrying outside the Calabrian clan. The worst crime, it seemed, was to have anything to do with the Irish.

After the Irish, the Italian immigration which followed was the most significant movement of people to the United States. Many within the Irish community soon forgot that they had once been immigrants themselves and did not immediately take to this new influx of short, swarthy, non-English-speaking foreigners. The fact that, ostensibly at least, they shared the same religion did not seem to matter.

The relationship between these two communities could be fraught, with the Irish often having the whip hand, particularly so as many of them in the larger northern cities had become policemen; almost half of the NYPD force in 1860 was Irish or of Irish descent and at the turn of the century it was nearer eighty percent.

That said, such negative Italian-Irish experiences were generally confined to those immigrants who came to America in the early part of the twentieth century. By the fifties and sixties, many third generation Italians and Irish had inter-married and for the new wave of immigrants there were fewer such conflicts, indeed often they went to the same schools.

Pasquale Vincenzo Fortino ended up with his own Irish troubles when he decided to leave Calabria just before he was conscripted in 1914. He went to Brooklyn first of all but settled in Queens and, ironically, ended up doing a stint in the American military.

By 1920 Pasquale was an American citizen and all seemed well with his world until he got into a bit of trouble with the family of a flame-haired woman he was courting, a family that did not like 'wops'. Teresa's parents were of Irish descent and, worse still, her father Pat was a larger-than-life policeman ... all the ingredients that soon spelled trouble for Pasquale.

Pasquale maintains that he was framed, that he never laid a finger on Teresa's father, but he had clearly gotten on his wrong side and so decided it was time to cut and run, to return to Calabria and find himself a Calabrian bride.

Later in life Pasquale, now a widower with grown-up children, decided to give America a second chance but he knew that he had left under a cloud, that his 'record' was not as clean as it might have been. Although he was an American citizen, he feared that revealing details of his citizenship would lead directly to him being refused entry—this was the sixties and the American administration was touchy about such things. Pasquale decided he would have to become someone else.

As luck would have it Pasquale's cousin Marco worked for the local *comune*—town hall—specifically in the *Anagrafe* department that dealt with such matters. It didn't take long for Pasquale to have all the necessary paperwork to get himself a new passport ... and when he did Vincenzo Fortino, born the year before Pasquale Fortino, had no difficulty in re-emigrating to the United States.

He kept well away from Queens.

In one small town with a sizable Italian population, a particular law enforcement officer was not over-sympathetic to the Italian community; when local laws were broken, as likely as not Kelly the Cop (no prizes for guessing his country of origin) could quickly come up with an Italian perpetrator. And, guilty or not, he enjoyed knocking his truncheon across their 'wop' heads. He took particular pleasure from abusing them verbally and knew all the ethnic slurs that hit the mark.

But person or persons unknown decided to give Kelly the Cop a taste of his own medicine and one night he was found slumped in an alleyway, a tell-tale piece of piping lying by his side. No-one knew who did it, nor did they ever find out who it was but, seventy years on, my informant told me that among the town's Italian community 'mum' was the word.

Marion Vaccaro, Lou Piezzo's second cousin, told me another Irish-Italian story about her grandfather Alessandro Tallarico—whose sister,

Marianna, was the wife of Lou's grandfather, Giuseppe. You may recall too that even one generation on within the extended Piezzo family, there were more than a few eyebrows raised when a distant cousin married an Irishman.

Marion's story of Alessandro Tallarico started off predictably but had an unexpected ending.

Alessandro was nearly twenty when he and fifteen-year-old Francesca Sirianni wed; like Alessandro, Francesca's family were from Casabona in Calabria.

In quick succession they had four additional mouths to feed and it became difficult to make ends meet, particularly when Alessandro found himself temporarily out of work. They had left a poverty-ridden region of Italy and now found themselves practically destitute in Brooklyn.

Someone told them about 'government assistance', what today would have been the equivalent of 'welfare', available at the government office in downtown Brooklyn. (Although in those days immigrants had to have a sponsor and a place to live in order to *enter* the United States if, after they were already residents, they fell on hard times, then they could apply for government assistance.)

The Tallarico family business on Classon Avenue, Brooklyn, in the late 1920s.

The first person they met at the government offices was an Irish-American who was singularly unhelpful and offensive; he dismissed their plea for assistance and was cruelly abusive about it too. Weeping and consoling each other at the same time, they huddled together in the corridor as they waited for the elevator.

Another official came by and seeing they were clearly distraught, took them aside and listened to their story. He brought them into his office where he helped them complete the paperwork and told them that they would receive money every month to make a new start in life. Before they left, he checked that they had enough money to feed the children until the first payment arrived and, when they told him they hadn't, he gave them some from his own pocket to tide them over.

This second government official was also Irish-American.

But the story didn't end there for, two years later, when Alessandro was working again and Francesca was supplementing the family income by doing sewing from home, Alessandro returned to the government offices and sought out the Irishman who had helped them.

The man recalled Alessandro but was surprised when he tried to pay back some of the money the government had paid him. Alessandro apologized for not yet having it all but promised to return the lot through regular payments until every penny was paid back in full. He also brought the gentleman a gallon of his home-made wine to show good faith.

The man was touched but explained to Alessandro that he didn't have to pay it back, that it wasn't a loan, rather money to help them get back on their feet, to get them started ... he suggested that he put it towards something for the family instead. Alessandro said he would indeed do that but before leaving he paid back the personal loan, with interest, that got them through those first few days.

Alessandro took the advice to heart and with the money he had saved he started up Tallarico Italian America Groceries on Classon Avenue, Brooklyn. Although an Italian grocery store in an Italian neighborhood should have been a runaway success, the business struggled. It was always competing with the men who came round to people's doors every day with cart-loads of fresh produce. Quite simply Alessandro Tallarico was ahead of his time.

His time *did* indeed come and he went on to found the fur business

NuWest which, as we have seen, was a very successful company with a fair, hands-on boss at the helm. What's more, he and Francesca never forgot this episode and how one Irishman turned him down while another dipped into his own pocket to help them get by and in later years, with their new venture doing well, the couple helped many others in similar predicaments.

•

Although it is clear from both anecdotal and documented evidence that Italian-Americans were often picked on and discriminated against, I met few families who recalled it as being a significant issue in their lives or the lives of their ancestors. I suspect that, then as now, people focused on the few well-publicized negative stories rather than the more commonplace non-stories of the majority.

Nationally there were social and political issues involving Italians that stole many a headline ... the Bread and Roses Strike in 1912 in Lawrence,

Handcuffed together, Bartolomeo Vanzetti and Nicola Sacco.

Massachusetts and the prolonged Sacco and Vanzetti affair in the twenties, which also had its roots in Massachusetts, were high profile at the time. For a time both divided opinion and, initially at least, had the capacity to whip up anti-Italian sentiment.

The strike hit the local textile mills who employed up to fifty thousand immigrants—men, women and children—of different nationalities. Until his arrest on trumped-up murder charges, Arturo Giovannitti of the Italian Socialist Federation of the Socialist Party of America was one of the joint leaders of the dispute.

Public sympathies that were initially against the workers' demands and which backed the use of the National Guard to police the strike, gradually swung the other way and a settlement generally favorable to the strikers was eventually reached.

But what later caught people's imaginations was the horrific testimony before a Congressional Committee of a fourteen-year-old Italian worker, Carmela Teoli, who described the unsafe conditions in mills that resulted in her scalp being removed by one of the machines.

As a teenager I read Howard Fast's moving book, *The Passion of Sacco and Vanzetti*, the story of two Italian anarchists, Nicola Sacco and Bartholomeo Vanzetti, who were accused of the murder of two men during an armed robbery in 1920. I was completely won over to the arguments that Fast so eloquently rationalized to illustrate the events —and particularly the legal shortcomings—that caused these men to be tried, convicted and ultimately executed because they were self-professed anarchists and, worse still, Italian anarchists. Their guilt or innocence, it seemed to me at the time, was almost a side-issue.

The case became something of a *cause célèbre*, mainly because the two were not executed until 1927 by which time the appeals process had run its course. In the American psyche of the time, an anarchist was just about the worst type of low-life to have in your midst so it was inevitable that for some people 'anarchist' and 'Italian' became one and the same.

Both men protested their innocence throughout the legal twists and turns which included two trials and several appeals until they were executed as the law of the time demanded.

Subsequently in 1977, fifty years on, Massachusetts Governor Michael Dukakis (the unsuccessful presidential Democratic candidate who stood against George Bush Senior in 1988) issued a proclamation in both English and Italian to the effect that Sacco and Vanzetti had been unfairly tried and convicted and therefore that 'any disgrace should be forever removed from their names'.

Dukakis' proclamation was careful not to mention guilt or innocence, only that the system let them down, which was undoubtedly the case. As it happens subsequent investigations into the affair and more recent forensic examination of the gun used would suggest that, in all probability, Sacco was indeed guilty.

Members of most of the families I met lived through one if not both of these events but few recall them ever being mentioned either as a subject of interest or as being the catalyst for anti-Italian sentiments. Few, but not all.

Mary De Luca told me how her mother's (Elizabeth Cortese) generation grew up in a politicized environment where both these events (and others) were talked about in terms of the place Italian immigrants had in the American labor movement. How, in the early days, the involvement of immigrants in disputes such as the Bread and Roses Strike initially spawned significant discrimination. But both her parents were also aware of just how far Italians had come *because of* the labor movement and the part they and other immigrants played in standing up for rights and dignity in the workplace. Elizabeth Cortese had experience of working in a garment factory and later, as a school cafeteria worker, served as an officer in her local union.

Mary reminded me that it was her Democrat grandfather, Bruno Cortese, who coined the phrase: "All politicians are crooks, but Republicans are crooks for the rich and Democrats are crooks for the poor".

Talk of Sacco and Vanzetti and their politics reminded me that two of the questions on some of the ships' manifests for would-be immigrants asked simply: 'Whether a Polygamist?' and 'Whether an Anarchist?' It is unlikely that anyone, whether or not an anarchist, would have answered 'yes' to the latter and gotten turned away at the door. It's therefore hardly surprising that both Sacco and Vanzetti lied when they entered the country in 1913 and 1908 respectively ... I checked.

It reminded me of a similar question on the visa application for the United States in the early sixties which asked if it was the applicant's intention to overthrow the government of the United States. According to a mutual friend, the Irish author and playwright, Brendan Behan, responded to this with characteristic, Guinness-fueled, irreverence when he wrote "Sole purpose of visit". His visa application was granted.

•

I was also curious to find out about the sort of criminal activity which, in the countless movies at least, has often become synonymous with Italians.

A Calabrian policeman of my acquaintance was pretty sure that most of his fellow Calabrians emigrated to escape the long arm of the law. Perhaps this was more prevalent in recent times but I wasn't sure if it applied to Calabrians a century ago or even in the fifties and sixties. The 'activity' he was alluding to was the Calabrian equivalent of the Sicilian mafia, the 'ndrangheda, though it is clear that in America a century ago no such distinction was made and all such activities came under the blanket term 'mafia' or, as they were often known, Cosa Nostra or Black Hand. The use of the word 'ndrangheda referring specifically to the Calabrian mafia seems to date from the mid-fifties.

It just so happened that these days one of the families I visited in America is known both in Calabria and further afield for standing up against the 'ndrangheda. In recent years Renato Cortese, a Santa Severinese and the brother of my friend Bruno Cortese, has been one of the high-profile policemen responsible for—and successful at—bringing many of the 'ndrangheda criminals to justice.

So it was ironic that one of the people who had some experience of such 'connections', albeit second-hand, was a member of the same Cortese family, Mary De Luca in Albuquerque. Her mother, Elizabeth Cortese, married into a family with Sicilian blood and her husband, Sylvester De Luca, used to tell stories about the mafia. He explained how they were seen initially by many as a kind of 'Robin Hood' organization but, when the extent of their criminality became all too clear, this was soon transposed into feelings of dread ... they became people to be avoided at all costs.

Sylvester's mother apparently got his older brother *out* of a job in Denver when they realized it involved people with mafia connections ... she pulled this off by invoking connections of her own and by using the name of a rival mafia boss whom she apparently knew when the family had lived in Wisconsin.

Someone else recalled how he had to repay his younger brother's debts with some Brooklyn loan sharks who were of southern Italian descent and therefore seen as 'mafia'.

Marion Vaccaro also had a story about her grandfather, Alessandro Tallarico, who was, if you recall, known to be the fair and respected boss of NuWest furs. So it is not surprising that when a local merchant came to tell him how he had been asked to pay protection to a small-time gangster with 'connections', his reaction was to ask "Protection from what, from whom?" Of course, the unspoken answer was protection from the man offering protection.

Alessandro went to see the man and turned the tables by telling him in no uncertain terms that if he didn't stop bothering his friends and relatives then he (Alessandro) would speak to some of *his* friends in the police and have him run out of town. Alessandro, it has to be said, was not only a well-respected member of the local community but also six feet tall, very strong despite being slight of build, and had steely blue eyes that, it was said, could stop a clock at ten paces. Not surprisingly the threat from the Black Hand evaporated and life for everyone—except the small-time racketeer—went back to normal

So, when I asked if, and to what extent, such criminal activity had

Prohibition Agents destroy cases of beer … what a waste.

emigrated to America *within* the Calabrian community, generally people had heard stories such as these but weren't directly aware of it impinging on their family. This could be interpreted as the classic fudge but I didn't think so.

When it was part of their family's experience, people were generally straight about grandpa dabbling in wine-making during Prohibition and losing a few barrels to the Prohibition Agents. Embarrassing, confusing even, for the family at the time but nothing more. Making wine when you're not supposed to would have been something of a badge of honor for most Calabrians.

However I did spend time with one Calabrian family where there was some potentially embarrassing fall-out from the predilection of two brothers for making the red nectar. The two brothers in question were Antonio (Tony) and Francesco (Frank) Tigano and the story came to light when one of the family found a newspaper clipping hidden in among other papers.

The year was 1931, almost a decade into the nonsense that was Prohibition. Both brothers had lived in pre-Prohibition America when it was as natural for them to make their own wine as it was to dry tomatoes in the sun or jar eggplants. For them the making of wine was not a commercial exercise, it was something they had done all their lives in both Calabria and America; the pleasure was as much in the making as the consuming, something to enjoy within the family and extended family and to pass on to friends. In America it was no more than a way of retaining some of the traditions of the homeland.

The Prohibition legislation did in fact acknowledge that people would and could make their own wine for their own consumption at home but this was the problem, the wording of the legislation was open to interpretation. Under the Act, two hundred gallons—about seven hundred and fifty liters or four standard barrels—of 'non-intoxicating cider and fruit juice' could be made each year at home. It was the interpretation of the word 'intoxicating' that was the loophole and allowed people to buy in grapes to make 'fruit juice' at home.

This in turn kept some of America's vineyards in business as did the huge increase in the sale of sacramental wine (supposedly for the church) which reportedly—and coincidentally of course—doubled during the Prohibition era. Even with these two outlets, over eighty percent of American vineyards closed during Prohibition.

Another anomaly within the Act was that it was not technically illegal to consume alcohol … it was the buying and selling that was against the law. It was this vacuum that people like Al Capone and others stepped into through making illegal liquor—especially spirits—available for sale below the counter.

It is against this backdrop that the apparent 'crimes' of Tony and Frank need to be judged.

At first the brothers lived in different cities, Frank a little closer to the Canadian border where bootlegging beer had become almost a way of life … until you were caught, that is. Frank was indeed caught and served a prison sentence of indeterminate length at Missouri's Leavenworth Penitentiary.

The newspaper clipping told the story of what happened some time after Frank regained his freedom:

FRANK TIGANO'S HEARING SET FRIDAY MORNING
He and son-in-law accused of giving liquor to brother's daughter; Tony faces sentence

The preliminary hearing for Frank Tigano and his son-in-law, Ralph Curtis, charged with giving liquor to a minor, the 14-year old daughter of Tony Tigano, a brother of the first-named defendant, has been set for Friday morning before Justice of the Peace, PC Wilson, the district attorney's office announced Tuesday night.

The men are on bond pending the preliminary hearing. The complaint against them follows a raid on the house of Tony Tigano resulting in the seizure in the basement of eight barrels of old wine and a quantity of whisky and beer all of which was destroyed by prohibition agents.

Deputy Prohibition Administrator Samuel B Richards revealed Tuesday that a suspended sentence of six months for violating the prohibition law is already hanging over Tony Tigano who was held to the next federal grand jury after a preliminary hearing Monday.

The suspended sentence was given by US District Judge Charles Nesbit last fall according to Richards. He announced that an investigation is being made which may result in a request that the court put the suspended sentence into effect.

The trouble between the brothers is said to have started when Frank Tigano returned recently from Leavenworth where he was placed on parole after serving part of a sentence for a liquor law violation. Officers say Frank Tigano alleges that his brother owes him $500 which the brother denies.

The raid by officers is said to be the result of the quarrel of the brothers, the last chapter in this row being the complaint against Frank Tigano and Curtis.

Clearly Tony had managed to accrue a fairly large quantity of wine in his basement and, depending on the size of his barrels, almost certainly somewhat more than the permitted two hundred gallons. It was in such cases that the Prohibition Agents had a measure of latitude and had to decide whether or not the wine was for personal use ... had to decide whether to destroy or not to destroy, to prosecute or not to prosecute.

When the family found this clipping they couldn't equate it with their more recent memories of the two brothers and their relationship. Whatever the quarrel was about, in later life it was resolved and the two became quite close and their families remain so. Nor was anyone aware of any local stigma that rubbed off on the family as a result of these events ... it was as if the fault lay elsewhere ... with the Prohibition Act itself.

Which, of course, it did.

•

Something else that came up in the stories of some of the families I visited was the problem of the Calabrian dialect, or rather the Calabrian dialects which were—and still are—localized. Despite the fact that today's mass media communicates in Italian, on the ground people still retain their local dialect—I live in such a town where people switch effortlessly from one language to another, a language which, to the untrained ear, sounds nothing like Italian.

A hundred years ago all uneducated Calabrians would have spoken only their local version of Calabrese, Italian would have meant next to nothing to them. And until immigrant Calabrians learned English they may not have been able to communicate with their fellow countrymen—apart from Sicilians, that is. Perhaps this explains why the families I visited all seemed to recall how their parents and/or grandparents picked up English so incredibly fast ... perhaps they had more reason to do so than other Italians.

One young man, who was born in the United States of Calabrian parents, told me how he had picked up from them their local Calabrian dialect under the mistaken assumption that he was learning Italian. When, nearly thirty years on, he visited his ancestral home for the first time, he recalled how he was scarcely able to communicate with anybody—they didn't speak English, he didn't speak Italian and the local dialect he had learned as a child had moved on in the forty years since his parents had grown up there and only the elderly recognized it.

Undaunted, he plans to return again soon having decided it's time he learned Italian—textbook Italian, that is.

•

All the immigrants I met—by which I mean those who actually emigrated, mostly in the fifties and sixties, as opposed to their children and grandchildren—spoke English with traces of an accent; some quite marked, others less so. Few of these ever actually wrote to me, preferring to do so through a younger family member ... I am guessing they were less confident with the written language.

English lessons for immigrants around 1925.

The one who did put pen to paper, did not write perfect English but the sense was always clear even if sometimes words were misspelled.

This got me wondering what it was like for those who emigrated in the early part of the twentieth century, those who gravitated at first to Calabrian enclaves in Brooklyn or North Adams or Kenosha; what it was like to have children who spoke better English than they did. I know from personal experience it is not easy to live in a foreign language but of course, unlike my experience, most immigrants at that time had youth on their side.

I wondered too whether the fact that so few passed on their experience of coming to America—the journey to Naples, the two-week crossing to New York, their Ellis Island experience and finding their way to their first American home—was because they experienced it all in their native language or dialect. All the anticipation, the fear, the degradation, the pain ... all these emotions were coped with and locked away in another language, a language that would soon become part of their past, a language their children would probably never speak.

The nearest I have come to a similar experience is being ill in another language—I felt the pain in English and could explain it in English but found the nuances of describing degrees of discomfort and pain in Italian very difficult. Was it, I wondered, the same for those early immigrants with their discomfort and pain—and worse—forever trapped in a language they were trying to forget as they single-mindedly strove towards American citizenship?

•

Languages, dialects and culture are always in a state of transition, changes that are barely perceptible at the time but which, over generations, evolves as new influences impinge and become the norm. So it was with the families I met—whether they came to America in the early twentieth century or fifty years later—the cultural transition from Calabrian to American began the moment they set foot on American soil.

Everyone, first and second generations, had grown up in this period of transition but never really recognized it as such. Like a snake, they were shedding their Calabrian skin—and with it the culture of their forefathers—and replacing it with a new American skin. Slowly, imperceptibly, they were assimilating the ways of their new home, filtering the past to modify the present and, inevitably, holding on to less and less.

Different families experienced this transition in different ways—some lived longer side by side with other Calabrians, some families soon lived more independent lives within more scattered Calabrian and immigrant communities while others moved away from their comfort zone within a generation. Some families quickly embraced the diversity of American culture and married into other cultures; others took their time and such unions were initially not encouraged.

Different people, different circumstances, different time frames, different ways of making the transition; but, it seemed to me, they all ended up at the same place—as Americans first and foremost. And proud to be so.

•

As I write, the Calabrian summer is waning. Soon deep blue skies and warm winds will be the exception rather than the rule. The annual influx of summer visitors returning to their roots has dissipated. Among them this year were people from Albuquerque, New Jersey and Long Island—Calabrian-Americans visiting family, friends, old haunts and enjoying an *aperitivo* in Santa Severina's *Piazza Campo*.

Next year, the one after and the one after that, the same scene will be repeated in every village, town and city in Calabria—in Stróngoli, Fossato Seralto, Marano Marchesato, Mesoraca, Casabona, Crotone and Roccabernarda—as the descendants of those who left this land fifty, eighty, a hundred years ago, return to share stories of people long gone, times long past and of newer, curious, internet-savvy generations on both sides of the Atlantic; to laugh, embrace, sit in a sunny square, drink a little wine ... and practice their Italian.

I look forward again to sharing some more of their time and listening to more of their stories ... and perhaps too, to uncovering a few more skeletons.

Afterword

I realize that not every Calabrian who emigrated to America passed through Ellis Island but, as the majority of Italian emigrants made their move between 1900 and 1925, then for most the Ellis Island experience would have been the last act of their long journey. The unique online archive that survives is a major source of information about these people; even those who emigrated in the fifties and sixties were often the descendants of families who had a history of emigration stretching back over half a century.

Ellis Island subsequently developed such an iconic status that even some of the children of those who emigrated in the sixties still believe that their parents entered the United States through the Ellis Island Immigration Center ... despite the fact that they probably flew TWA.

If you conduct an internet search on the following, '29 questions'—nothing more, nothing less—within the first half dozen links on offer there will be at least one described in terms similar to the following: 'What were the 29 questions at Ellis Island?'

This heading alone contains two errors and is misleading. It is also a reminder—if one were needed—that nobody should believe everything they read on the internet.

The information that would-be emigrants supplied became two pages of a ledger-like manifest that was completed *at the port of embarkation* and *not* at Ellis Island. These manifests came to America aboard the ships that carried the emigrants listed in them.

The number '29' that is so often bandied about refers to the number of *columns* in most manifests though even this is misleading as the number of columns varied depending on when people actually emigrated—some of the ship's manifests had fewer than twenty-nine columns, others had more.

In *Appendix One* I have listed the headings and sub-headings of a typical 29-column, two-page, manifest from 1912; there is also a facsimile of part of an actual manifest. As can be seen, its twenty-nine columns include two (columns 1 and 13) which are just the number (normally one to thirty) of each passenger entry that spans the two pages. In addition, within several of the other columns there are two or more additional questions.

The instructions for inspection officers and registry clerks regarding how the manifests had to be completed were quite detailed and precise—see *Appendix Two*—and are an example of how organized the whole process was, right down to the distinction between various races and nationalities, including northern and southern Italians.

For most southern Italians the port of departure was Naples and it was here that the first medical inspection took place and not on Ellis Island. This was a less rigorous examination—though it could include disinfection of both passengers and their belongings—and was carried out under the supervision of the ship's surgeon who provided the answers for columns 23 to 28 of the manifest. There was, of course, a more thorough medical examination on arrival at Ellis Island.

Not only had the ship's surgeon a duty of care to the passengers but he also had to fulfill the shipping company's obligation to arrive in New York with a ship-load of ostensibly healthy would-be Americans.

Those weeded out at Ellis Island could be sent back to their homeland at the shipping line's expense and the company could also be fined. The captains and surgeons of all vessels had to sign affidavits to confirm that they had done their duty in this respect—see *Appendix Three*.

•

It is, of course, the information contained on these manifests or passenger lists that form the backbone of the documentation available on the Ellis Island website.

Whatever the number of questions each individual had to answer, it nevertheless remains the case that most southern Italians emigrants answered the two questions in column 7 with 'No' and 'No' again—they could neither read nor write.

Illiterate they may have been but somehow they got together the information that was necessary to leave Italy and enter the United States including, after 1900, a passport which itself would have included some of the information required for the ship's manifest.

To facilitate this the shipping companies employed agents who not only travelled within Calabria selling passages to the United States but they also helped with the logistics of when would-be emigrants should arrive at Naples and when they could expect to set sail. Part of their sales pitch— apart from the land-of-milk-and-honey bit—also included assistance with acquiring passports and other information, both locally and at Naples, information that the shipping companies were obliged to detail in their manifests.

The arrival of an agent in a town could soon result in the mass exodus of its menfolk. On May 1, 1910, for example, the *Batavia* docked in New York. On board were forty-six people from Petilia Policastro, a small Calabrian village in the foothills of the Sila mountains; all but three of them were men. Two days later another eight arrived on another ship and the following week a further thirteen.

Each had paid between $12 and $20 for their passage and each was expected to have between $18 and $25 in their pockets. Although column 16 of the manifest suggested that the American authorities would have preferred immigrants to have at least $50, it was clearly recognized that this was not going to happen.

One of the most important pieces of information required for the manifest was the answer to the question in column 18—the name and address of the person they were meeting up with at the other end.

The resourcefulness required to arrange and co-ordinate everything at both ends was mind-boggling. Communication between rural Calabrian villages and, say, New York was reliant on the telegraph service (if it existed at the Calabrian end), the postal service and/or messages carried to and from America by *paesani* (those from the same town or village) and other family members. While those emigrating needed to have a name and address in the United States, that named person also needed to know whom to expect, when to expect him, her or them and on which ship ... and all with the most basic means of communication.

•

For me, the ships' manifests available on the Ellis Island website proved to be a particularly bounteous source of further information but how that information was originally transcribed could make things very simple or incredibly difficult ... this was usually done by hand and the range of legibility could be anywhere between classic script and a scrawl; thankfully some later manifests were typewritten.

The shipping lines operating between Italy and the United States were responsible for compiling these manifests—companies could be fined if this was not done properly—and of course they were written up at the port of embarkation. Any anomalies, misspellings, mistakes or confusion therefore originated in the home port and not, as has often been implied, on arrival in the United States.

When, for example, the town of Roccabernarda appeared as R.Bernardi, Roccekemanto, Roceadevandro, Roccaberuarda, Roccabuniere, even Bocca Cernardo, or the seemingly more straightforward surname Fonte as Fonti or Fante, it was the inevitable result of the interplay between the emigrant and the scribe, between the former's dialect and the latter's hearing and handwriting. And sometimes all of this was complicated even further by the more recent intervention of those whose unenviable job it was to decipher the original handwriting for inclusion in the Ellis Island archive.

•

Family memories can be capricious—sometimes firm facts, at other times flights of fancy. But thanks to online archives like, among others, the Ellis Island Foundation and census information available through sites such as Ancestry.com, it is now possible to dovetail family memories with the actual detail of what happened and when. As far as was possible I checked every piece of information I could and often was able to add to the story, sometimes amend it and at times refute it.

Occasionally too the information in such sites is open to interpretation, to making it fit the story. So, tucked away in these pages, there are a couple of dates I believe to be incorrect but I decided to leave them as the family preferred only because they did not impinge on the rest of the story.

Appendix One

The ship's manifest

MANIFEST for the SS HAMBURG
Genoa-Naples-Palermo-New York
Departed Genoa February 2, 1912
Arrived New York February 17, 1912
Carried 959 passengers

First Page
1   Number on List
2   Name in Full: Family Name / Given Name
3   Age
4   Sex
5   Married or Single
6   Calling or Occupation
7   Able to: Read / Write
8   Nationality (Country of which citizen or subject)
9   Race or People
10 Last Permanent Address: Country / City or Town
11 The name and complete address of nearest relative or friend in country whence alien came.
12 Final Destination

Second Page

13 Number on List

14 Whether having a ticket to such a final destination

15 By whom was passage paid? (Whether alien paid his own passage, whether paid by other person, or by any corporation, society, municipality, or government)

16 Whether in possession of $50, and if less, how much?

17 Whether ever before in the United States, and if so, when and where: Yes or No. If yes—year or period of years. Where?

18 Whether going to join a relative or friend, and if so, what relative or friend, and his name and complete address

19 Ever in prison or almshouse or institution for care and treatment of the insane, or supported by charity? If so, which?

20 Whether a Polygamist

21 Whether an Anarchist

22 Whether coming by reason of say, an offer, solicitation, promise, or agreement, expressed or implied, to labor in the United States

23 Condition of Health, Mental and Physical

24 Deformed or Crippled. Nature, length of time, and cause

25 Height: Feet / Inches

26 Complexion

27 Color of: Hair / Eyes

28 Marks of Identification

29 Place of Birth: Country / City or Town

Appendix Two
Instructions for filling alien manifests

Column 3 (Age)—The return of age in column 3 should be expressed in years or months, the latter applying only to those under 1 year of age.

Column 4 (Sex)—The entry in column 4 should be either M (male) or F (female).

Column 5 (Married or Single)—The Entry in column 5 should be either M (married), S (single), Wd (widowed), or D (divorced).

Column 6: (Calling or occupation)—The entry in column 6 should describe as accurately as possible the occupation, trade, or profession of each alien arrival, as for example: Civil engineer, stationary engineer, locomotive engineer, mining engineer, brass polisher, steel polisher, iron molder, wood turner, etc., and not simply as engineer, polisher, molder, turner or other indefinite designations.

A distinction should be made between *farmers* and *farm laborers*, regardless of the amount of money shown, as follows:

A *farmer* is one who operates a farm, either for himself or others.

A *farm laborer* is one who works on a farm for the man who operates it.

Column 7 (Able to read, and write)—Column 7 is subdivided and the entries therein should be either Yes—Yes (can read and write), No—No (can neither read nor write), or Yes—No (can read but not write).

Column 8 (Nationality)—Column 8 should be constructed to mean the country of which immigrant is a citizen or subject.

Column 9 (Race or people)—The entry in column 9 should show the race or people as given in list on reverse side of alien manifest. Special attention should be paid to the distinction between race and nationality. and manifests should be carefully revised by inspectors and registry clerks in this regard. For instance, "France" appearing on a manifest does not necessarily mean "French" by race or people, and similarly, "French" appearing on a manifest does not necessarily mean "France" by nationality. An alien who is Irish, German, or Hebrew by race might properly come under the heading of United Kingdom or any other country by nationality. In this connection the following distinctions should be specially observed:

[Clarification of distinctions as they relate to specific racial groups: Cuban / West Indian / Spanish-American / African (Black). Followed by ...]

Italian (North)

The people who are native to the basin of the River Po in northern Italy (i.e., compartments of Piedmont, Lombardy, Venetia and Emelia) and their descendants, whether residing in Italy, Switzerland, Austria-Hungary, or any other country should be classed as "Italian (north). Most of these people speak a Gallic dialect of the Italian language."

Italian (South)

The people who are native to that portion of Italy south of the Basin of the River Po (i.e., compartments of Liguria, Tuscany, the Marches, Umbria, Rome, the Abruzzi and Moise, Campania, Apulia, Basilicata, Calabria, Sicily, and Sardinia) and their descendants should be classed as "Italian (south)."

Column 10 (Last permanent residence)—The entries in column 10 should show the *country and city or town* of last permanent residence. It is important for statistical purposes that country of last permanent residence independent of country of temporary residence, nationality, or race.

Aliens who are permanent residents of the United States and are returning from a visit abroad should be recorded on manifests as United States for country of last permanent residence.

Column 11 (Name and complete address of nearest relative or friend in country whence alien came)—The entry in column 11 should give name and address of such relative. If no such relative living, give name and address of friend.

Column 12 (Final Destination)—The entry in column 12 should show definitely the place (city or town) of final destination if within the United States; country, if outside the United States.

Column 13 (Number on List)

Column 14 (Whether having a ticket to such final destination)—The entry in column 14 should be either Yes (ticket) or No (no ticket).

Column 15 (By whom was passage paid)—The entry in column 15 should show definitely by whom passage was paid, as self; husband, father, brother, or other relative; friend; steamship company, etc.

Column 16:(Whether in possession of $50; and if less, how much)—The entry in column 16 should give in each case (individual or family) the exact amount of money shown. Money brought by head of a family should not be divided among the several members of the family.

Column 17 (Whether ever before in the United States; and if so, when and where)—The entries in column 17 should show whether or not (Yes or No) in the United States before; and if so, the year (or period of years), place; as, 1894-97; Philadelphia.

Column 18 (Going to join relative or friend; and if so, what relative or friend)—The entry in column 18 should show whether going to join either a relative or friend; and if so, what relative or friend, with name and complete address.

Column 19 to 29—The answers in these columns are subject to revision by any inspection officer in the examination of aliens.

Appendix Three

Captain's and Surgeon's affidavits

AFFIDAVIT OF THE MASTER OR COMMANDING OFFICER, OR
FIRST OR SECOND OFFICER

I, ..., Master of the .... from ...., do solemnly,
sincerely and truly swear that I have caused the surgeon of said vessel
sailing therewith or the surgeon employed by the owners thereof, to make
a physical and mental examination of each and all of the aliens named in
the foregoing Lists or Manifest Sheets, ... in number, and that from the
report of said surgeon and from my own investigation I believe that no one
of said aliens is an idiot, or imbecile, or a feeble minded person, or insane
person or a pauper, or is likely to become a public charge, or is affected
with tuberculosis, or with a loathsome or dangerous contagious disease,
or is a person who has been convicted of, or who admits having committed
a felony or other crime or misdemeanor involving moral turpitude, or is
a polygamist, or one admitting belief in the practice of polygamy, or an
anarchist, or under promise or agreement, express or implied to perform
labor in the United States as a prostitute, or a woman or girl coming to
the United States for the purpose of prostitution or for any other immoral
purpose, and that also, according to the best of my knowledge and belief,
the information in said Lists or Manifests concerning each of said aliens
named herein is correct and true in every respect.

AFFIDAVIT OF SURGEON

I, ..., Surgeon of the ...., do solemnly, sincerely and truly swear that I have had .... years experience as a Physician and Surgeon and that I am entitled to practice as such by and under the authority of the University of ...., and that I have made a personal examination of the aliens named herein and that the foregoing Lists or Manifest Sheets, ... in number, according to the best of my knowledge and belief, are full, correct, and true in all particulars, relative to the mental and physical condition of such aliens.

Selected Bibliography

Calabrian Tales by Peter Chiarella (Regent Press, 2002)

Old Calabria by Norman Douglas (various editions 1915 to present)

Italians in Albuquerque by Nicholas P Ciotola (Arcadia Publishing, 2002)

The Italian American Family Album by Dorothy and Thomas Hoobler (Oxford University Press, 1994)

Boston Italians by Stephen Puleo (Beacon Press, 2007)

Niall Allsop ...

... was born and educated in Belfast, Northern Ireland, but began his working life as a primary school teacher in London and in 1971 took up his first headship.

He left teaching in 1981 to pursue a career as a freelance photo-journalist specializing in the UK's inland waterways and wrote extensively in this field both as a contributor to several national magazines and later as author of a number of related titles, one of which, in a fourth edition, remains in print.

By the early 1990s he was a graphic designer and the in-house designer for an international photographic publishing house in Manchester before becoming a freelance graphic designer based in the south-west of England.

In September 2008 he and his wife, Kay, moved to Calabria, the toe of Italy, where they enjoy a sort of retirement and where they continue to struggle daily with the language in a small hilltop town where they are the only English-speaking people.

Since moving to Calabria he has written several books with Italian themes and also a memoir relating to his teaching career.

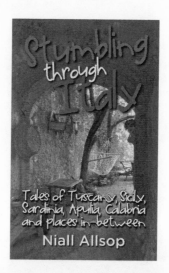

Stumbling through Italy

Tales of Tuscany, Sicily, Sardinia, Apulia, Calabria and places in-between

In September 1999 Niall Allsop and his wife Kay flew to Pisa and stepped onto Italian soil for the first time.

Within six months they returned and thereafter they visited Italy at least twice a year, usually to the most southerly provinces of Apulia and Calabria and the islands of Sicily and Sardinia.

They knew they holidayed differently to other people and in Italy, despite the lack of language, they found themselves somehow drawn into people's lives and homes; they had experiences and encounters that seemed to pass others by.

Stumbling through Italy is the prequel to *Scratching the Toe of Italy* and is the irreverent chronicle of their Italian travels and the many remarkable and colorful people they met there up to the summer of 2008 ... when, finally reconciled to the inevitable, they returned to Italy one last time. Which, as they say, is another story.

Also includes chapters on the idiosyncrasies of the Italian language and the Italian driving experience.

... above all else, an entertaining book, a book packed with characters, stories and anecdotes, frequently amusing, often enlightening, sometimes thought-provoking, never dull.

... it's fun and informative ...

It's the people of the different regions that we get a real sense of with Stumbling—their daily lives, their families, their feuds, their celebrations.

Niall Allsop ... brings to life with affection and humour a whole cast of characters ... against a background of the glorious colors of southern Italy and Sicily.

Amazon Reviews of *Stumbling through Italy*

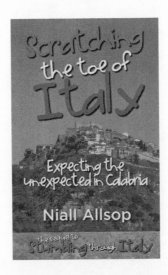

Scratching the toe of Italy
Expecting the unexpected in Calabria

In July 2008 Niall Allsop and his wife Kay returned to the UK after their third holiday in Calabria near the small hill-top town of Santa Severina; the plan was to return the following summer.

Ten weeks later, their left-hand drive Renault Clio bursting at the seams, they left their home in south-west England and headed for the coast on the first leg of their journey back to Calabria to live.

Scratching the toe of Italy continues the story from where **Stumbling through Italy** left off and explains how their move to Italy came about, the logistics of the move itself and what happened next.

It is the story of two adventurous pensioners adapting to being the only English-speaking people in a small Calabrian town, of the new friends they made and the home they created there.

Scratching the toe of Italy is a heart-warming chronicle of perseverance and optimism, of the struggle to come to grips with a new language and a new culture, of starting each day with the certain knowledge that it will not turn out as expected.

... Santa Severina will be on my next Journey ... it was a very vivid account of the area and the people and the Italian way of life ...

This was a pleasant surprise. It's characters were well presented and I could just envision what was happening in this small village. Some very typical Italian politics rear their ugly heads, too.

This is a great book to learn the good and challenging parts of moving away from home.

If you haven't met Niall and Kay in the first book ... I strongly suggest you do. They are both so refreshingly down-to-earth, you'll wish they were your closest friends.

Amazon Reviews of *Scratching the toe of Italy*

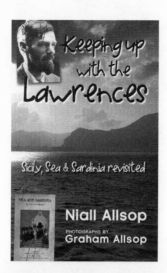

Keeping up with the Lawrences
Sicily, Sea and Sardinia revisited

In January 1921 DH Lawrence and his wife, Frieda, left their Taormina home in north-east Sicily and set off on a nine-day excursion to and through Sardinia and back to Sicily via mainland Italy. Lawrence's account of their journey, *Sea and Sardinia*, was published later that year in New York.

Keeping up with the Lawrences is a contemporary account of making the same journey, as far as possible keeping to the same route, the same time scale, the same mode of transport and the same overnight stops as Lawrence and the queen-bee, his pet name for Frieda.

Like *Sea and Sardinia*, *Keeping up with the Lawrences* is written in the present tense but there the comparisons end for the irascible Lawrence was not a tolerant traveller, was not what the Italians would call *simpatico*.

Lawrence travelled at a time of heightened tensions in Europe after the Great War and these are reflected in his outlook and the people he encountered, most of whom he gave appropriate nicknames such as Hamlet, the Bounder, Mr Rochester and the Sludge Queen.

Niall Allsop and his nephew traversed the same route in a different world, a brave new world of iPods and tele-communications masts, and here they met Julius Caesar and Cicero, Wonderwoman, Red and Mr Irritable ... and many more colorful and interesting characters brought to life on the pages of this unique travelogue.

Also includes over forty black & white images and four maps, including the original drawn by Lawrence himself.

... more than once [I] wished they'd taken me along with them.

... hugely entertaining ...

[Niall's] penchant for the odd glass of wine or three ... had me reaching for my own glass as his journey rattled along. I learned a lot and laughed a lot.

The journey fairly rattles along as [they] encounter all sorts of interesting characters ... and have as many off-the-wall encounters in their nine days as I do in a year

Amazon Reviews of *Keeping up with the Lawrences*